Chassidic Ecstasy in Music

Shmuel Barzilai

Chassidic Ecstasy in Music

PETER LANG

Frankfurt am Main · Berlin · Bern · Bruxelles · New York · Oxford · Wien

Bibliographic Information published by the Deutsche Nationalbibliothek
The Deutsche Nationalbibliothek lists this publication in the Deutsche Nationalbibliografie; detailed bibliographic data is available in the internet at http://dnb.d-nb.de.

Cover Design:
Olaf Glöckler, Atelier Platen, Friedberg

Cover Illustration:
Dancing Chassid (1999) Dvora Barzilai

ISBN 978-3-631-58452-1

© Peter Lang GmbH
Internationaler Verlag der Wissenschaften
Frankfurt am Main 2009
All rights reserved.

All parts of this publication are protected by copyright. Any utilisation outside the strict limits of the copyright law, without the permission of the publisher, is forbidden and liable to prosecution. This applies in particular to reproductions, translations, microfilming, and storage and processing in electronic retrieval systems.

www.peterlang.de

*In Everlasting Memory of
My Mother, Frieda Lea Barzilai z"l,
and my parents-in-law,
Menachem Dov and Lea Rat z"l.*

Every lock has its own key,
but the artist has a master key that opens all locks,
and this is the melody.

(Rabbi Shalom Dov Ber Shneersohn (1860–1920),
Sefer Hanigunim, Likutei Reshimot, p. 41).

Table of Contents

Acknowledgments	13
Chapter 1 – Music in Judaism – General Review	17
1. Reading the Torah	21
2. Prayer	22
Chapter 2 – Chassidism	27
1. Chassidism – Modes and Methods	27
2. Music in Chassidism – The Manifestation of Joy	31
3. The Innovative Aspect of Song in The Chassidic Perception of Serving G-d	35
4. Joy as the Remedy for Sorrow	38
Chapter 3 – The *Niggun* (Melody)	53
1. What is The Niggun?	53
2. The Wordless Melody	58
3. The Niggun and Formulated Prayer	66
4. The Inspirational Power of the Niggun Before and During Various Activities	68
5. Niggunim for the Bridal Canopy, Marriage Festivities, and First & Second Year Chedder Pupils	70
Chapter 4 – Dance	71
1. Dance in the Bible	71
2. The Importance of Dance in Chassidism	72
3. Dancing before the Bride	76
Chapter 5 – The Shabbat and Music	81
1. The Shabbat and Music	81
2. Welcoming the Shabbat	83
3. Shabbat Songs	85
4. The Shabbat Table in the Admor's Court	88

Chapter 6 – Music in Mysticism ... 93
1. Mysticism (Kabbalah) and Chassidism ... 93
2. The Importance of Music in Kabbalah ... 95
3. Excerpts from the Kabbalah relating to Music ... 97
4. Use of Kabbalistic Writings as Texts for Melodies ... 102
5. Kabbalistic Composers ... 102
6. Tunes of Meron ... 103

Chapter 7 – Musical Expression in Chassidic Courts ... 107
1. Modzitz Chassidism ... 107
2. Chabad Chassidism ... 111
3. Bratzlav Chassidism ... 112

Chapter 8 – Composers and Lyricists ... 115
1. Tzaddikim and the Amud haTefillah ... 115
2. Rebbe-Composers ... 117
3. Court Composers ... 118
    Modzitz Chassidim ... 118
    Gur Chassidim ... 119
    Chabad Chassidim ... 120
4. Singers and the Choir ... 120
5. Chassidic Chazzanim [Cantors] ... 121

Chapter 9 – Famous Niggunim: Legends and Examples ... 123
1. ha'Ezkerah (Niggun haYissurim) – Rabbi Israel Taub of Modzitz (1849-1921) ... 123
2. The Four Babas Niggun – The Alter Rebbe of Chabad (1745-1813) ... 126
3. Niggun haMalachim (El Adon March) – Kozenice Chassidic Court ... 128
4. Yah Echsof – Rabbi Aharon of Karlin (1736-1772) ... 129
5. Ani Ma'amin – Rabbi Azriel David Fastag – Chassid Modzitz ... 130
6. The Shepherd's Niggun – The Kalev Rebbe (1744-1821) ... 130
7. Niggun haMalachim – Rabbi Yaakov Yitzhak, Seer of Lublin ... 132

Chapter 10 – Adages referencing Chassidic Music ... 133
1. Song ... 133
2. Niggun ... 134
3. Dance ... 138
4. Joy and Sadness ... 138
5. The Chassid and Chassidism ... 140

Chapter 11 – The Chassidic Approach to non-Jewish Music 143

Chapter 12 – Musical Instruments used in Chassidic music 149

Chapter 13 – Neo-Chassidic Movements 151
– Rabbi Shlomo Carlebach 151

Chapter 14 – Interviews 157
1. Rabbi Aharon Catorza, Vienna 157
2. Rabbi Chaim Eisenberg, Vienna 159
3. Mr. Israel Katzover, Jerusalem 164
4. Mr. Yaakov Mazor, Jerusalem 169
5. Mr. Saul Meizlish, Kfar Saba, Israel 172
6. Rabbi Yishaya Meshulam Feish Halevi Rattenburg, Jerusalem 175
7. Professor Eliyahu Schleifer, Jerusalem 179
8. Rabbi Moshe Shur, New York, USA 183

Chapter 15 – Appendices 187
1. The First Meeting between the Besht and Rabbi Yaacov Yosef 187
2. The Besht's Role as Kindergarten Teacher's Assistant 189
3. Legends and Tales 192
   (i) The Diamond – For Chabad's Day of Redemption 192
   (ii) The Holy Thief – A Life Story 194
   (iii) The Flute 195
   (iv) The Se'udah Shlishit Meal at the Rebbe 197
   (v) The Soul of the Musician 200
   (vi) The World of Music 200

Epilogue 203

Sheet Music and Manuscripts 205

Notes 209

Photographs 215

Glossary of Rabbis and Cantors 221
   Rabbis by date of birth 221
   Chassidic Rabbis by Location 222
   Disciples of the Besht 225
   Cantors 225

References 227

Acknowledgments

I wish to warmly thank all those who assisted me in writing this book, whether by providing me with information, critical remarks or helpful suggestions. In particular, I would like to thank the following:

The teaching staff in the Department of Jewish Studies at Vienna University: specifically, Prof. Kurt Schubert, *z"l*; Prof. Klaus Davidowicz and Prof. Gunther Stemberger for their help and guidance from the outset of my studies at the Faculty.

Mr. Yakov Mazor, Prof. Eliahu Schleiffer and Dr. Gila Flam from the Institute of Musicology; the Music Department of the Hebrew University, Jerusalem.

The Jewish National and University Library; for their help, information, good suggestions, and permission to use and photocopy the records of A. Z. Idelsohn and M. S. Geshuri.

My mentor and friend, Rabbi Chaim Eisenberg, the Chief Rabbi of Austria, for his help from the moment I arrived in Vienna, and for suggestions that led to the writing of this book.

The author and journalist Mr. Saul Meizlish; the Chabad Vienna representative Rabbi Aharon Catorza; author and journalist, Mr. Israel Katzover; the son and heir of the Kosson *Admor,* Rabbi Yeshaya Meshulam Faish Halevi Rottenberg; and Prof. Eliyahu Schleiffer, all of whom gave of their unique and fascinating ideas and improvements.

The photographer, Shuki Lerer, for allowing me access to photographs of the great Chassidic leaders (Admorim) playing violins during the lighting of Chanuka candles.

My father, Rabbi Moshe Zvi Shlomo Barzilai, for his encouragement and support. My dear brother, Rav Mordechai Barzilai, for assistance in collecting pictorial material, receiving approbation from the Modzitz Rabbi, and so much more.

My dear and wonderful wife, Dvori, and my beloved children, Yair, Chaya and her husband Chaim, Efrat, and Daniela, whose encouragement supported me throughout.

In compiling a list of names and places where Rabbis appearing in this book served, together with their dates of birth and passing away, I was greatly assisted by Mr. Zvi Rabinowicz's book *The Encyclopedia of Chassidism.* Dates of birth and death of cantors appearing in this book were taken from Mr. Akiva Zimmerman's *B'ron Yachad.*

*Printed with the assistance of
The Ministry for Science and Research, Vienna
and
Family Benedek of Vienna*

*Translated by Byron Translations, Israel –
Seree Cohen Zohar*

Chapter 1 – Music in Judaism – General Review

The Midrash says[1]:

Ten songs were sung in the world: the first was sung by Adam, when his sin was forgiven, and Shabbat came to protect him: and he sang: "A Song for the Sabbath Day"[2].

The second song was sung by Moses together with the Children of Israel when G-d split the Reed [Red] Sea, and they all chanted: "Thus Moses and the Children of Israel shall sing...."[3].

The third song was sung by the Children of Israel when they were given the well of water: "Spring up, O Well, sing unto it"[4].

The fourth song was sung by Moses when he was about to depart this world, and proved the worth of the Children of Israel: "Give ear, Heavens, and I will speak, and let the Earth hear the words of my mouth"[5].

The fifth song was sung by Joshua ben Nun, as war at Givon approached, and the sun and moon stood still for thirty-six hours, and ceased to sing; and instead, he sang: "Thus Joshua speaks to G-d, on the day that the Lord delivered the Amorites unto the Children of Israel"[6].

The sixth song was that of Barak and Devorah, when G-d delivered Sisera and his camp into the hands of Israel: "And Devorah and Barak son of Avinoam sang on that day, saying."[7].

The seventh song was sung by Hannah when the Lord blessed her with a son: "And Hannah prayed and said:..."[8].

The eighth song was that of King David, for all the miracles G-d performed to help him: "[A psalm] of David [...] who spoke to the Lord the words of this song"[9].

The ninth song was sung to G-d by Solomon, King of Israel, and guided by the spirit of G-d: "This is the Song of Songs, from Solomon"[10].

The tenth song will be sung in the future, by the redeemed ones, when they leave the exile as explained by the Prophet Isaiah: "Ye shall have a song as in the night when a feast is

---

1   Aharon Elhanan Wasserman www.vbm-torah.org/vtc/0055480.html, cited in Mechilta, Yalkut Shimoni, Midrash Tanhuma, and translation of the Song of Songs.
2   Psalms 92
3   Exodus 15:1
4   Numbers 21:17
5   Deuteronomy 32:1
6   Joshua 10:12
7   Judges 5:1
8   Samuel 1:2
9   Psalms 18:1
10 Song of Songs 1:1

hallowed; and gladness of heart, as when one goes with the flute, coming into the mountain of the Lord, to the Rock of Israel"[11].

And of the tenth song, King David said: "Sing a new song to the Lord, sing to the Lord all the Earth, sing to the Lord, bless His name, proclaim His salvation from day to day [...] Then all the trees of the forest will sing for joy, before the Lord for He is come, He is come to judge the earth"[12].

Rabbi Meir added, saying: "From where do we understand that even the unborn in their mothers' wombs sang at the [splitting of the] Sea? Because it is said: "In assemblies, bless the Lord, G-d, all who are from the fountain of Israel" (Psalms 68:27)[13].

In the Bible, music is first mentioned at the beginning of the book of Genesis, when Yuval, the mythological father of music, says: "he was the father of all such as handle the harp and the pipe"[14]. The harp was a stringed instrument, the pipe a form of wind instrument[15]. The book of Genesis also mentions a type of drum: "that I might have sent you away with mirth and with songs, with tabret and with psaltery"[16]. This instrument is connected with the songs to which women danced, such as Miriam's Song, by the Sea of Reeds [Red Sea]: "and all the women followed her with timbrels and with dances"[17].

It is possible that the silver trumpets of the Tabernacle were similar to those found at Egyptian burial sites, rather like other musical instruments that came from Egypt during King Solomon's reign.

We also find, in Midrash Otiot D'Rabbi Akiva[18]:

And from where do we understand that the Holy One, Blessed be His Name, did not create the world if not for song and music? As it is said: Glory and splendor are before him[19]. And from where do we understand that the Holy One, Blessed be His Name, did not create the heavens if not for song? As it is said: The heavens declare the glory of the Lord[20]. And from where do we understand that since the day that the Holy One, Blessed be His Name, created the world, song is sung before Him? As it is said: From the wings of the earth have we heard songs[21]. And from where do we understand that even the seas and rives sang? As it is said: From the voices of many waters[22].

---

11 Isaiah 30:29
12 Psalms 96:1-2, 12-13
13 b. Brachot 50a
14 Genesis 4:21
15 Ibid, Onkelos
16 Genesis 31:27
17 Exodus 15:20
18 *Otiot D'Rabbi Akiva, 1:* also *Sefer Perek Shirah*, pg. 70
19 Chronicles 1:16-27
20 Psalms 19:2
21 Isaiah 24:16
22 Psalms 93:4

The Gemarra notes that every day, angels are created only for the sake of playing music; when their work is fulfilled, they are immediately consumed by fire[23].

The songs of Israel originate chiefly from the services performed in the Temple and were a foundation for subsequent rites, as Rabbi Judah quoted in the name of Samuel:

> From where do we understand that the principle of song is derived from the Torah? As it is said: Then he shall minister before the Lord his G-d as all his brothers the Levites do who stand there before the Lord[24], what ministration is this in the name of the Lord – this is song[25].

In the Temple, song was the domain of the Levites and poets. They sang songs of thanksgiving and praise while sacrifices were being offered, as is said: "And to stand every morning, to thank and praise the Lord, and likewise at evening, thus singing".[26] They sang songs of praise and thanks-giving. Singing in the Temple was accompanied by musical instruments such as the flute, lyre, harp and timbrel, with cymbals, and drums. This song of the Levites was not intended to be some form of background accompaniment but rather, an integral part of the holy service, inspired by the Shechina.

Rabbi Judah Halevi describes this succinctly in his book *The Kuzari*:

> Understanding music is important to the nation who respects the songs and allows the greatest among the people this honor, these being the Levites who are steeped in music in the consecrated house at consecrated times. They were not expected to involve themselves in matters of livelihood but received [their sustenance] from the tithes and were involved in nothing other than music.[27]

Although King David was not permitted to build the Temple, according to tradition, it was he who laid the foundations for the music of the First Temple', with lyres, psalteries and cymbals, as noted in 1 Chronicles 23:5.

> And four thousand Levites shall praise the Lord with the instruments which I made to praise therewith.

David organized the Levites[28] into twenty-four Watches comprising singers and players, headed by lead players recalled in the Scriptures by name. David

---

23 b. Hagiga 14a
24 Deutoronomy 18:7
25 b. Arachin 11a
26 I Chronicles 23:30
27 The Kuzari 3:64
28 Compare with: Nehemia 12:27

was also considered the inventor of musical instruments[29]. The instruments played in the Temple were the harp and psalter (apparently a small stringed instrument), and the cymbals. There were no wind instruments in the Temple other than the shofar (ram's horn), and trumpet. These instruments were kept in special chambers beneath the Temple assembly area.

During the Second Temple period, a choir consisting of at least twelve Levites stood on a special dais intended for the singers. The orchestra comprised two to six psalters, two to sixteen flutes, at least nine harps and a pair of cymbals. The players were joined by at least two priests blowing trumpets[30], as is recorded: "Also in the day of your gladness, and in your appointed seasons, and in your new moons, ye shall blow with the trumpets[31]. There was a further instrument known as "rake" whose nature is unclear, which generated a loud sound and was used to indicate the commencement of prayers that comprised part of morning sacrificial services. During King David's reign, 120 priests would play trumpets. In processions that brought first fruits to Jerusalem, the "flute would sound out before them"[32].

Song was an inseparable aspect of service, and according to Rabbi Meir, even postponed offering the sacrifice, as noted in Gemarra, in Tractate Arachin: "The song postpones the offering, so said Rabbi Meir"[33].

From the Temple, song moved into the Synagogue. The synagogue is a place of public gathering for prayer. Worshippers assembled three times daily, on Sabbaths and Festivals, to study Torah, Mishnah, Talmud and so on), and for various meetings and gatherings. The synagogue became the crowning glory and essence of spiritual, ethical and public life for the nation, and served as a fortress guarding the perpetuation of these aspects. To this day, it is a place of dignity and majesty for Jews. In those times, every public event, meeting of Torah scholars, people involved in public affairs, or assemblies of a joyous or tragic nature, revolved around or were conducted in the synagogue.

Apparently, the first synagogues were established during the Babylonian exile at the end of the First Temple period. From records that have been discovered, we learn that in Egypt synagogues already existed during the reign of Talmei (Ptolemy) III, the most renowned being the Alexandria synagogue which was especially magnificent, and of which it was said: "Whoever has not seen the Grand Synagogue [Stoa style] of Alexandria, has not seen the glory of Israel"[34].

29 Amos 6:5
30 b. Arachin 2:3-6
31 Numbers 10:10
32 Mishnah Bikurim 83:44
33 b. Arachin 11:71
34 b. Succah 51b

The Germarra goes on to describe the synagogue in Alexandria as being exceedingly large, and for this reason, the synagogue's beadle would stand in the center and wave a marker when the cantor would commence or end a section of prayer, so that worshippers in the other half of the synagogue could also prayer with the whole public[35].

After the destruction of the Temple, the synagogue became the central and most important place for the Israelites. The connection between the individual and the public, and between Israel and her G-d were all conducted in the synagogue. The nation acknowledged prayer and study of Torah as being in place of the Temple's sacrificial offerings, and they referred to the synagogue as the "small Temple", based on the verse: "I have been to them as a little sanctuary in the countries where they are come from"[36], so much so that the Sages said: "For as long as Jacob's voice is heard in the synagogue, the hands will not be those of Esau"[37]. They added: "If there are no synagogues or study houses, the Blessed One's presence shall not be found in the world"[38].

In the synagogue, music is of two kinds: that used for reading of the Torah scroll, and that used for prayer.

1. Reading the Torah

During the Babylonian exile, Ezra the Scribe instigated ten measures to ensure that the Torah would not be forgotten. Among these were reading portions of the Torah on Mondays and Thursdays, and as part of the Mincha [afternoon] service on the Sabbath[39]. The reading of the Torah in the synagogue uses melodies known as cantillation notes.

Chanoch Avenari, in his article on Torah reading melodies, noted:

> Reading the Torah aloud and to a tune is already mentioned in the Talmud as an established and accepted[40] custom, and chanting was incumbent on each reader and instituted as a Halachic [religious law] obligation (Avenari, 1971: 577).

Following completion of the Talmud, the Masoretic sages established the method of written cantillation notes to ensure that the reading would be correct

---

35 b. Succah 51b
36 Ezekiel 11:16
37 Midrash Rabbah Bereshit 65:20
38 Midrash Rabbah, Esther, Introduction 11
39 b. Baba Kama, 82a
40 b. Megilla 32a: "Rabbi Yochanan said: Whoever reads without cantillation or song, of him it is said 'I gave them statutes that were not good', etc." Ezekiel 20:25

and understood (Dotan, 1967). When the cantillation notes became inseparable from their musical motifs, they became known as 'music'.

The forms that these notes adopted were apparently passed from one generation to the next; only in the beginning of the 16th century were they recorded using musical notes. The first to publicize these musical notes included Johannes Reuchlin (1518), Sebastian Muenster (1524) and Johannes Valensis (1545). As Avenari noted further on, "Since the 16th century, humanists commenced publishing Old Testament grammar books in Latin, and included chapters on voweling and cantillation. "The musical notes", as they called them, that is, the melody for reading the Torah, held special interest: three of the earliest grammarians printed the Ashkenazi Jews' Torah melodies using musical notes. Avenari recorded the books titles of the three grammarians, and noted further that "The three versions of melody recorded in these books were sung by different Jewish readers".[41] In Chapter 3, the author's article states that "After the mid-16th century, Ashkenazi melodies ceased to be recorded until the early 19th century. Since then and to date, some thirty independent records have been made. It was not easy to locate them, even among the abundant libraries in Israel". Avenari then lists some twenty different forms of Torah reading, according to geographic location.

From the above, we see how important it was for the Torah to be read with a melody, and the variety of opinions on just how the melody should be chanted.

2. Prayer

Prayer is the heart's emotion, the heart's attitude towards a person's G-d. Prayer serves as the source of a person's life, and strengthens a person's heart.

In the past, there was no fixed prayer formulation, and prayer was the outcome of an individual's inner need to pour his or her heart out to the Creator, and without those outpourings being heard by anyone else. This is clearly stated as regards Hannah: "And she prayed to G-d and wept intensely"[42], moreover, "And it came to pass, as she prayed lengthily before the L-d... Hannah spoke within her heart, only her lips moving but her voice never heard..."[43]. This is said, too, of King Solomon and others. Only during the period of Ezra the Scribe, Nehemiah the Prophet, and the members of the Great Assembly were the first prayers set with fixed form; norms for public praying were determined which included reading portions of the Torah and the Prophets, reciting Psalms. Further norms for obligatory prayers were

---

41 Chanoch Avenari, *Torah Melodies in Ashkenazi Tradition*, Tel Aviv: 1976:8
42 I Samuel 1:10
43 I Samuel 1: 12-13

established that included saying the "Shema" (Hear, O Israel) prayer every morning and evening, and the first blessings of the Amida (silent prayer).

No musical instruments were used in the synagogues. A cantor, chosen by the people attending the service, led the prayers. The music consisted of several genres of song such as psalmody, cantillation, and recitative. It was either performed by a cantor leading and the community responding, or by two groups who sang in alternating rounds[44].

Recitative and special melodies were set for synagogal use, which came to be known as "Nusach". These melodies came to be used almost exclusively for specific prayers, so much so that some were even termed "melodies from Sinai" as a mark of honor for the long tradition of melodies, as though these too had been passed down from Moses when he received the Torah at Mt. Sinai.

Liturgical recitative was, and still is, the cantor's special art. Traditional melodies are used, some of which are fixed while others are flexible or modular.

This is what Israel Ta-Shma states, quoting Rabbi Judah the Hassid:

> Rabbi Judah the Hassid related utmost and even decisive importance to the role of the Shaliach Tzibbur [the communal representative]. Particularly on Sabbaths and festivals throughout the year, the 'Shatz' [Shaliach Tzibbur] must be acceptable to the whole community; he is not chosen by a majority but rather, unanimously. Thus the candidate for this role must satisfy each and every member of the congregation. A Shatz who is not on good terms with even one congregant endangers that congregant's welfare; how more applicable to a Shatz who is not supported by the majority of the public. The religious responsibility which he bears is indeed great, and his very approach to this role contains weighty personal precariousness, to the degree of endangering life itself. This may even occur through changes he introduces, possibly without any intention, in the familiar prayer Nussach, or with one of the accepted melodies. The Shatz must be fluent with and understand all the hymns and melodic forms required. He must be able to cope well with his main function, as intermediary between the public and its G-d, and if he is capable of bringing the praying community to correcting its ways through yet does not do so, then his prayers on their behalf endanger his very own life".[45]

This kind of song integrated into synagogal praying became recognized as "the song of the precepts" and became connected with prayer, as noted in the Gemarra[46]: "We learn in a Braitta [Mishnaic material not included in the compilation by Rabbi Yehuda Hanassi] that Abba Benjamin said: A person's prayer is not

---

44 b. Succah 38: "...He says 'Halleluja' and they say 'Halleluja'... he says 'Praise the L-d's servants' and they say 'Praise the L-d's servants', and so on".
45 Israel Ta-Shma, *haTefillah ha'Ashkenazit haKdumah*, Jerusalem, 2003. Ch. 6: "The Cantor's Status", pg. 52
46 b. Brachot 6a, & ibid 31a, "to hear the song and the prayer' – song is prayer.

heard except in the synagogue, as it is said, 'To hear the song and the prayer'."[47] And Rashi's interpretation notes: "Instead of song – in the synagogue where the congregations pronounce their songs and praises in pleasant voice".[48] Joshua Weizmann offers the following explanation:

> Abba Benjamin is responding to the question, 'Why does public prayer need to be in the synagogue, especially when the bulk of it is whispered, each person to himself, and why does it need to be conducted in a congregation?' And Abba Benjamin's reply is, 'Wherever there is song, there prayer should be'. Song means singing and praises, and they can be conducted only as a public. Singing 'with pleasant voice' derives from there being a public which sings to praise G-d, thus the voice of the entire public is pleasant. From this stance of singing as a public, the individual approaches his own praying. The song that precedes the prayer thus causes the silent prayers to become public, a prayer derived from within that public. Reciting 'Psukei Dzimra' [verses from Psalms] as a public, aloud, in pleasing voices, constitute an appropriate introduction to the Amidah said individually and silently.

Weizmann concludes thus:

> As we can see, communal prayer appears in three dimensions: place, time and person. All these turn each individual's silent prayer into public prayer. When the individual prays during the **time** that the whole public prays, in the **place** where the congregation is praying, this becomes public prayer. The dimension of the soul, the **person**, completes the songs and praises chanted by the public as one, which forms them into a congregation; thus the silent prayers become part of the public prayer.[49]

The Mishnah, in Tractate Avot, says: "The world stand on three things, on Torah, on service, and on good deeds".[50] The Sages[51] interpret 'service' as indicting the sacrificial rites of the Temple but once the Temple was destroyed, service became prayer, as the Sages explain with the verse, "And serve Him with all your heart".[52] What kind of service is in the heart? Prayer.[53] Thus the Jewish people said, 'I am sleeping although my heart is awake[54], meaning, Lord of the Universe, I sleep as far as sacrifices, yet my heart is awake to praying[55], the prayer in the heart is the heart's song".

47 I Kings 8:28 – this verse is also a chorus in *Slichot* prayers before the New Year
48 Rashi, b. Brachot 6a
49 Retrieved from www.yemalot-co-il/shiurhtml/malot256.html on Sept. 21, 2004
50 b. Avot 1:2
51 Read Tosafot on Brachot 31a, 4, 5 – In a place of joy, trembling will occur, as quoted from the Yerushalmi: 'Serve G-d with fear, that is, with prayer, the essence of service'.
52 Deuteronomy 11:13
53 b. Taanit 2a
54 Song of Songs 5:2
55 Based on Shmot Rabbah 33: 'I sleep as far as sacrifices but my heart is awake and the Holy One, blessed be He, engages me'.

Maimonides wrote: "And the one praying should turn to the Blessed One… enjoying with heart and lips… and should not turn away from pleasant voices".[56]

The cantor filled the role held by the Levite in the Temple, and according to a Gemarra in Tractate Taanit, "No one could come before the Ark unless he was known as being able to sing, knowing a melody, and possessing a pleasant voice that attracts the heart".[57]

Rabbi Judah the Hassid (1150 – 1217) advised:

> Seek melodies and when you pray, say [the prayers] with whichever melody you find pleasant and sweet, with that melody say your prayer, then prayer with great purport, and your heart will follow that which comes from your mouth: for a request or wish, a melody that makes the heart weep; for praise, a melody that makes the heart joyful, that your words should be those of love and joy to whomever sees your heart's intent, that you should bless him with great affection and gladness, as these things prepare the heart.[58]

My father, Rabbi Shlomo Barzilai, showed me the interpretation offered by the Baal Haturim on the verse, "And I sought the Lord" (Deut. 3:23): The single Hebrew word *Va'et'chanan* (And I sought) has the same numerical value as *Shira* (song), that is, Moses sang to G-d to hearken to his prayer.

The power of song is the soul's mode of developing the heart's tendencies, towards strengthening devotion, arousing fervor, uplifting the congregants' mood, purifying their thoughts, and raising them higher in their service of G-d.

---

56 Maimonides on success, pg.7, retrieved from www.toravoda.org.il/14shevi.html
57 b. Taanit 16a
58 Judah Wistinsky, *Sefer Hassidim*, Jerusalem, 1969:8-9. See also Note 7; and also, *Sefer haTefillah beIsrael beHit'patchutah haHistorit* Tel Aviv: 1972, pg.377

Chapter 2 – Chassidism

1. Chassidism – Modes and Methods

Chassidut [Chassidism] is a movement of widespread popular religious renewal established in eastern Europe during the second half of the 18th century, and is still prevalent. Its founder was Rabbi Israel ben Eliezer (1700-1760), who became known as the Baal Shem Tov.

The movement grew and spread rapidly among Jews in the Ukraine, Poland, Galicia, Hungary, and Romania. The background to the growth of Chassidism were the political and economic crises in Poland, which had a direct influence on Polish Jews.

Following the decrees and carnage in the Ukraine and Poland in the 17th and 18th centuries, and their seemingly ceaseless wars, a change began to take place among the Jewish population. In addition to the generally declining economic level, and the heavy taxes demanded by cities and land owners from the community, living conditions declined severely and social tension increased, placing emphasis on moral distortions in the behavior of the rabbis and the community leaders, and undermining their prestige. This caused deep tension and rift between the philanthropists and community leaders, and the Torah scholars, on the one hand, and the general populace who were forced to cease their Torah learning in order to earn their livelihood, and came to despise the scholars who scorned the people. This state of affairs together with the messianic religious crisis of the time created fertile ground for new ideas and for leadership which was not based on scholarly status alone. Changes even occurred to the familiar mode of learning: prosaic study for the sake of Torah knowledge was no longer considered the main aspect of religion, but was expanded to a new mode of devotion to G-d. This approach swept through one community after another, offering a new state of mind and enthusing the hearts of the people.

Chassidism stressed the importance of the person's intentions and religious fervor more than scholarship and meticulous fulfillment of religious precepts. The religious experience, and the aspiration to adhere to Godliness, were the focal aspects: the 613 commandments should be fulfilled through negating or voiding the evil inclination rather than overcoming it. Should one be unable to attain this level of devotion of his own accord, it was attainable through the

Tzaddik [the righteous leader], the Rebbe who was both religious and community leader, concerned with – and involved in – the lives of fellow Jews.

The movement founded by Rabbi Israel ben Eliezer came to call him the Baal-Shem-Tov, simplified to 'the Besht', in light of his exemplary care and concern, his healing of the ill, and the many miraculous acts surrounding him. A group of Torah scholars and other rabbis became his followers and disciples, believing in him by virtue of his unique, enthusing personality. They studied with him, and witnessed a new kind of leadership, that of the figure of the Tzaddik-rabbi, commonly known as 'the Rebbe'. The Besht indeed shaped the image of the 'followers' who became known as Chassidim and who consolidated around the central figure of the Tzaddik, a charismatic leader who provided counsel and guidance to each and every one of his Chassidim.

Shmuel Ettinger noted that:

> The ultimate change that the Besht instituted with his new mode was that he diverted the individual mystic [kabbalist] away from the path of self-isolation and asceticism for the sake of the self, towards the people and guiding the people, thereby shaping the model of the new leader of the Jewish people, that of the Chassidic Tzaddik. This new figure brought changes to the manner of Jewish leadership: *Mishnat haChassidut* states that "The righteous one [Tzaddik] is the foundation of the world"[1] – the world was created for none other but him, who can direct [G-d's] abundance (both material and spiritual) and even cancel decrees of the Holy One, Blessed be He; that is, the destiny of the Tzaddik is to lead the people, and should he not do so, his mission [in life] loses its significance".

Ettinger added:

> Therefore, there is singular meaning to 'devotion', as perceived in the *Mishnat haChassidut*: the Tzaddik cleaves to the Holy One, Blessed be He, on one hand, and is devoted to the people, on the other hand, thereby becoming 'the mean, the mediator between the people and their G-d. Thus, he bears responsibility for the whole community, and is obligated to lower himself from his personal, lofty spiritual station (the Tzaddik's descent) in order to raise His people. To descend [successfully], the Tzaddik must adopt the simple appearance of the populace, mingle with folks in the market, involve himself in seemingly everyday chatter, yet all the while remain in a state of devotion with the upper world, his sole purpose in lowering himself being to raise the whole community to a higher [spiritual] level'.[2]

Only after the Besht had passed away did the principles of Chassidism became unified by his closest disciples, such as the Great Seer Rabbi Dov Ber, known as the "Maggid of Mezhirech" (1704-1772), and his son Rabbi Avraham the Angel (1741-1776); Rabbi Jacob Joseph haCohen (?-D.1782) whose work, *The History of Jacob Joseph [Toldot Yaakov Yosef]*, the first book in Chassidic

---

1   Proverbs 10:25
2   Shmuel Ettinger, *Toldot Am Israel B'et Hachadasha*, Tel Aviv: 1969, Vol. 3:56

literature, was highly influential in shaping Chassidism; Rabbi Yehiel Mikhel from Zloczov (1731-1786); Rabbi Pinhas from Korzec (1726-1791) and his disciple, Rabbi Raphael from Bershad (?-D.1825); and the famous folk-Tzaddik, Rabbi Leib ben Sarah (1730-1791), known as Rebbi Leib Sarah's.

The figure who most closely followed the Besht's leadership was Rebbe Dov Ber of Mezhirech, who endowed Chassidism with its system of mystical concepts and most of its organizational functions. It was during his time that Chassidism strengthened throughout the Ukraine, established roots in Lithuania and Belarus, and began sprouting in central Poland. One of the renowned Rabbis of the time who joined Chassidism was Rabbi Aharon the Great of Karlin (1736-1772). After the death of the Maggid of Mezhirech, no single personality was found who was acceptable as a leader to the general populace, and together with the rapid growth and spread of the movement, Chassidism split into multiple factions, each headed by its own independent Tzaddik.

Disciples of the Maggid of Mezhirech were sent to other communities for the purpose of spreading Chassidism. Among the most renowned 'messengers' were the saintly brothers, Rabbi Elimelekh of Lejask (1720-1791) and Rabbi Zusya of Annopol (1717-1786). Some of these disciple-messengers settled in the locations that they had merely intended to visit, becoming the Tzaddik of that village. In this way, they were able to spread Chassidism [throughout the surrounding villages], giving rise to additional Chassidic leaders.

Despite Chassidism splintering into numerous streams and manifold courts, its teachings stayed true to its deeply enshrined seminal concepts, which continually revealed themselves in later generations, up to the present time, insofar as basic perceptions and central themes. No dispute of any kind has ever violated their central ideological unity.[3]

Chassidism sought to uphold full observance of Torah law while continuing the tradition of Torah study and performance of commandments, yet developed a unique core to its religious practice: it positioned the emotional elements of devotion and fervor as central to serving G-d. This element could be achieved through the new kind of leader, the Tzaddik, who embodied diligent devotion to G-d and sweepingly attracted all those who came in contact with him and accepted his mastery, into this kind of devotion. Chassidism, then, was a populist movement and anyone who acknowledged the Tzaddik's preeminence was invited to join it.

The historian Shimon Dubnov (1860-1941), in *The History of Chassidism*, viewed Chassidism as a movement with a socio-political message. He explained its formulation towards the end of the 18th century as a response that provided for the mental and spiritual needs of the people in general. Dubnov noted that

---

3   Yoram Yakobson, *Toratah shel haChassidut*, Tel Aviv: 1985, Introduction.

Chassidism filled the people with joy, expanding the religious lifestyle that focused chiefly on the burdensome aspect of observance and prosaic scholarship.

The principles of Chassidism include:

1. G-d is in everything, filling all space in the world, and reciprocity exists between the upper and lower world.
2. Prayer, which is the service of G-d, is the mediator between these two worlds and must derive from joy, as it is written: "Serve the Lord with gladness"[4] – therefore, one must pray with fervor in order to bring about the "negation of material existence" and adhere to the G-dly source.

   The prayer of the Chassidim was highly vocal and enthused. They prayed with songs, with body movements and rocking. The Tzaddik, who was usually the person acting as the Shatz (cantor), sometimes achieved ecstasy or transcendence.
3. It is forbidden to disdain sin. Instead, the hidden spark must be drawn out from its shell. Drawing out these sparks weakens the evil force: the sparks that had been concealed within it were part of the evil force's strength, and revealing them weakens it.
4. One should conduct oneself with humility, negating pride. Meekness creates an attitude of fraternity, equality and love with others. Thus, in their own hearts, Chassidim disdained scholars who related to their Torah scholarship with conceit.
5. Because devotion to G-d was considered of utmost importance, not attainable by all but only by one who possessed the highest spiritual level, it was therefore important to adhere to the saintly leader, the Tzaddik, who was like a man of G-d, having the power to influence G-d's providence, and alter or negate G-d's decrees.

It is no wonder that a great many opponents began to appear in these same environments. They included disciples of the Vilna Gaon and others, who held the view that Torah should be studied at degrees of self mortification to the extent of "working themselves to death in the tent of Torah"[5] whereas, by contrast, what they considered as the 'cult' of Chassidism claimed that serving G-d must derive only from a state of joy. Not only did the Chassidim alter the formula of prayers to that known as *Sefarad*, they also wore white on Shabbat, raising the suspicion of their opponents who saw them as too closely resembling the false Shabtaian messianic cult.

---

4   Psalms 100:2
5   Numbers 19:14

2. Music in Chassidism – The Manifestation of Joy

Serving G-d with joy is one of the ideas that strongly influenced the external nature of Chassidism, and Chassidic literature is replete with guidelines for achieving this state. This concept is often quoted as being Chassidism's innovation, and one of its most typical aspects. Even though this view must be related to with some degree of limitation, it is clear that Chassidic teachers sought the negation of sorrow and promoted the positivity of joy.

Chassidism, noted Horodezky (1871-1957), is the teaching of life, unlike the teachings of The Holy Rabbi Isaac ben Shlomo Luria (1534-1572), who was known by his initials, "The Ari". Horodezky added that "not only are you allowed to live, but you are obligated to live, as it is written, 'Do not ignore your flesh'. Nor does one just live, but one must 'live with joy always', and even 'when one fails through transgression, do not dwell on sadness'[6]".

Shmuel Ettinger states the following:

> Emphasis on joy in serving G-d arose both from opposition to, and fear of the outcome of, asceticism, as the Besht himself wrote: 'The physician does better by healing with a beverage that is sweeter than honey'. Joy is a principle foundation in Chassidic doctrine. Asceticism and melancholy of the ultra-devout minority arouse the trait of judgment in the world, in that the whole world is judged for not behaving according to their manner, but the world cannot withstand the trait of judgment, thus joy brings Israel's transgressors back to their Creator, thereby arousing the trait of mercy. In fact, it is possible that emphasizing joy and the uniqueness of the Chassidic way of life deriving from this principle assisted in attracting so many, especially among the young.[7]

The interpretation of Ezekil of Kuzmir (1812-1856), grandfather of Reb Israel Taub who founded the Modzitz Chassidim, on the verse "serve G-d with joy"[8] is well known. [Phonetically, the Hebrew reads thus: *Ivdu et Hashem besimcha*, literally, *serve to G-d with joy*. The word 'et' is comprised of the Hebrew letters alef and tav, being the first and last letters of the alphabet]. Ezekil of Kuzmir asks,

> Why does the word 'et' appear here? Wherever it appears, it indicates that something additional is implied. What can be additional [to G-d] here?

---

6 S. A. Horodetzky, *HaChassidut vehaChassidim*, Tel Aviv: 1951, Book 1:LIV
7 *Toldot Am Israel B'et Hachadasha*, Vol.3:56-57
8 Psalms 100:2

And he provides the response:

The word 'et' consists of the letters alef and tav, that is, a person must always be joyful, no matter what happens in life, from beginning to end [in all things], one should be in a state of joy.[9]

Yitzhak Alfassi (b.1929) wrote that:

Chassidism expanded the issue of joy in performing commandments, and turned joy itself into an exceedingly important value in serving G-d, accordingly 'the Torah commanded' us to pleasure the body on Sabbaths and festivals with meat and fish and wine, so that the body will rejoice in physical pleasures, satisfying the soul which can then rejoice in devotion to the Holy One, Blessed be He. For this reason, Chassidim allowed themselves to drink liquor at every opportunity, in order to increase their joy. Incidentally, this, too, was one of the claims of the "Mitnagdim" [the opponents] against the Chassidim 'who sit every day as though it is a festival', and 'whose days are always spend in laughter, humor, joy and wantonness'.[10]

In the weekly Torah portion of *Vayigash* [Gen. 44:18 to 47:27], the narrative describes how the sons of Jacob went down to Egypt to buy food due to the famine in the land of Canaan. In Egypt, it was known that a famine would occur, thus preparations had been made during seven plentiful years, for the duration of seven harsh years. The Egyptian Pharoah's deputy at the time was none other than their brother. Joseph received them, sold them provisions in sacks, and in the sack of the youngest brother, Benjamin, Joseph hid a goblet with the intention of ensuring that Benjamin would remain with him. Judah, who accepted responsibility for returning Benjamin to their father Jacob, realized the problematic situation, and said: "How can I return to my father, without the lad!"[11] Chassidism interprets these words as follows: "How can I return to my father" means how will I return to my Father in heaven when I have died; "without the lad", means without the joy of youthfulness within me.

Why is joy so important to Chassidim? In the introduction to his article, *The Power of Melody in Chassidic Contemplation and its Role in Socio-Religious Existence,* Yaakov Mazor wrote:

Researchers of Chassidism and musicologists are of the same opinion regarding the important place held by music in the Chassid's life. However, they do not share the same view when offering an explanation for the phenomenon. The most common elucidation relies, on one hand, on the perception of music as the manifestation of happiness while on the other hand, others see its importance as being the fulfillment of a directive from the Chassidic leaders who shaped Chassidic ideology, to worship G-d from a state of joy. This is how

---

9   *Imrei Saul*, Tel Aviv: 1960, page 412 section 25.
10 Alfassi, *Bisdeh haChassidut,* Tel Aviv: 1986:54
11 Genesis 44:34

Yishayahu Tishbi and Yosef Dan, for example, reach their conclusions concerning the doctrine of joy in Chassidism: 'One of the significant results of Chassidism riding on the wave of joy is the development of ways to worship G-d through **melody and dance** [bold as per original] which penetrated into the religious life of the people and changed their customary ways. Wertheim, by contrast, sees [the importance of music] as a result of Chassidic leaders recognizing that *awakening that leads to an outpouring of the heart and the negation of material existence and the soul cleaving to higher worlds can only be achieved through melody*. Since devotion is one of the foundations of Chassidic doctrine, it becomes obvious that music is central to it.

Two of the most esteemed researchers of Jewish music, Idelsohn and Avenary, adopt both of the above explanations. They feel that the centrality of music is a result of the connection between music, and the dual traits of joy and devotion.

Towards the end of the introduction, Mazor concludes that:

> Any attempt to explain the centrality of music in Chassidic society through one perception alone is doomed in advance to fail. It is presumable that music was seen by Chassidic leaders from more than just one angle, though music per se was common to all views.[12]

Perhaps the idea derives from the Germarrah which relates how Rava would preface his lectures with some light-hearted remarks. The commentator Rashi (1040-1105) explains this to mean that Torah scholars' hearts open up to wisdom out of joy.[13] Thus, notes Yoram Yakobson, joy is the principle behind awakening the heart, the factor that allows elation in both study and fervor. This joy is the joy of mitzvas. At all times, even during the most difficult hours that the world knows, and in all places, we are commanded to be joyful always, thus we must enthuse our hearts in the service of G-d, that is, we must arouse joy.[14]

Expanding on this approach, the Chabad Chassidic movement relates to the following verse: "Then they will say among the nations, 'The Lord has done great things with these; the Lord has done great things with us, we are rejoiced'."[15] Chabad explains that *then* means *when the Messiah comes*; *they will say among the nations* means *the nations of the world will ask: why did the Children of Israel merit miracles and wonders? Why did 'the Lord do great things with these'?* And the people of Israel will respond: Do you know why *'the Lord has done great things with us'?* Because *we are rejoiced* – we were meritorious by virtue of our joy.[16]

---

12 'Yovel', Vol.7, Jerusalem: 2002. *Research in Honor of Israel Adler*, pg.23
13 b. Shabbat 30b
14 *Toratah shel haChassidut*, pg.78
15 Psalms 126:2-3.
16 From *The Collection of Chabad Sayings*, (*Otzar Pitgamei Chabad*), Brooklyn, NY: 1994:184, in the name of the last *Admor* Rabbi M.M. Schneersohn

Moreover:

It is explained, in Chassidism, that joy breaches barriers; if a person faces difficulty, it is joy that can help the person create the inner energy that will remove the barrier and even negate it. Then even the Holy One, blessed be He, assists that person, because of that person's joy, which causes joy in the spiritual worlds, and makes the Holy One, Blessed be He, go out of His way, as it were, to change the ways of Nature into good and blessed ones. Many people who approached the last Rebbe of Chabad, Rabbi Menahem Mendel Shneersohn (1902-1994) for advice and a blessing in matters medical or other difficulties in their lives, received his response that they should be in a state of joy, which would help breach the barriers of Nature and alter the evil decree. And this follows the renowned saying of the *Admor Tzemach Tzedek*, "Think good thoughts, and indeed things will be good".[17]

Along these same lines, Chabad relates the following parable: In the times of the Besht, there lived in the township of Lubavitch a Jew whom everyone called 'Reb Israel the Happy One', for he was accustomed to saying, "A mitzva with no intention is like a body with no soul. The intention behind the mitzva derives from another mitzva: *I am the Lord your G-d who took you out of the land of Egypt*. The Creator, blessed be He, rescues humans from all kinds of tricky situations, and if I, Srulik, a mere nothing, am considered meritorious for upholding a commandment given by G-d, then I should be jumping and dancing with glee".[18]

It was commonly known that in the Mir Yeshiva, the joy and dancing on Simhat Torah went far beyond the customary level. Rabbi Yeruham Leibowitz, a *Mashgiach* [spiritual supervisor] there, wondered about which of the two states was more important to G-d, the fasting and seriousness of Yom Kippur, or the joyful worship of Simhat Torah.[19]

Music holds an exceedingly important position in Chassidism, and is one of the typically Chassidic norms introduced by the Besht as part of his Chassidic methodology. One of the principles of Chassidism states the following:

A joyous heart, and fervent soul, longing and yearning for our Father in Heaven, and all these manifestations can be reached by the Chassid through melody, which has the power to uplift the soul along the rungs of G-d's ladder and bring the Chassid to higher planes.[20]

Joy breaks through all boundaries, even the barrier of exile. Joy bears the special attribute of being able to bring about the redemption, and even the Hebrew letters of the word 'joy' – *Sa'me'ach*, being *sin-mem-khet*, are the same letters as those of Messiah – *Mashiach*, being *mem-shin-khet* with the addition of the letter

---

17 Ibid.
18 From *The Collection of Chabad Sayings,* pg.185 from *Likutei Dibburim 1*, pg.115.
19 Rabbi Yoel Schwarz, *Perek Shirah*, Jerusalem: 2003:77
20 Shmuel Zalmanov, *Sefer haNiggunim*, Kfar Chabad: 1985:19

yud. The late Rabbi M. M. Shneersohn used to declare, announce, suggest, ask, even demand, that joy would be added to all our actions, in order to bring the full and true redemption of the righteous Mashiach.[21]

Joy was so important that Rabbi Israel Friedmanof Ruzhyn (1797-1851) would quip: "I fear that Israel's sinners are also invited to the world to come, as they are always, throughout their lives, in a state of joy!"[22]

3. The Innovative Aspect of Song in The Chassidic Perception of Serving G-d

In reviewing ideas presented thus far, it is apparent that Chassidism related to song as an inseparable part of prayer which leads to worshipping G-d. When perusing the daily prayer texts, some of which are comprised of Psalms and sections fixed by the Great Assembly or liturgical poets, innumerable references to song and singing are manifest throughout all the prayers. Here are several examples:

In the *Shacharit* morning service are the phrases:

A Song at the dedication of the House [...] I will extol you, Lord, for you have raised me up [...]. Sing praise to the Lord, you Godly ones, and give thanks to His holy name.[23]

Further on, in the *Baruch She'amar* blessing, we find: "And in the songs of David your servant, we praise and exalt and glorify and recall Your name, Our King, [...]".

A song of thanksgiving [...] Serve the Lord with joy, come before Him with gladness [...].[24]

In the *Yishtabach* prayer, we find:

Song and praise, glory and singing.

In the *Yotzer Or* prayer of the angels:

And all open their mouths in holiness and purity, in song and melody, and they bless and adore [...], they utter hymns and chant praises.

---

21 Explanation to Melody 12 in Joyous Melody 2, on the disc of *Collected Chabad Melodies*
22 Simha Raz, *Sayings of Chassidim*. Jerusalem: 1989:179
23 Psalms 30: 1-2, 5
24 Psalms 100: 1-2

In the blessing for redemption:

> For this, the loved ones praised and uplifted, companions offered chants and songs and praises.

And:

> To You they responded with song and great joy [...] with a new song, the redeemed extolled.

There are a great many other such examples.[25] In light of this, it would be reasonable to question what the Chassidic approach innovated when determining that song should be an integral part of serving G-d, as we clearly see that song did hold a place in prayer.

It seems clear that even prior to the existence of the Chassidic movement, song was clearly an integral part of serving G-d, used to glorify, praise and extol G-d's Name, through chants and singing. Song became a part of the expression of prayer, having the sole purpose of praising and glorifying G-d's greatness: this designation became its most important aspect. However, the impact of singing and offering praise was directed towards G-d rather than people.

This, then, is the approach presented by Chassidism: while song and praise to G-d are an important objective per se, song contains the no less important goal of allowing worship of G-d with joy, because it is impossible to serve and pray to G-d out of sorrow. Before serving G-d, one must prepare oneself. This is done through negating the sadness within us, thereby allowing joy to exist. Song is needed to help us negate our sadness. The role of song is to bring about joy, and only serving G-d joyfully is considered perfect worship. Thus song and chant assist in reaching the ability to serve G-d joyfully. In my meeting with Professor Schleifer (also see the section on Interviews), the latter noted that because Chassidim integrated playing of music into their doctrines relating to the soul, and that all service of G-d is within the human soul, therefore music influences the soul.[26]

In an article by Idelsohn, *Chassidic Music,* the author states:

> Not only did this movement influence synagogal music but created a new form, a new type of Hebrew music known as "Chassidic music". It developed not only as a result of the movement's doctrines which, like the doctrines of any movement, bears influence on the creation of new musical forms, but chiefly because these doctrines applied exceedingly great

---

25 See also, among others, Psalms 95:1, 96:1, 98:5, 81:2, 27, 104, 33.
26 The son of *the Admor of Kassan*, Rabbi Yishaya Meshulam Feish Rattenburg of Jerusalem, drew my attention to the fact that it is possible to find proof of music being able to change a situation's status to its opposite, with a quote from the Kuzari, 2:65 : "[...] of it (music), it is said that it shifts the soul from **one dimension to its opposite.**"

importance to music, raising it to the level of an avenue through which one can attain the fundamental goal of Chassidism: to the plane of boundless joy and fervor.[27]

Let us consider the explanation offered by the Admor of Slonim in his book, *Talalei Orot*,[28] on a section of Midrash:

> Whoever recites song is forgiven all his transgressions. Whoever recites song daily indicates his pleasure in the way the Holy One, blessed be He, conducts the world existence, however He may choose to do so, whether by mercy or by judgment. Whoever **receives it with joy** and believes that the Creator leads the whole wholly for the good is worthy of the next world, in that already in this world he is immersed in the next world.

Let us once again look closely at the texts of the songs and prayers referred to above: we find that their language is very specific, for example;

> And with the songs of David your servant.

How can we use the songs of David? The following examples offer a range of responses:

> We praise and extol and glorify You and recall Your name, our King.
> Sing to the Lord, the whole earth.
> For this, the cherished people praised and uplifted G-d.
> To You, we offer song.
> And they all open their mouths, in song […] and bless and praise and glorify the Name of G-d.
> Go sing to the Lord.
> With song we extol Him.
> Sing to G-d with the lyre.

The author of *Yesod veShoresh ha'Avodah* (The Foundation and Root of Service) claims that the essence of song is to praise G-d. Thus, he offers an explanation for the verse, "For it is good to sing praise to our G-d":[29]

> It is appropriate that a person be profoundly joyful and deeply acknowledge the Creator, may His name be blessed, and be uplifted for being merited the opportunity to sing to, and extol, the Creator.[30]

In other words, we offer praise for being considered worthy of praising G-d, and this is the essence of our song.

---

27 A. Z. Idelsohn, *Haneginna haChassidit,* NY: 1931, Chapter 1, pg.1.
28 Jerusalem: 2003:401
29 Psalms 147:1
30 *Talalei Orot,* pg.200

In *Rashi's Siddur* (prayerbook), the explanation offered regarding the *Psukei D'zimra* (Verses of Song) is very direct:

> Rabbi Shamlai interpreted (Talmud Bavli, Brachot 32b) that a person should always relate first to praise of G-d, and only thereafter pray, which is why the Sages instituted the *Psukei D'zimra* and *Hodu La'shem* prayers, and all the songs before and after them, so that first G-d is praised, and only then does one stand and pray.[31]

In conclusion, song prior to Chassidism was intended to glorify G-d, while song in Chassidism served not only to praise the Holy One, blessed be He, which is an act aimed at something external to us, but also to act internally on ourselves, on improving the nature of service to G-d. In later sections of this book, we come to realize the extent to which the Chassidic approach of dance, melody and song influences fervor.

4. Joy as the Remedy for Sorrow

"The main value of music is its ability to bring about awakening and joy, as sorrow comes from the *Sitra Achra* ('Other Side')", said Avraham Zvi Idelsohn (1882-1938).[32]

The conceptual foundation for the doctrine of joy in Chassidism is the determination that sadness derives from evil forces, and that joy indicates a person's ability to overcome the evil temptation. The state of sorrow and the state of falling into sinful behavior are interconnected, and the evil inclination attempts to bring sorrow into the human through feelings of sadness over even the lightest of transgressions. Chassidism instructs the individual to ignore this sorrow, and become awakened to serving G-d joyfully, which is of greater importance than the sorrow induced by regret over that transgression.[33]

It is said that the Besht spoke at length and in great praise of joy, denouncing sorrow. The Besht wrote:

> [...] to always be in a state of joy, and to think and believe in absolute faith that the *Shechina* (holy Presence) is in [the individual] and is guarding [him].[34]

---

31 Shlomo Buber, *Siddur shel Rashi*, Jerusalem: 1999, Ch.6, pg.6
32 In *haNeginah haChassidit*, pg.4
33 Hebrew Encyclopedia, *Chassidut*, pg.810
34 *Baal Shem Tov on the Torah*, Jerusalem, Portion of *Ekev*, section 38.

And the Besht adds:

> The main thing is that one should always be joyful, especially so when cleaving [to G-d]. For without joy, it is impossible to cleave to the Holy One, blessed be He.[35] [...] When the leaders of the generation are joyful, it arouses joy throughout the whole world.[36]

The story is told of an incident that occurred at the end of Yom Kippur. It is the custom to bless the moon at the end of the Fast day. But one year, it happened that the heavens were overcast, and clouds filled the skies, so that the moon could not be seen, nor was there any chance of seeing it due to the stormy weather. The Besht was deeply sorrowed, for he saw, with his holy spirit, that if the moon would not be blessed, there would, G-d forbid, be uprisings against the Jews during that year, and he wished with all his might to prevent that situation. But the moon could not be seen, and the Besht entered his room with great sadness. His Chassidic followers, unaware of the reason for his sorrow, were joyful, just as they were every year at the end of the Fast, having experienced their Rabbi's holy service of G-d. They danced happily, and gradually managed to draw the Besht into their dancing. Suddenly, in the midst of all that joy, some Chassidim came to say that they had been outside and seen the moon. It was now possible to utter the blessing. The whole gathering went outside, recited the blessing, and the Besht related that what he had sought to achieve through his own deep concentration did not succeed, whereas the Chassidim, through their joy alone, merited a successful result.[37]

The very fact that a person merits the chance to serve G-d should be enough to fill that person's heart with joy. Joy is the foundation of unceasing hope, of faith in the world, of belief in good deeds, of faith in the ability to correct the self, which is the light of life. In contrast, sadness is the source of despair and negative actions.[38]

On this same matter, the Midrash *Shokher Tov* relates, in the name of Rabbi Ievo, to the verse, "Serve G-d with joy, come before Him with gladness".[39] The explanation offered is that "when you stand to pray, your heart should be glad that you are praying to G-d [...] for that is the real joy".[40]

---

35 Ibid, section 41
36 Ibid, Portion of *Ki Tavo*, section 6.
37 Ibid, in Note 6, and in *Ohr Haganuz*, Jerusalem: 1979, Introduction, pg.17-18.
38 Aharon Aescoli, *haCHassidut bePolin*, Jerusalem: 1998:31
39 Psalms 100:2
40 Shlomo Tzofioff, author of the *Scroll of the Song of Songs*, pg.14

Rabbi Chaim Eisenberg, the Chief Rabbi of Austria, refers to a specific verse and interpreted it thus:

> Draw me, we will run after you, [...] we will be glad and rejoice in You,[41] means that by virtue of 'being glad and rejoicing in You', that is, being in a state of joy, we will be worthy of being drawn by G-d and being able to run after Him.

Sadness per se is not a transgression, notes Rabbi Hanoch of Alexander, but the heart rending that sadness can cause, cannot even be caused by a transgression. When we say 'joy', we do not mean the joy derived in performance of the mitzva, which refers to one of the levels. Rather, we mean 'anything but sorrow'. A Jew who is not joyful in being a Jew, is in fact ungrateful.[42]

An anecdote is told of the Seer of Lublin who would travel as little as possible, being unable to fall asleep anywhere but in a bed prepared by a G-d-fearing beadle. He was invited once by Rabbi Joseph of Ostilla to the latter's home. Rabbi Joseph asked a G-d-fearing carpenter to prepare a worthy bed for the guest. The carpenter cleansed himself and prepared a bed worthy of the Tzaddik. When the Tzaddik went to lie down on the bed, he immediately jumped again, crying out "It jabs, it's jabbing me!" Rabbi Joseph was left wondering. The Tzaddik requested that the carpenter come to him. "When did you build this bed?", the Seer asked. "During the Three Weeks", answered the carpenter, "and tears streamed from my eyes over the destruction of the Temple". Then the Seer said, "I cannot sleep in this bed, as it reeks of sadness and gloom".[43]

In the *Book of Customs* of the Hatam Sofer, the following appears: "His joy, always visible on his face, became far greater when he learned, which he did with wonderful, boundless exhilaration and fervor". In footnote 110, we find: "When he began learning, one could feel no sadness in him whatever [...] as sadness is improper, especially when seeking wisdom and attunement, for nothing prevents such attainment as sadness!".[44]

An anecdote is told of a Chassid who came to his mentor, Rabbi Yitzhak of Nechsiz. The Chassid told the Rabbi how sad he was that the wheat for his supervised unleavened bread [*matzah shmurah*] had soured ant that he would have to eat matzah made from regular flour. The Rabbi responded, "Matzah shmurah is an adornment of the mitzva, while joy on a festival derives directly from the

---

41 Canticles 1:4
42 Aaron Aescoli, *haCHassidut bePolin*, Jerusalem: 1998:107
43 B'Oholei Tzaddikim: Sippurim uMashalim al Hagaddah shel Pessach, Shalom Meir haCohen Wallach, Bnei Brak: 1989:283
44 *Sefer Minhagei heCHattam Sofer*, published by Juda Leib Shielel, Pressburg 5750.

Torah, therefore it is better to eat simple matzah with joy than matzah shmurah with sorrow".[45]

"Chassidism teaches that sadness is a demonic act", stated Yoram Yakobson. "Chassidism even goes so far in denouncing sadness, that it rejects the sadness involved in moral religious reckoning over sins and transgressions as an ingenious prank on the part of the Evil Inclination". Yakobson refers to an excerpt from the testament of the *Riba"sh* found on page 11:

> Sometimes the evil inclination misleads a person, convincing that person that he has committed a terrible misdemeanor, even though it is nothing but an arbitrary stringency or not a misdemeanor at all. When a person is sad, this force gains the ability to negate one's serving of the Holy One, blessed be He. This deceit needs to be understood; then the person should tell the Evil Inclination, 'I do not pay any attention to the stringency of which you speak, where you seek to negate my service of G-d, and you are lying to me. Even if it were slightly true, it would be more satisfying to my Creator if I did not keep this stringency about which you inform me, causing me sadness while serving Him. On the contrary, I will serve him in gladness, as this is the great rule, for my service is not meant for myself, but to please the Holy One, blessed be He. […] for this is the greatest rule: anyone who can, should beware of sorrow".[46]

Further to the above, a wonderful interpretation is offered by Rabbi Moshe Yehuda Taub of Kuzmir, in his book *Divrei Mosheh*, for the verse: "And Melchizedek king of Salem brought forth bread and wine; and he was priest of God the Most High".[47]

'Bread' is the Torah, as it is said, "Come, eat of my bread,[48] while 'wine' alludes to joy, as it is said, "And wine gladdens the heart of Mankind'[49]; which indicates that engagement with Torah must be out of joy and not out of sadness. Only then can one be 'a priest of G-d Most High', that is, only in this manner can one's service of the Holy One, blessed be He, be of an innocence that rises upon high.[50]

The power of a lively Chassidic tune can banish the heart's dolefulness and sorrow – both these characteristics are utterly despised in the Chassidic doctrine; yet how valorous it is in replacing them with the new light of joy, exhilaration and gaiety, desirable traits of the soul, and so highly praised in Chassidism.[51]

---

45 Ibid, pg.27
46 Toratah shel Chassidut, pg.73-74. See also, Sefer Toldot haChassidut, Tel Aviv: 1930:56
47 Genesis 14:18
48 Proverbs 9:5
49 Psalms 104:15
50 In *Simchu Tzaddikim*, Bet Shemesh: 2004:27
51 Shmuel Zalmanov, *Sefer haNiggunim*, Kfar habad: 1985:19

Rabbi Eliyahu Munk (1900-1980) explained the importance of the songs of Simhat Torah:

> With the singing of these Simhat Torah songs, the joy of the day peaks. This mood, at the end of the sequence of festivals during the month of Tishrei derives in the long run from a deep awareness of the atonement of misdeeds of Yom Kippur, but also has a purpose: to strengthen us as we return to routine, and give us the power, confidence and courage we need before the joyless wintery days. For the *Shechina,* which we hope will be among us, does not reside among us 'out of laziness nor out of sorrow nor out of mockery nor out of lightheadedness nor out of nonsense, but out of the joy in performing a mitzva, as it is said: 'But now bring me a minstrel.' And it came to pass, when the minstrel played, that the hand of the LORD came upon him'.[52] Therefore hilarity is related to with severity, as is pride that prevents expressing any kind of happiness, and true joy is found in the joy of the mitzva.[53]

With regard to the above, my dear friend the Chief Rabbi of Austria, Chaim Eisenberg, referred to *Ben Ish Chai,* written by Rabbi Yosef Yitzhak, and the verse: "Go eat your bread with joy"[54], [translit: *Lech echol besimcha lachmecha*], where the letters comprising the word *besimcha* are the same as those of *machshava* [ie: thought], which indicates that even joy must derive from a thoughtful state: in other words, through self-control rather than through hilarity.[55]

During the festival of Sukkot, it was customary to pour the water with joy, according to the verse: "And you drew water with gladness from the wells of salvation"[56]. The use of two words describing happiness, *sasson* [joy] and *simcha,* [happiness] need to be understood: is there any difference between them? The Malb"im, in his interpretative book on Isaiah (35:1) explains as follows:

> *Simcha* is in the heart, and *sasson* is its manifestation. There can be *sasson* without *simcha,* such as when a person wears festive clothes, when violins and drums play, yet that person's soul is in a mournful state. There can also be *simcha* without *sasson,* such as when a person wears the garb of mourning but is inwardly happy. The Torah aspires to original *simcha,* deriving from a person's heart, thus used the expression "*simcha*", as is written: 'And you rejoiced in your festivals, and you were happy'[57] while the Prophet Isaisah said: 'And you drew water with *sasson* [joy]', where the expression '*sasson*' indicates that such joy is connected to externality. Thus our Sages determined that the water must be poured with great joy.[58]

---

52 Kings II 3:15
53 *Olam haTefillot,* Jerusalem: 1994, Part 2, pg. 325
54 Ecclesiastes 9:7
55 *Ben Ish Chai,* Jerusalem: 1986, Section on Laws, pg.189
56 Isaiah 12:3
57 Deuteronomy 17:14-15
58 See Avraham Orenstein, *haNe'un vehaDarosh,* Bnei Brak 1969:146

Rabbi Saul Yedidyah Eleazar Taub (1882-1947), the second Admor of Modzitz, also related to the difference between joy and happiness. Concerning the blessing "May the barren one surely rejoice and be glad as her children are restored to her in joy" from the *Sheva Brachot* [Seven Blessings] recited over the bride and groom, Rabbi Taub formulates the following question: it is obvious that if her children are restored to her, she would be glad; why, then, should she be glad, if she is barren? What cause for joy could there be? After all, she does not yet have children! The Rabbi provides the interpretation: there is a difference between joy and happiness. The first indicates the hope directed towards the future, as is found in Psalms 19:6 – "He will rejoice as the strong man who is able to run his course". Why should one rejoice before the wreath of victory is achieved? Does it not say, "Let not he who girds himself in armor, boast as he who removes it".[59] Indeed, if he is mighty and strong, he will rejoice even before the final outcome, in the hope and confidence that he will overcome and be victorious, as is written, "I rejoice at Your word, as one who finds great spoils".[60] Over a statement or promise, one might rejoice as though the outcome is already determined. But happiness indicates that the outcome has already been achieved, as is written: "For You, Lord, have me glad through Your work; I will exult in the works of Your hands", etc.[61] In other words, once the action has been completed, the person is happy. Thus the interpretation of "May the barren one surely rejoice and be glad" is that although she is still childless, she is joyful over the hope that the future promises, but once her children are gathered to her, that is, once the state of having children already exists, and her children are with her, then she can certainly be happy.[62]

Concerning this very same blessing, Rabbi Israel Taub (1849-1921) of Modzitz stated: What is the meaning of "Who created joy and happiness"? 'Created' [*bara*] shares the same linguistic Hebrew root as 'health' [*bri'ut*], thus, joy and happiness in performing a mitzva brings the person good health.[63]

Orenstein relates to the importance of happiness in his elucidation on the difference between the festivals of Passover and Sukkot, where the former is called 'The time of our freedom' and the latter, 'The time of our rejoicing'. Orenstein explains:

> The festival of Passover and all the miracles performed there were the work of the Holy One, blessed be He, and Israel was not required to take any action; on the contrary, in Exo-

---

59 Kings I, 20:11
60 Psalms 119:162
61 Psalms 92:5
62 *Imrei Saul,* Tel Aviv: 1960, pg.415 section 38.\
63 *Atkinu Se'udata,* Jerusalem: 1992: 71, referencing "Divrei Israel".

dus 14:13, Moses approaches them and says, 'Stand still and see the salvation of the Lord'. The meaning of 'salvation' refers only to salvation of the Lord, and not of Israel. However, regarding Sukkot, all the activity reflects 'after you have gathered in from your threshing floor and your wine press'.[64] In other words, the activities are undertaken by the people themselves. We see that during Passover, we are joyful because of another's joy (that is, the Holy One, blessed be He), and during Sukkot, our joy is for ourselves. Therefore Sukkot is called 'the time of our rejoicing'. Further to the above, the moralists (opponents of Chassidism) interpret the verse, 'But as for me, I trust in Your mercy; my heart will rejoice in Your salvation; I will sing to the Lord, who has dealt bountifully with me'.[65] In other words, I am happy over G-d's salvation. As for 'I will sing to the Lord', when am I able to sing? When 'the Lord has dealt bountifully with me', that is, when G-d assists people by virtue of their trying to assist themselves through their own actions.[66]

True happiness can be reached through song, according to a response given by Rabbi Matana to the question put by the Germarra, and already mentioned: "From where do we understand that song derives from Torah?" Rabbi Matana responds: "Rav Matana said : 'Because you did not serve the Lord your G-d with joy and gladness of heart, by reason of the abundance of all things'.[67] What does serving with joy and glad-heartedness mean? It refers to song.[68] On this issue, Rashi adds his explanation: "A person does not sing except in a state of joy and glad-heartedness, as is written, 'Behold my servants shall sing for joy of heart'."[69]

From the verse "Because you did not serve the Lord your G-d with happiness"[70], Rabbi Simha Bunem of Przysucha (1767-1827) understood the great importance of happiness, and said:

> The transgressions that would lead to curses of rebuke were not listed in the Torah: the only transgression noted specifically is 'Because you did not serve the Lord your G-d with happiness'. The explanation, then, is as follows: in the weekly portion of *Ki Tavo*, Moses commands six tribes to stand on Mt. Gerizim, the mountain of blessing, in order to bless the people, while the six remaining tribes stand on Mt. Eval, the mountain of curses, in order to curse the people. The Torah then details all that will happen to anyone who does not listen to G-d's word, and enumerates the many curses and penalties, but does not provide the name of any specific transgression which results in these punishments. At the end of this list, the Torah states the reason for these punishments as being 'because you did not serve the Lord your G-d with happiness'. Thus we learn how important happiness is to the Holy One, blessed be He.[71]

---

64 Deuteronomy 14:13
65 Psalms 13:6
66 Avraham Orenstein, *haNe'un vehaDrosh,* Bnei Brak 1969:138-139
67 Deutoronomy 28:47
68 b. *Arachin,* 11a
69 Isaiah 65:14
70 Deuteronomy 28:47
71 See *Sefer Iturei Torah,* Tel Aviv: 1970, A. J. Grinberg, Vol.6, pg.167

Rabenu Bachyeh, in his interpretation of the Torah, notes that from the above verse we learn that we must perform mitzvas with happiness, and that performing the mitzva happily is a mitzva in itself. Therefore, in addition to the merit received for performing the mitzva, we are also merited for doing it happily. Thus, G-d will punish the person who has undertaken a mitzva, but does so without happiness.[72]

Chassidism used the motif of happiness widely, and the Chassidim held many celebrations. They related in particular to the three Sabbath meals, or other meals that mark the completion of a mitzva, with song, dance and drinking liquor, thereby negating and avoiding all acts of self-mortification.

Two kinds of happiness are predominant: one is innovative, motivating service of G-d, and the second is the psychological state reached while serving G-d. According to most books on Chassidism, the second form is the correct one, as this kind of happiness integrates with fervor.

> One of the most important consequences of Chassidism launching its doctrines on song is the development of ways to serve G-d through music and dance, which penetrated the religious life of the populace and changed its ways.[73]

Rabbi Ezekil of Kuzmir (1812-1856) concludes this concept in three words: *Ki besimcha tetzu* – "for in joy, shall you go forth".[74] The explanation offered is that through happiness, it is possible to overcome all obstacles and troubles. The main thing is to be happy, and through this happiness, it is possible to extricate oneself from any grim situation.[75] Furthermore, the Rav explained as follows:

> A person must be happy, for even artificial happiness, enforced and despite oneself, is better than sorrow and bitterness though they may be true.[76]

Rabbi Dov Ber, the Maggid of Mezhirech (1704-1772) wrote a great deal in praise of song and happiness. In one instance, he referred to a person who is praying but is surrounded by others who are discussing everyday issues, rather than matters of prayer. If those everyday issues are joyous ones, the person praying can uplift them, and by virtue of doing so, increase joy in the Upper Worlds while creating great fervor in himself. If the everyday issues are sorrowful, however, it is difficult to uplift them.

---

72 Booklet *Otzar haYediot,* Part I , pg. 171
73 *Encyclopedia Ivrit*, on Chassidut, pg. 810
74 Isaiah 55
75 *Imrei Saul*, pg. 412, section 26
76 Ibid, section 27

The power of such prayer generates lights. The Maggid adds an explanation of the verse: "Light is sown for the righteous, and happiness for the upright of heart".[77] It is worth reviewing this interpretation thoroughly.[78]

Rabbi Moshe of Kozenice, quoting Rabbi Zusya (1717-1786), stated that it is indeed possible to serve G-d through weeping and sorrow, but this is only appropriate during the Days of Repentance, when it is worth increasing the number of plea-prayers offered that request G-d's forgiveness for all of our unacceptable acts during the year that passed. For the greater part of the year, the opposite is true. We should increase the amount of happiness and lessen our tears. He draws this understanding from the verse: "Those who sow with tears shall reap with gladness. Though he goes out with weeping, the measurer of the seeds, he shall surely return bearing his sheaves with gladness".[79] Rabbi Zusya offered the following explanation of the above verse:

> There are two kinds of service of G-d. There are those who serve through weeping and tears, always crying over the destruction of the Temple, over the sorrow and the exile of the *Shechina* [Divine Presence], while others serve G-d with gladness, with happiness, song and praise. This is the meaning of 'Those who sow in tears will harvest with gladness', that is, those who serve G-d with tears and those who serve Him with joy will both receive merit from the Holy One, blessed be He, for their service. Yet there is a difference between them: 'he who goes out weeping' refers to those who serve G-d through their crying, but are no more than 'bearers of the seed' and receive their merit according to the measure of their service. However, 'he shall surely return with gladness' refers to those who serve G-d with happiness, and receive unmeasured merit, which is understood from 'bearing his sheaves', that is, bearing a great amount of good merit for their service.[80]

Concerning the passage, "Blessed is the man who trusts in the Lord and the Lord will be his security"[81], Rabbi Saul Yedidyah Eliezer Taub of Modzitz (1882-1947) explores the doubling of language in "who trusts [*bote'ach*] in the Lord" and "the Lord will be his security [*mivtacho*]". He explains as follows: there are people who think they have security, saying to themselves that it surely cannot hurt to say they are secure, even though in the depths of their hearts they are not truly secure and instead, are sad and worried over their lowly state. This is an incorrect attitude: through expressing security, one should be able to leave

---

77 Psalms 97:11
78 Rivka Shatz Oppenheimer, *Maggid D'varav keYaakov*, Jerusalem: 1990, section 29; and see sections 95, 109, 118 on song.
79 Psalms 126:5-6
80 Eliezer Lippa Cahana, *Birkot Avi*, Jerusalem: 1995, quoting the Admor of Spinka, pg.119. See also, lengthy exploration of the service of G-d in sorrow during the days of repentance.
81 Jeremiah 17:7

sorrow behind and be in a state of joy and hope for salvation. This is why the verse states "Blessed is the man who trusts in the Lord"; and what, then, is the security realized? "The Lord will be his security". The term "will be" is none other than a synonym for happiness, as is noted in *Vayikra Rabbah*:81. Thus, happiness is one's security.[82]

Elsewhere, one of the seven blessings at the *chuppah* [bridal canopy] states "Happily gladden these beloved". Rabbi Saul of Modzitz once again pointed out the duality of language in "Happily gladden", explaining that this alludes to the concept of joy causing greater joy, one happy state leading to another, and that the proximity of these two joyful situations is the beloved pair itself.[83]

When Rabbi Shmuel Eliyahu Taub of Modzitz (1906-1984), on whom the glow of joy could always be seen, was asked why worry never seemed to color his face, he answered:

I, too, worry, and many concerns encompass me, but I have packaged all these into a 'suitcase' which I open once a day, and from which I take forth the bunch of concerns for an hour, then return them, and close the suitcase well, as though it no longer existed. Why should I be concerned over all my worries throughout the whole day?[84]

Geshuri (1897-1977), in his article, *Concerning the Doctrine of Music in Chassidism*,[85] wrote:

The Chassidic movement seemed to many people like a new revelation in Judaism. With every new, popular spiritual movement connected to Torah or a new method, renewed interest in folk music arises. This is a generality applicable to all popular movements, and all the more so in regard to Chassidism, in which music was not only influenced and renewed, but became an important tool for contemplating Godliness and simplifying materialism. Its main goal was to distance depression and despair from the Jewish home and instruct congregants in how to serve the Creator from a state of happiness and exhilaration. This is the vital position that music and song held in the lives of the Chassidim.

Further on in the article, Geshuri relates to types of music. He states, on page 73:

Music expressed happiness and exhilaration, in line with the approach propounded by the Besht that the *Shechinah* does not rest upon a person except out of joy, and 'even if that person has failed through a transgression, he shall not be sorrowed but shall be truly regretful over what has occurred and then must continue to be happy in the blessed Creator'. This Chassidic approach of happiness and pleasure is highly conspicuous in songs of the Besht, songs that bear the mark of joie de vivre and happiness in nature.

---

82 *Atkinu Seudatah*, pg.69, cited from *Imrei Saul*.
83 Ibid, pg. 71
84 *Mor miBsamim*, 1983, pg. 18
85 Rabbi Y. L. Meimon, *Sefer haBesht*, Jerusalem: 1960, pg.70

The above attitude can be seen in the Talmud commenting on Psalms written by King David: commencing as they do with "A song of David" indicates that he first sang, and only thereafter did the *Shechinah* make itself felt. This teaches that the *Shechinah* cannot be felt when one is in a state of sorrow or laziness, of lightheadedness or hilarity, or commonplace thoughts, but only in a state of joy when performing a mitzva, as is said: 'But now bring me a minstrel.' And it came to pass, when the minstrel played, that the hand of the Lord came upon him'.[86,87] Elsewhere the Talmud relates to the verse, "I said of laughter: 'It is mad'; and of mirth: 'What does it accomplish?'"[88]. Referring to 'Of mirth, 'What does it accomplish?', the Talmud states that this is not joy deriving from performing a mitzva but rather, indicates that the *Shechinah* cannot be felt when one is in a state of sorrow or laziness, of lightheadedness or hilarity, or commonplace thoughts, thus this is joy for joy's sake, as is said: 'But now bring me a minstrel.' And it came to pass, when the minstrel played, that the hand of the Lord came upon him'.[89] Rashi relates to this same verse and interprets the Germarra to mean that 'Bring me a minstrel' indicates that it is a good deed to cause the *Shechina* to be present.[90]

The Rabbis therefore teach that one cannot lead the prayer service when one is in a state of sorrow or laziness, of hilarity or idle conversation, of lightheadedness or commonplace thoughts, but only from joy per se.[91] The Rabbinic interpreters known as *Baalei Tosafot* explained this to mean "it was customary to recite *Psukei Dzimra* [Verses of Song] and *Ashrei* prior to praying".[92] In Ecclesiastes[93] we also find the verse, "For to the man that is good in His sight He gives wisdom, and knowledge, and joy". In this way, the Torah makes a connection between joy, wisdom and knowledge.

Eliezer Steinmann, in the introduction to his article *On the Threshold of His Temple,* related to the innovative approach of the Besht and wrote:

> He discovered that life is an eternity. In this way, he merited continuing the majesty of eternity in life. He succeeded where so many others who attempted to bring about widespread change in the lives of the populace did not: he truly gave the people a life style without attempting to maintain an 'upper hand', nor presenting himself with pride, but achieved

---

86 II Kings 3:15
87 b. Pesachim 117a
88 Ecclesiastes 2:2
89 II Kings 3:15
90 b. Shabbat, 30b
91 b. Berachot 31a
92 Also noted in *Sefer Talalei Orot*, Part 2, pg.1
93 Ecclesiasters 2:26

this through the power of music and dance, song and prayer, with the force of faith and confidence, with tremendous joy.[94]

Rabbi Nahman of Bratzlav (1772-1810) viewed joy as central to worshipping G-d according to the Bratzlav tradition, as noted by Zvi Mark,[95] who added:

> Rabbi Nahman's battle against sadness and his declaration that 'it is a great mitzva to be happy always'[96] represent further development of the great importance with which the Besht related to happiness and warned against being sorrowful; so much so that 'A person cannot be a believing person without joy'. Not only is 'joy the product of faith', but the reverse is equally true: 'faith is the product of joy', and without joy there can be no faith. Sorrow and misery lead the person into godlessness and idol worship.[97] [...] Rabbi Nahman's explanation of this issue [...] expand our understanding of why he became one of the flag-bearers of the concept of happiness in Chassidism.

The Rambam (Rabbi Moshe ben Maimon, 1135-1204) relates to joy with great importance, and finds a connection between joy and prophecy, claimed Mark.[98] It was Rabbi Nahman's view, by contrast, that the requirement of joy related to each and every person, and not only to the spiritually advanced who saw themselves as designated for prophecy and holiness. The Rambam noted that:

> Active participation in the happy event of the *Simchat bet haSho'evah* [the water drawing festival] was only for the greatest of Israel's wise, the heads of its Rabbinic academies, the Great Assembly and the elders, and those whose active service was required (*Mishneh Torah*, Laws of the Lulav 8:14).

Mark thus concluded:

> It appears, from this passage, that the Rambam perceived this group of people as the religious elite who aspired to reaching prophecy and holiness, for which joy is a necessary condition, while others who do not belong to this elite group and its objectives are warned against actively participating in joy. This separation between the elite of society and everyone else can also be found in the Rambam's approach to music. Even though it arouses joy which in turn enables prophecy, it is for destined prophets, for whom the harp and cymbals, the flute and the lyre, should be played when they seek prophecy, from which can be understood that music is therefore absolutely forbidden for the populace.[99]

---

94 *Be'er haChassidut,* The Book of the Besht, Tel Aviv: Introduction, pg. 13
95 In his book, Mystics and Mania in the Works of Rabbi Nahman of Bratzlav, Tel Aviv: 2003:94
96 Likkutei Moharan Tanina, 24
97 In Mystics and Mania in the Works of Rabbi Nahman of Bratzlav, Tel Aviv: 2003:98-99
98 Ibid, pg. 97-98
99 Ibid, pg.98

In his interpretations of Rabbi Nahman's lessons, Rabbi Itamar Eldad noted the importance of happiness in removing the sorrow within us. This is the approach that Rabbi Nahman used to explain the verse from Psalms 104:31, "I will sing unto the LORD as long as I live; I will sing praise to my God while I have any being": in just the same way that one should relate to another with benefit of the doubt, so should one relate to oneself. Rabbi Nahman emphasizes the aspects of psychological awareness that accompany a person who commits a wrongdoing. It usually involves sorrow, despair, and desperation which overcome the person and do not allow praying and serving G-d properly. Thus the most urgent resolution is to eradicate the paralyzing, depressive mood. This can be achieved, claimed Rabbi Nahman, by finding the meritorious aspect in the reality of that specific act which, to the perpetrator, may seem like an absolute liability. Even when a person's actions involve some ulterior motive, it is not possible that no point of merit whatsoever can be found, some positive aspect that motivates the whole process. The greatest wisdom, Rabbi Nahman taught, is the ability to identify that aspect and pinpoint it, highlighting it against the negative aspects with which it is surrounded.

This is the meaning of "I will sing praises to the Lord for as long as I have my being [*azamra ... b'odi*]". According to Rabbi Nahman, this is understood to mean 'for as long as the being [*od*] is within me'. "*Od*" is that very point which is not negative, and which infuses the face with color, brings a smile to one's lips, joy to one's heart, and fills the music with Godliness.

Happiness, in Rabbi Nahman's opinion, is a necessary condition for achieving the uplifting needed towards Godliness. Sadness is a silencing and repressive force, while happiness, by contrast, drives adrenalin into the blood and provides us with vitality. Once again, Rabbi Nahman's explication demonstrates that happiness can be acquired through a person's ability to choose and sift between the good and bad frames of mind; this is how music can be created. Rabbi Nahman stresses here that 'sanctified music' comes from a lofty position, and mediates or reveals the positive spirit, the constructive aspect, causing happiness that uplifts us, thereby allowing us to serve G-d.[100]

Indeed, the remarks note:

> The trait of happiness constitutes a topic of its own, and various approaches in Jewish thought can be identified in this regard. On one hand, happiness can be viewed as another force of the many existent in the individual that can be used to serve G-d. This force, however, like others, must not be allowed to breach its boundaries and must remain in balance with the other forces.

---

100 www.vbm-torah.org/vtc/0055480.html

On the other hand, we find, especially in Chassidism, that happiness is an 'absolute value' constituting a vital condition for serving G-d. It represents the single avenue that carves a channel through to spiritual uplifting, and all spiritual service must pass through it. In light of the above, then, it seems that Rabbi Nahman supports the second method. Further on, in the third note, he states:

> Serve G-d with joy, come before Him in gladness.[101] Thus there can only be one possible path which a person can take in reaching the highest levels of standing before G-d.

Elsewhere, Rabbi Nahman discussed the importance of happiness from another perspective altogether. In the chapter dealing with the topic, *Dream, Devil or Angel*, Zvi Mark[102] refers to Rabbi Nahman's explanation that dreams derive from a combination of two sources that come together: angel and demon. Mark provided the following explanation:

> The dream of a person whose mind is pure is mediated by an angel, while a person who exists at the level of beast receives a dream via the demon.

Mark further explained Rabbi Nahman's view:

> This does not imply two separate channels whereby the angel visits the righteous, and the demon, the wicked; rather, both angel and demon dwell together in each person and preside over each dream. Through our minds and powers of imagination (which Rabbi Nahman calls 'the force of imagination'), we mediate the way in which our dreams will come to us; the dream itself, however, is comprised of both components, angel and demon. At this point, Rabbi Nahman states that the main way of strengthening the angel and weakening the demon is through happiness [...] which is why the place where angels exist is called *shekhakim*, recalling merriment [*s'khok*] and joy. Thus we understand that joy strengthens the angel.[103]

Rabbi Nahman continues in this vein, offering an explanation of the corrective fast to be undertaken by one who has experienced a bad dream. The fast is related to the aspect of joy, as is written: 'Make us glad in equal measure to the days wherein You hast afflicted us'[104]. In other words, the fast causes happiness, and happiness causes a strengthening of the angel, correcting and subduing the aspect of the bad dream.

In the chapter exploring *Melody*, I will delve further into the importance of music according to Rabbi Nahman, based on the above concept.

---

101 Psalms 100:2
102 In *Mystics and Mania in the Works of Rabbi Nahman of Bratzlav*, Tel Aviv: 2003:91-92
103 *Likkutei Moharan Tanina*, 5:10, as quoted in *Mystics and Mania in the Works of Rabbi Nahman of Bratzlav*, Tel Aviv: 2003:92
104 Psalms 90:15

Additional light is shed on the aspects of happiness and opposition to fasts and self-mortification by Rabbi Y. L. Meimon in his book, *Sarei haMe'ah*.[105] It contains a fascinating account of the first meeting between Rabbi Jacob Joseph (?-1782) and the Besht. The former authored *Toldot Yakov Yosef* and was the Rabbi of Sharigrod, was a Gaon, a righteous person and a wise Torah sage, but did not agree with the Besht's approach. The Besht had wanted very much to meet him in order to try and persuade him of the justness of his method, but somehow never seemed to attain that preliminary stage. At some point, Rabbi Jacob Josef came to the Besht's home to evaluate the latter and argue against the Besht's approach. During their encounter, the Besht succeeded in proving to the Rabbi that the latter was in a state of sorrow and despair rather than one of happiness. Towards the end of their meeting, Rabbi Jacob Josef noticed that the Besht's eyes were filled with a special kind of tranquility, and a ray of light that seemed to be sourced in upper splendor shone from his face with a heavenly blaze. At that point, the Rabbi indeed decided that the way of the Besht was the proper one, and became his outstanding disciple.[106]

From the many quotes and examples offered thus far, we see that from a Chassidic approach, the entire goal of music is none other than to cause joy, which is our obligation in this world.

Over time, Chassidism came to hold an exceedingly important position in the lives of Jews, or, as Rabbi Eliezer Shach of blessed memory (1894-2001) said: "It is said that I oppose Chassidism. I cannot even begin to imagine how the world would look without Chassidism".[107]

---

105 Rabbi Y. L. Meimon, *Sarei haMe'ah*, Jerusalem: 1951, Part 3, pgs. 42-43
106 See the full narrative in the Appendices.
107 Natan Anshin in the weekly *laMishpacha*, 20 Adar II – 31 March 2005, pg. 18

Chapter 3 – The *Niggun* (Melody)

1. What is The Niggun?

Rabbi Shalom Dov Ber (1860-1920), the second *Admor* of Chabad, known also as *Moharsh"ab*, said:

> Every lock has its own key, but the locksmith has a master key with which he can open all the locks. This is the niggun.[1]

With this brief and precise sentence, Rabbi Shalom Dov Ber responds to the question of what the niggun is, summarizing the essence of the power embedded within it.

Known as the *Chatam Sofer* following the name of his book, Rabbi Moshe Sofer (1762-1839) referred to the importance of the niggun by noting that he "would be willing to give half of his Torah knowledge in order to acquire the wisdom of melody" (as cited in *Sefer Binah veShir*).[2]

Rabbi Eliyahu ben Shlomo (1720-1797), known as *The Gaon of Vilna*, wrote, concerning music, that:

> It is highly praiseworthy, being used for reading the Torah, containing the secrets of the Levites' songs and the secrets of the *Tikkunei Zohar*, and knowledge cannot be attained without it. Indeed, a person's soul may expire because of its great pleasantness.

Of the Vilna Gaon, it was said that "he prayed, word by word, in a pleasant voice, with a delicate melody".[3]

The importance of melody is clearly reflected in this saying: "It was better for one who has a pleasant voice yet does not use it to bring pleasure to the Holy One, Blessed be He, not to have come into this world".[4]

---

1 *Sefer haNiggunim*, Collated Lists, pg. 41 Section 80
2 Rabbi Joel Schwarz, Jerusalem: 2003, *Shira veNiggun baRe'I haYahadut*, pg. 71
3 See Rabbi Meshkalow in the Introduction to *Pe'at haShulchan*: pg.70 – www.toravoda.orgil714shevi.html
4 Idelsohn, citing *Sefer Charedim*, Chassidic Melody, pg. 2

The opinion held by the Modzitzer Rabbi was that song is considered equal to learning Torah, as found in his book *Yissa Berachah*, where he discussed the Torah portion of Beha'alotcha, chapters 4 and 5:

> Song is considered as equating the Five Books of Moses, and I have already explained that the voice of song is like Torah, and for both of them we recite a similar blessing. Over the Torah we say, 'Who chooses the Torah', and for song, we say "Who chooses song". That song can be compared to the Five Books of Moses follows my explanation that, in music, the scale of tones contains five notes of joy: two can be changed from major to minor, the third and sixth, as is known; thus the main tones of joy total five.[5]

Rabbi Chaim of Brisk is known to have considered song so important as to be sacred and requiring a *minyan* [quorum] of ten men. He interpreted the verse, "And Miriam answered them, 'Sing to the Lord'" as meaning that because women do not join the minyan, they could only answer, while the men, being ten or more, chanted the songs.[6]

The Chassidic melody, the niggun, is described by teachers of Chassidism as also expressing the most secret whisperings of the heart, which cannot be expressed verbally, even through the holiest of words, prayer. Thus the niggun acts as an auxiliary tool which the Tzaddik can use to reveal the latent aspects of a person towards achieving the aspired for fervor, whether that person is wicked or a Torah disciple. Even the simplest of people, whose virtues are far from those of the Tzaddik, can find the niggun effective, whether actively through singing, uplifting the soul, or passively by listening. Listening to a niggun sung by a Tzaddik can be likened to hearing anecdotes about Tzaddikim, allowing the simple person a handhold on the edge of the world of sanctity. This allows the Tzaddik to redirect the person's soul, and raise it higher.[7]

Geshuri has noted that Chassidic melody is a treasury of religious energy. The annals of Chassidism relate not only to the personalities and actions connected with it, but also to its niggunim. Ever since the establishment of Chassidism by the Besht, the niggun served as a mirror to the soul and a source of spiritual uplifting. Rabbi and disciple, old and young, all found interest in the Chassidic niggun. All experienced great revelations of some kind. Many Chassidim tried to explain or interpret the Chassidic aspirations through the language of notes, each person according to how he perceived the concepts, each seeking greater self-cognizance. Niggunim and the musicians who played the melodies became a very expansive phenomenon in Chassidism, reflecting a world of figures and

---

5   Rabbi Joseph Moshe Kahana, *haMachaneh haCHaredi* newspaper, 20 Shvat 5767 – February 8, 2007, Section: *Korei Oneg*, pg. 8
6   Eliach Dov, miShulchan Gavohah, on Shemot
7   Yaakov Mazor, *haNiggun haChassidi befi haChassidim*, Jerusalem: 2004, in the chapter titled 'Music in Chassidic Society', pg. 6

creations. Each stream of Chassidism in each country developed its own style of niggun, with its shades and tones. Just as each stream of Chassidism had its own atmosphere, so the niggunim became attached to various figures in that stream. Every Chassid who was connected to the court of a Tzaddik was able to identify the unique sound of the music associated with that court.[8]

An anecdote relates to Rabbi Schneur Zalman of Liadi (1745-1813), who established the Chassidic stream known by its acronym of *Chabad,* and who was its first *Rebbe* [honorific title]. When he returned to Vitebsk after visiting Mezhirech for the first time, the whole city came to greet him. When asked what he 'took' from Mezhirech, he answered:

> In Mezhirech, I became acquainted with three things: what the Holy One, Blessed be He, is; who the Children of Israel are – "Israel, the Torah, and the Holy One, blessed be He, are one"; and what niggun is.[9]

Who was the first to discover the niggun? M. S. Geshuri, in his article, *The Besht – Decipherer of the Chassidic Niggun,* stated:

> Who revealed the first niggun? The Besht, or his acquaintances, disciples and adherents? Who are they? From where did the Besht draw the power to consolidate the premise that singing can ease pain and manifest joy, a concept that served as the foundation for several discourses ascribed to him? [...] In his youth, when the soul of the Besht longed for the expanses of nature and he spent some years in such surroundings, he found – in every place and every period throughout the generations of Jews – that a lively interest in song and singing had existed, and felt that people would be charmed by the beauty and tranquility of the niggun, by its force and its ability to comfort. The spiritual leaders of the time, however, attempted to bottle up this emotion, for various reasons. The Rabbis related to cantorial music and to the cantors themselves either with apathy, or with hatred and contempt, while others saw them as targets of ridicule.

Geshuri then related to the developments in which the Besht was pivotal:

> The Besht delved into the factors causing opposition but found no clear prohibition against singing and playing music. What he found was that since the destruction of the Temple and the Exile, it had become customary to decrease the scope of song and music, using them for the most only in the sphere of the synagogue or religious life. However, as one who was enthralled by Nature, who loved to seclude himself among the forests and fields, among trees and green growth, he realized that Nature itself was replete with an abundance of sounds like the playing of music, and that Mankind had been born into, and placed within, a world full of sounds.
>
> The Besht found fascinating examples relating to the influential force of music on Mankind in the *Tanach.* King David, while yet young, played his lyre to help allay King Saul's

---

8   Negginah veChassidut b'Beit Kuzmir uBnoteha, Jerusalem: 1952, Introduction, pg. 5
9   *Sefer haNiggunim,* Collected Lists, Section 84

harsh mood.¹⁰ The Prophet Elisha used music to arouse the power of prophecy.¹¹ The Besht could only ponder: why should we, too, not derive benefit from the music that dwells in the soul of each of us?

Chassidism disclosed the hidden archives of joy. It unlocked the song which had been ceased, and returned it to the Jew who followed its path. The poetic song, the singing and the music had disappeared from Israel. Song had remained accessible to all other peoples but removed from Jewish life; yet it fills the whole world and is produced by every creature, every tree and plant in the field, by the mountains and hills, all overflowing with thanks for the Creator. What had been inhibited among Jews suddenly resurfaced through the phenomenon of Chassidism and its focus on joy.¹²

Rabbi Abraham Jacob Friedman (1820-1883) of Sadegura was known to have said:

> Every nation has its own melody. None plays the music of any other. Only Israel plays all the melodies, in order to raise them higher before the Holy One, Blessed be He. In the *Perek Shirah* [Chapter of Song], all the animals and all the birds sing, each with its own form; but Israel makes one song of them all, uplifting that song to G-d.¹³

Niggun went arm in arm with Chassidism like a helpmeet, branching out as Chassidism did, its branches reaching ever higher until the heavens were breached on the wings of these melodies, and the pure, Jewish souls rose to the G-dly Throne to chant and sing with the angels of G-d.¹⁴

Rabbi Yehoshua Heschel of Apta said of Rabbi Mordechai from Kremnitzer that his soul derived from the chambers of music, thus he is able to bring Jews to repentance through his melodies.¹⁵

It is told of Rabbi Zusya of Annapoli (1717-1786) who heard the Cantor in the synagogue on the eve of Yom Kippur sing the verse, "And we forgive the whole congregation of Israel"¹⁶ with such a wonderful melody that he immediately called out to G-d, saying, "Sovereign of the Universe, if Israel had not sinned, would this melody have ever come before you?"¹⁷

---

10 I Samuel 16:23
11 II Kings 3:15
12 *Machanayim,* Magazine 46, 5720 (1960).
13 *Ohr Haganuz*, Jerusalem: 1979:288
14 Yitzhak Alfassi, *Basadeh haChassidut*, Tel Aviv: 1986: 500
15 Yitzhak Alfassi, *Tzaddikim and Chassidim,* Israel: 2003:214
16 Numbers 15:26
17 Ohr haGanuz, pg. 227

From Geshuri's article, we come to realize the tremendously important role that the Besht placed on melodies. In it, he describes how the Besht commenced working as an assistant teacher of toddlers and very young children, before his destiny became revealed:

> Every time that he took the infants to the synagogue, a melody accompanied them, with pleasant voice and great zeal, which could be heard at a distance.

The melody was so special that it became compared to the songs sung by the Levites in the Temple. The full story appears in the Appendices.[18]

In fact, the source of this tale derives from the book, *Shiv'chei haBesht* [*In Praise of the Besht*], which briefly relates how the Besht went with the children to the *Chedder* [lit: room; a schoolroom for Jewish studies for young children] to teach them Torah and sing with them, causing them to be happy and want to learn. The children loved to go with him so much that *Satan* decided to put an end to it. He disguised himself as a wolf, and chased the children away into the forest. Of course they returned, and then continued on their way, as on every day, with the Besht. The anecdote states the following:

> The whole time that he walked with the infants, he would sing with them in a pleasant voice and with great zest, and from a distance it could be heard how his service rose ever higher, there being great satisfaction in the Upper Worlds such as that brought about by the songs that the Levites sang in the Temple, and it was a time of goodwill in Heaven.[19]

Idelsohn referred to the importance of melody prior to the appearance of Chassidism, but adds:

> Chassidism raised music to such an important position that without music, it became impossible to conduct focused meditations and reach awakening towards performing the service of G-d.

Idelsohn added:

> The founder of Chassidism, the Besht, imbued music with this measure of importance. It is said of him that he was able to understand the thoughts of the instrumentalist while the latter played (as cited in *Likkutei Moharan*). Legend has it that he would collect folk-tunes and teach them to his students.[20]

Chassidism is like poetry to Judaism, it is the Song of songs of the Jewish soul. It is for very good reason that song and music hold such a high place in

---

18 *Machanayim* Magazine, 46, 5720 (1960)
19 Shiv'chei haBesht, Ch.9H pg. 13
20 A. Z. Idelsohn, *haNegginah haChassidit,* pg. 5

Chassidism. Through song, the Chassid can rise to higher worlds, reach the wings of the Shechinah and the Throne of Glory, and merge with worlds beyond the world of Nature in which we are bound.[21]

2. The Wordless Melody

Another innovation attributable to Chassidism, and indeed one of the greatest innovations ever, is the wordless melody. Until the period of Chassidism, music was connected to a text, thus the music was also limited by that text. Furthermore, certain songs were customarily sung only on certain occasions, that is, when that text was relevant. With the advent of Chassidism, the wordless niggun was created. This form of song developed only in Chassidic streams, and did not exist prior to that time (see A. Z. Idelsohn).

The niggun contains the totality of the Chassidic approach: for this reason, the Chassidim sing a great deal, thereby explaining the essence of Chassidic doctrine through niggun to those who have not fully understood the concept as expressed with words. Rabbi Nahman of Bratzlav would say to his disciples:

> Can it be possible to serve G-d with words alone? Come, let me show you a new way to G-d, not through talking but through singing. We shall sing, and He Above will understand us.[22]

What is so unique about wordless melody, and why does it seem to be far more important in Chassidism than music combined with words? In principle, the answer is that the wordless niggun became more important because it is not directly linked to any text and can therefore be sung at any time. Explaining Rabbi Nahman of Bratzlav on the wordless niggun, Zvi Mark wrote:

> The niggun can exist without words. Its independent force and vitality do not require dependence on a defined text. Rabbi Nahman describes the niggun as having the characteristic of being a lifegiver, thus a person who feels 'lifeless' can be assisted by the niggun.

Mark quoted Rabbi Nahman:

> It is good when a person accustoms himself to enlivening himself with a niggun, as the niggun is a great tool with superlative traits having the power to arouse and draw a person's heart towards G-d. Even if a person cannot play [a musical instrument], at least in his own

---

21 M. S. Geshuri, haNiggun vehaRikkud baChassidut, pg. 18-19
22 Geshuri, *laChassidim Mizmor*, Jerusalem: 1936, pg. 11-12

home and when he is alone, he can revitalize himself with a niggun, in whichever way he is capable of singing it, for the value of the niggun is immeasurable.[23]

Rabbi Israel Taub of Modzitz commented as follows:

> Music – its notes and nuances – is the language of the soul; the language of the soul is contraction, and what one niggun can express cannot be expressed by even a thousand words.[24]

Perhaps it is possible to say that an additional reason exists for the importance placed on the wordless niggun: it has a unique language of its own, a language expressed in a certain way by the one 'saying' it, that is the 'singer', and which is understood in an individual manner by the 'listener', but not every person listening hears the exact same language in the niggun being aired. The special influence latent in the niggun depends on who is singing it, how he sings it, before which audience the niggun is being sung, and under which circumstances. In other words, I would say that while performing a niggun, a dialogue is created between the 'singer' and the 'listener/s'. Furthermore, when listeners join the singer during a niggun, they become enthused as they sing. This is very common among Chassidim, such as when they gather at their Rebbe, for example, when a *Tisch* is held, or when there is some other kind of gathering. Their enthusiasm increases constantly until the sense of the material world is lost. This is the great force embedded within the niggun.

Perhaps this is what Rabbi Shmuel Eliyahu (1828-1888) of Zwulen, father of Rabbi Israel Taub of Modzitz, referred to when he said:

> A person takes great responsibility upon himself when he airs a melody, as the ascending and descending of the soul and the spirit are dependent on the niggun: everything depends on the player, what he plays, and how he plays. And the niggun may raise him to the greatest heights, but may also, G-d forbid, bring him to the lowest abysm.[25]

An alternative and quite interesting answer to the question of what exactly the wordless niggun is, can be found in Mordechai Steinman's *Niggun*. He commenced the introduction with the question, "When does a Jew sing?" And offered the following response: that this question was put forward by someone he termed "an Israeli author", who responded: "When he is hungry!" Steinman continued:

> In truth, the Jew is always hungry, and for most Jews, the niggun (without words, of which there are no need) is the most expeditious way to satisfy that hunger.

---

23 *Mistika veShiga'on beYetzirat R' Nahman miBreslav*, pg. 193, as cited in "Sichot Moharan', Section 273, page. 169
24 *Imrei Saul*, pg. 316:43
25 *Imrei Saul*, pg. 316:41

Hungry! The Jew is constantly seeking, because the Jewish soul will never rest until it hears what needs to be heard, and say what must be said.

Steinman added:

The niggun is a combination of the voices of parents and children, who understand each other even though a stranger cannot. For example, when a babe says 'ya ya ya' or 'na na na', typical of the syllables that an infant forms, we see that G-d created intimate feelings within us that are able to understand the child, yet a stranger cannot understand that same infant. Thus, a baby that speaks in languages (ya ya ya, na na na) uses that language perfectly. Only after the child grows up and learns the language used by the parents, does the child forget the baby talk. Then the time comes when the person is old, and his abilities to understand are far greater: the niggun that he sings from within him recalls once again that language spoken as an infant, to his parents.

Thus the niggun is the ya-ya language of childhood, and according to Steinman, while singing the niggun, a person feels as though he is communicating with his father; and that makes him feel good.

What, however, happens to a person who is not a father and has never felt his own sensations about the infant's form of language, as noted above? Steinman provided this answer:

Every person has a sense of hunger. We need someone to feed us and feed our children, including the child within us and even that as-yet unborn child. The niggun we hear fills us with beauty, light and spirit, and most of all, with the information that satisfies our hunger.

Steinman then questioned:

What is the niggun? [...] Why do I ask this question a second time? Because the significance of the niggun is different for the 'singer' and for the 'listener'! G-d, who hears the niggun, which is the 'ya ya ya, na na na' of the child, safeguards His love and longs for the child who is performing the niggun. There is, however, a bi-directional movement. G-d moves towards the lower level of the experience, that is, the child; and the child approaches the true experience of the universe and the world of language. According to this theory, the niggun appears to equate to the most important part of the prayer, which is the *Amidah* [Standing Prayer]. In summary: 'Niggun is the fastest way to reach G-d's inner ear'.[26]

Schleifer, as cited in Vinaverger, related to wordless music:

The most important among Chassidic melodies is, without a doubt, the wordless niggun. The Chassidic doctrine relates extensively to the importance of the wordless melody and there is yet much which can be said of it. It is worthy of further study.

---

26 *Niggun*, USA: 1994, Introduction, xiii

Schleifer, referencing Geshuri, stated that according to the first Chassidim, every wordless niggun alludes to a narrative, and the true Tzaddik can hear the narrative's words within the niggun. He further referred to Zalmanov, quoted in the introduction to *Niggunei Chabad*, which states:

> The main characteristic of the Chabad niggun is emotion. It is constructed entirely on the heart's feelings and the soul's fervor, thus does not require words and notes as other songs do. On the contrary: words limit it, as the niggun is of a much higher [spiritual] level than speech.[27]

In the anecdote presented at the commencement of this chapter (and fully presented in the Appendices), which relates to the Besht prior to becoming revealed to the populace, when he was employed for a salary as an apprentice teacher and would lead the children to the *Chedder*, we are told that "he led them with song and a pleasant voice, with joy and gladness" and so forth. The purpose of the story, noted Y. Dan, was to emphasize the greatness of the way the Besht served G-d through the songs of very young children. It is not told which songs the children sung on their way to the *Chedder*, but from the emphasis on "with a pleasant voice and great zest" we can understand that the singing itself, even when not during designated times for prayer or study, was considered an [integral] part of the way in which the Besht served G-d.[28]

Mazor presented a commentary ascribed to Rabbi Mordechai (Mottele) (1770-1837) of Chernobyl which states:

> In earlier times (prior to Chassidism) it was customary for the angels to sing songs in the Upper Worlds with a niggun, and later the niggun was played at the tables of Tzaddikim. From our generation onwards, however, matters are conducted differently: first, the niggun is played at the table of the Tzaddik, and then the angels sing using this niggun.

Mazor elaborated further to the above, noting that the purpose of this statement was used by the proponents of the Chassidic approach to contrast with their Tzaddikim with pre-Chassidic Tzaddikim; yet we can nonetheless learn about how music was perceived at the outset of the Chassidic period. Firstly, there is a clear distinction between 'song' which is textual music, and the 'niggun' which is melody. This distinction relates to music even when it is not tied into a sacred text, or even when it is sung outside of the synagogue. Secondly, the sanctity emanating from the tables of the Chassidic Tzaddikim is alluded to, as well as the value of singing as a real part of holy service: for if this were not so, why

---

27 *Anthology of Chassidic Music*, Jerusalem: 1986:224
28 Yaakov Mazor, in Yuval, Vol. 7: *Mech'karim lichvod Israel Adler*, pg. 32

should the angels use the Chassidic niggunim sung at the table, for the purpose of serving G-d?[29]

The extrapolation provided by the Rabbi of Chernobyl indicates, first and foremost, the Chassidic perception that it is possible to serve G-d in many ways including through material avenues, (or, as the Besht put it, "Through all your ways, know Him"). Simultaneously, however, it promotes the Chassidic custom of singing niggunim at the Sabbath and Festival meals set out at the Tzaddik's table (*Tisch*). By comparing views of pre-Chassidic Tzaddikim to the approach of the Besht and others of his generation, the differences between them become apparent. While pre-Chassidic views related the theurgic power to the textual songs of praise known as the Hallel, the Song at the Sea, Pslams and passages of prayers in line with the accepted views of the 14th and 15th centuries, later Chassidim viewed singing and melody, even when disconnected from all textual content, as an act with theurgic potential. Such potential may then be realized not only by those who were imbued with holy spirit such as Moses or King David, or those whose roles incorporated such as, as with the Levites who served in the Temple, but by every single member of the Jewish people.[30]

All the views stated above strengthen what has already been presented in the chapter on Chassidism: if it can be said that Chassidism innovated the use of melody in order to reach a state of joy and nullify sadness, then it is clear that in order to reach a state of joy, there is no need to sing melodies with texts. Rather, any melody, even one having no words, and perhaps especially one with no words, can bring a person to the desired state.

Rabbi Shmuel Eliyahu Taub (1906-1984) of Modzitz found greater advantage in serving G-d through melody than through devotion: serving G-d through intellectual devotion holds a disadvantage, as one person's service does not incorporate others. Devotion through speech does admittedly connect others but its disadvantage is that speech can cause schism. By contrast, the niggun contains both values without any of the disadvantages: that is, the niggun can sweep others into participating, and enthuse them without causing division. On the contrary: when delving deeper into the niggun, one achieves fervor.[31]

It is known that Rabbi Nahman of Bratzlav perceived niggun as holding a central role: in his view, the niggun derives from the same source as prophecy. There is an affinity between the cantor [*chazzan*] who sings a niggun, and the vision [*chazzon*] of prophecy. He pointed to the connection between the two

---

29 Yaakov Mazor, in Yuval, Vol. 7: *Mech'karim lichvod Israel Adler*, pg. 32
30 Ibid
31 Rabbi Shmuel Eliyahu Taub of Modzitz, *Pe'er miKdoshim*, Jerusalem: 1996, commentary on Psalms, pg. 19

words, chazzan and chazzon, the latter meaning prophecy: prophecy derives from the place where prophets draw their inspiration.[32] As he would say, the value [ie: heights] of niggun is immeasurable.[33]

Zvi Mark noted[34] that the niggun, in Rabbi Nahman's view, is formed by gathering the scattered parts of the good spirit of joy, which are parts of the spirits of holiness and prophecy and which, when brought together into a complete niggun, can lead the person to holy spirit and prophecy:

> The player should know how to bring and gather and find the parts of the spirit, one at a time, in order to structure the niggun, that is, the joy, which means structuring a positive spirit, the spirit of prophecy, which is the opposite of sorrow, for his hand must move up and down the instrument that he plays with the intention of structuring whole joy. And when the prophet hears such a niggun from one who truly knows how to play it, he receives the spirit of prophecy through the one who gathered [joy] into his hand from the sad mood, and 'he shall play with his hand, and you shall be well'.[35] 'You shall be well' occurs precisely when one gathers and joins together the good from the bad, [...] as is said, 'And it came to pass, when the minstrel played, that the hand of the LORD came upon him'.[36]

Rabbi Aharon Katorza quoted Rabbi M. Schneersohn, who would say that in Chabad, when a niggun that had been composed by someone who was no longer alive was sung, the soul of the composer would come down to this world. The Chassidim would say that with the [last] Rebbe this was not interpretation or imagination. They could see that the Rebbe could sense the soul there.[37]

An incident relating to the Tzemach Tzedek describes how, during the period of the High Holy Days, he was in a state of great distress and ordered that the whole book of Psalms be said every morning upon rising, in a *minyan* [quorum of ten men] and how, on the 19th of Kislev, he was found to be in a state of immense joy, and asked that the niggun of the *Four Babas* be played. Then he relayed the following:

> On the night of Rosh Hashanah, a powerful denunciation was directed against all Israel, and I tried to speak to the *Baal haTanya* to no avail. At the festive meal of *simchat Torah*, when the niggun of the Rabbi, *The Four Babas*, was played, I saw my elder, and said to him: 'A cup of blessing is held one *tefach* above the table, and King David's cup of blessing is the book of Psalms, which rises up one *tefach* and nullifies all accusations. Thus, he commanded that the Psalms be read.

---

32 See Zvi Mark, *Mystica veshiga'on beYetzirat Rabbi Nahman miBreslav*, pg. 88
33 Ibid, pg. 192. Citing discourses by Rabbi Nahman, 273, pg. 169
34 Zvi Mark, *Mystica veshiga'on beYetzirat Rabbi Nahman miBreslav*, pg. 190
35 I Samuel 16:16
36 II Kings 3:15, as cited in *Likutei Moharan*, 141: 54:6
37 See Chapter on Interviews

See in depth.[38] In any event, the narrative relates how the niggun succeeded in allowing the Rabbi to speak to the soul. Rabbi Nahman of Bratzlav referred to the verse, "And their father Israel said unto them: 'If it be so now, do this: take of the choice fruits of the land in your vessels, and bear a gift down to the man, a little balm, and a little honey, spices and labdanum, nuts, and almonds; [...] and God Almighty give you mercy before the man, that he may release unto you your other brother and Benjamin. And as for me, if I be bereaved of my children, I am bereaved'.[39] Rabbi Nahman offered the following interpretation:

> Our Father Jacob, who sent his sons, the ten tribes, to Joseph, sent them with a melody from the land of Israel: and this is the source: 'Take of the choice fruits [*zimrat*] of the land in your vessels'. This refers to song [*zemer*] and melody. For you should know this: that every single shepherd has his unique tune, according to the grasses and the place where he herds, that each and every beast has a special kind of greenery which it needs to eat [...] that each and every kind of green thing has its own song, which says [...] and from the songs of the grasses the shepherd's niggun is formed. This is what he said to his sons: 'Take of the *zimrah* of the land [...] and bear a gift down to the man, a little balm, and a little honey, spicery and labdanum, nuts, and almonds', which refers to the aspect of the rhythms and measures of the music, for the meldoy is formed from the growth of the land of Israel.[40]

On this same verse, "Take of the choice fruits of the land", Rabbi Israel (1849-1921) of Modzitz raised a question: in this portion of Torah, after the first visit of Jacob's sons in Egypt, the text states that Jacob gives his sons various advice before their second visit. Thus it is surprising that Jacob ends by saying to them, "Do this: take of the choice fruits of the land in your vessels, and bear a gift down to the man, a little balm, and a little honey". Initially he refers to 'the choice fruits of the land' as an appropriate gift, and then he continues with 'a little balm and a little honey'. The question also arose as to why the word 'gift' in the form *mincha* rather than *matanah* is used. Rabbi Israel offers the following fascinating explanation:

> This is similar to comparing someone who seeks the Tzaddik on any weekday to request a blessing for a good livelihood, and so forth, or someone who comes to the Tzaddik on Shabbat, out of awe of the Heavenly One and in service of the Creator, especially when he partakes of the three Sabbath meals with the Tzaddik. The brothers' first visit was during a weekday, and they said to him [Joseph], 'We have come to buy food'. In other words, they had come on matters of livelihood rather than for the sake of Torah. For this reason, they saw nothing, that is, they were unable to recognize Joseph, as is written: 'And Joseph knew his brethren, but they knew him not'.[41] On their second visit, however, it was Shabbat, as is

---

38 *Sippuri Chassidim,* Section *Mo'adim,* Anecdote 414, pg. 350-351
39 Genesis 43:11, 14.
40 Likutei Moharan Tanina, 63
41 Genesis 42:8

written: 'and slaughter a beast, and prepare it'.[42] Such preparations indicate that it was for the Sabbath, thus the brothers joined Joseph for the Sabbath meal. We can presume that on this opportunity, they indeed recognized him and acknowledged his lofty position as a great, holy Tzaddik, as is said: 'and the men marveled with each other'[43], meaning that they were amazed at Joseph's righteousness and holiness, as is written: 'And they sat before him, the oldest according to his birthright, and the youngest according to his youth'[44] , in other words, each according to his attained [spiritual] level. Jacob indeed saw, through his holy spirit, that the sovereign was a great, holy, righteous person.[45]

Rabbi Avraham (1820-1883) of Sadegura used to say:

> In the *Song at the Crossing of Reed Sea*, it does not say that the people sang immediately after crossing the Sea: first, they reached a perfect level of faith, as is written: 'And they believed in G-d and in Moses, His servant'[46] and only thereafter, does it say, 'Then Moses and the Children of Israel sang'[47], indicating that only one who believes is able to chant such songs.[48]

The following narrative indicates, more than anything else, the magical importance of the niggun in Chassidism. A certain *Beit Midrash* [center of Torah study] became famous for the brilliance of the Torah disciples who learned there. One of those regularly attending the Beit Midrash was a simple man who did not know how to study, but aspired merely to be in the presence of the scholars. Unable to actively study with them, he would stand in a corner and hum, together with them, the niggun that they voiced while learning: he was an object of ridicule to the scholars. Eventually he passed away and was forgotten. Shortly after his death, the scholars began to sense that they had lost their keenness. Over time, it became known that this Beit Midrash had lost its prestige, and no longer produced great Torah luminaries. One day, Rabbi Zusya (?-1800) of Annapoli passed by. He was informed of the scholars' woes. On delving into the matter, he realized the proximity between the plight of the Beit Midrash scholars and the man's death. He told the scholars that their brilliance had derived from the holy sparks that the Jew had created in his soul through the pureness of his niggun, for it is through the power of the niggun used for learning that one merits heavenly awe; only then, can one's Torah study rise to the Throne of Glory and the scholar does not forget what he learned.

---

42 Genesis 43:16
43 Genesis 43:33
44 Ibid
45 Atkinu Seudata, Section Pninim Yekarim, pg. 113-114
46 Exodus 14:31
47 Exodus 15:1
48 *Ohr haGanuz*, pg. 287-288

This narrative indicates the forceful influence of music which can reveal not only directed intentions of the person using it, but also reveal music's power when used by someone out of sheer innocence.[49]

3. The Niggun and Formulated Prayer

The importance of formulated prayer has already been related to in the chapter on "Music in the Synagogue". Prayer leaders [*Baal Tefillah* – a lay person who leads prayer service] and cantors integrated a great many niggunim into prayers. As far as both the formulation [*nussach; pl. nussachim*] of prayers per se, and the integration of niggunim into prayer, we can presume that Chassidism contributed greatly.

Indeed, the three streams of Chassidism had somewhat different prayer formulations, but all integrated niggunim.

Eliyahu Schleifer, in his notes to a book authored by Vinaver, related to the special *nussach* of Chassidim:

> Usually, researchers of Chassidic music devote a great deal of attention to Chassidic niggunim, and while these do indeed possess great value, it directs attention away from the other aspect of Chassidic music, being Chassidism's special *nussachim*.

Schleifer refers here to the forms of Chassidic nussach and how they differ to those of the accepted Ashkenazi formulations.[50] Further on, he stated:

> The approach of the Chassidim to the old Ashkenazi nussachim is disputed. Some researchers felt that the new Chassidic niggun of the 18th and 19th centuries led to the rejection of the old nussachim. Idelsohn (*Otzar*, Vol. X page ix) claimed that because their [own] singing was the result of improvisation and inspiration, the Chassidim scorned the synagogal musical traditions. Idelsohn further presents objections voiced by one of the greatest Chassidic leaders, Rabbi Mendel of Kotzk (Menachem Mendel Morgenstern, 1787-1859) to the prayers and tunes "of yesteryear". On the other hand, others, such as M. S. Geshuri (*haNiggun vehaRikkud*, Volume 1, page 24) claimed that "the Chassidic cantors did not change tunes from [the time of Torah-giving at] Sinai, but sang new niggunim alongside the old".

Schleifer referred to the collection of Chassidic nussachim presented by Vinaver and concluded that in the Chassidim's view, they indeed introduced changes, "and sang new niggunim instead of the old melodies", and "the Chassidic prayer leaders used their own melodic formulations which sounded no less ancient than those of the Ashkenazi world".

---

49 Yaakov Mazor, *Yuval*, Vol. 7, *Mechkarim lichvod Israel Adler,* pg. 35-36
50 *Anthology of Chassidic Music*, pg. 33

Schleifer then posed the question:

> Did the Chassidim abandon the Ashkenazi nussachim – just as they abandoned the Ashkenazi *Siddur* [prayer book], replacing it with the Sephardi nussach of the Ari – and compose new melodic nussachim that sound to us, currently, as though they are ancient, or did they use an ancient melodic repertoire common to Eastern Europe simultaneously with Ashkenazi nussachim, but emphasizing the former in order to emphasize their uniqueness?

He concluded: "It is possible that we shall never find the answer to this question".[51]

An anecdote concerning Rabbi Levi Yitzhak (1740-1810) of Berditchev relates how he came to the home of Rabbi Dov of Mezhirech for the first time, and stood in the Beit Midrash to pray *Shacharit* [the morning service]. From his room, Rabbi Dov could hear the chanting of the *Psukei Dzimra* [verses of song] and especially, the intonation of the phrase "Sing to the Lord a new song, and His praise in the assembly of the pious [*Chassidim*]".[52] He then declared:

> We should now sing 'a new song' to the Creator, as 'His praise', which we had customarily sung up until now 'in the assembly of *Chassidim* [pious], is already known by the Chassidim![53]

Rabbi Yeshayahu Halevi Horowitz (1565-1630), known as *The Shl"ah* from the initials of his book, *Shney Luchot Habrit* [*The Two Tablets of Stone*] related to the nation that does not have a special melody for each kind of prayer, nor distinguishes with their voice between praise, plea or confession. He presented the example which he himself was taught by one of the generation's great scholars, who during the *Eyzehu Mekoman, baMeh Madlikin* or *Pitum haKtoret* prayers, would use the same tune as that for learning a Mishnah.[54]

The Chassidim did indeed renew the wordless niggun and imbued it with immense importance as a way of serving G-d. As already noted, they saw no contradiction in adapting some of these niggunim to the nussach of prayers or integrating liturgical texts into the niggunim. Many cantors or those who served as *Shatz* sought tunes appropriate to expressing prayer.[55]

---

51 Ibid
52 Psalms 149:1
53 Menachem Guttman, *Ma'ayan haChassidut*, Jerusalem: 1965, Vol. 2, Year 2, 5725 [1965], pg. 3
54 Booklet *Otzar haYediot*, Part 1, pg. 234
55 M. S. Geshuri, *laChassidim Mizmor*, pg. 22

4. The Inspirational Power of the Niggun Before and During Various Activities

Music, containing the immense power that it does, served in many roles. King David, for example, used the forces aroused by playing the lyre to ascertain when midnight occurred, as is noted in the Germarra[56] which refers to the King's lyre:

> It is relayed by Rabbi Acha bar Bizna, who quoted Rabbi Shimon Chassida, that a lyre hung above David's bed, and at midnight, a northern wind blew through it and caused it to play notes. Immediately, David would arise and occupy himself with Torah until the first light of the morning, etc.

Rashi interpreted this to indicate that the handhole in the lyre faced north and at midnight, the breeze from the north would stir the strings which would begin to emit musical sounds. In this way, King David was able to know the time and rise accordingly. The Germarra[57] ends by asking how we know that it was the lyre hung above his bed which would arouse him from his sleep? The response given states that we learn this from the verse: "Awaken, my glory; awaken, lyre [...], awake the dawn".[58] Rashi added that the words "awake the dawn" mean "I have wakened the dawn, unlike those kings where first, the dawn's light rises and only then, they rise". In regard to the playing of the lyre, it refers to King David rising and remaining awake until sunrise.

As I have previously noted, many instances exist in the Scriptures where playing of music is recalled as a remedy to calm a person's mood or arouse that person, as with David who played his lyre to help dissipate King Saul's negative mood, according to the verse:

> And it came to pass, when the [evil] spirit from God was upon Saul, that David took the lyre, and played with his hand; so Saul found relief, and it was well with him, and the evil spirit departed from him".[59]

Elisha the Prophet employed music in order to arouse the power of prophecy, according to the verse:

> But now bring me a minstrel.' And it came to pass, when the minstrel played, that the hand of the Lord came upon him.[60]

---

56 b. Sanhedrin, 16a, and also Berachot, 3b
57 b. Sanhedrin, 16b, and also Berachot, 4a
58 Psalms 57:9
59 I Samuel 16:23
60 II Kings 3:15

Samuel the Prophet invokes the power of music when speaking with King Saul:

> After that you shall come to the hill of God, to the garrison of the Philistines; and it shall come to pass, when you approach the city, that you shall meet a band of prophets coming down from the high place with a psaltery, and a timbrel, and a flute, and a harp, before them; and they will be prophesying. And the spirit of the LORD will come mightily upon you, and you will prophesy with them, and be turned into another man.[61]

We find similarities to the court of the *Admor* of each Chassidic group, where music was used to alter moods. The music was played by *klezmers*. *Klezmer* is a combination word derived from the Hebrew *klei* [instruments] *zemer* [of song] and refers to a small band of players. The group usually included a violinist, a clarinetist and an accordionist, who played and sang at the Rebbes' gatherings. Their main role was to gladden the Rebbe and arouse a good mood. When the atmosphere was at its worst, the klezmers would play a plaintive tune if the Rebbe felt it necessary. A great many anecdotes and examples relate to such situations.

Another way of reaching joy was through jesting. Professional merrymakers existed for the sole purpose of bringing happiness to the Rebbe, or to the bride and groom on their marriage day. These merrymakers acquired a reputation for famous jokes which were usually peppered with nuggets of knowledge from the Torah, the Midrash and Aggadah. The merrymaker performed his work on different occasions, in addition to bringing happiness through the *Mitzvah Tanz* [dancing before bride and groom] where his role reached its peak: he would joke and sing at the wedding celebration itself, including before the bride's veil was lowered, he would flatter the groom, and would enliven the festivities when invited to join the groom's celebratory meal prior to the marriage ceremony, or the festive *Sheva Brachot* [seven blessings] meal after the ceremony.

The merrymaker would take part in the *Purim Spiel* [jesting play] and the festive Purim meal which the Rebbe would conduct, and in any other activities as requested by the Rebbe. The merrymaker required the ability to create rhymes, use *gematria* [numerology], be fully proficient with Scriptures, have a sense of humor and music, and of course possess a personality that was accepted by the community.

Merrymakers were nonetheless known for their great awe of G-d, and were right-hand men to the Rebbes. Among the most famous were Rabbi Hershel of Ostropol, who was the merrymaker in the court of Rabbi Baruch (1753-1811) of Medzhibozh. Rabbi Hershel was one of the Besht's grandsons, was a very accomplished scholar and knowledgeable on Kabbalah. When Rabbi Baruch would become disheartened, Rabbi Hershel would distract him and cause the sorrow to dissipate. His form of jest was extremely well loved among Chassidic circles, so

---

61 I Samuel 10:5-6

much so that whole books were published containing quips and jokes attributed to him.

Yitzhak Isaak was another merrymaker, from Homil, a disciple of the 'Middle Admor', the Tzemach Tzedek of Lubavitch; Yonah Aharon of Ostrodetz was the favorite of the Rebbe of Neschitz; Rabbi Yossel Brader was active in the court of Rabbi Uri of Sterlisk, and when the latter passed away, moved to the court of Rabbi Israel of Ruzhyn.[62]

5. Niggunim for the Bridal Canopy, Marriage Festivities, and First & Second Year Chedder Pupils

Many tunes found their way to being associated with performance of a certain activity, such as the niggun that Chassidim sang when they accompanied the groom on the way to synagogue on the Sabbath prior to his wedding. On such a Sabbath, the groom is called up to the reading of the Torah. His family prepares a festive meal to which the synagogue community is invited. The groom's family and friends would lead him from his home to the synagogue in an impressive parade, singing a special accompanying niggun used only for this occasion. There were also special niggunim sung by the Chassidim to lead the groom, and then the bride, to the wedding canopy [*chuppah*]. These and certain other niggunim became traditions in the general populace for leading the bride and groom to the chuppah. One of the most famous, which has become traditional throughout the Jewish world not only in Chassidic circles but is equally popular throughout Jewish society, derives from an unknown composer.

The Chabad Chassidic stream uses the *Four Babas* niggun composed by the *Alter Rebbe* for leading the groom to the chuppah.

A special niggun was sung when three year old boys were brought to start their Torah study: the child was draped with a *Tallit Kattan* [fringed prayer shawl], then lifted onto his father's shoulders and, in song and dance, brought to the *Chedder* to start learning *Chumash* [Pentateuch].

---

[62] Yaakov Mazor, *haBadchan baChevrah haIsraelit*, Jerusalem: 2000, in *Duchan,* Journal 15:45-47

Chapter 4 – Dance

1. Dance in the Bible

Dance appears in the Bible in two main forms: as part of victory celebrations following war, or as a religious act.

Dance following victory is seen when "Miriam the Prophetess, sister of Aharon, took a timbrel in her hand; and all the women went out after her with timbrels and with dances".[1] The same thing occurs when Yiftach returns victorious over Ammon: "And behold his daughter came out before him with timbrels and dancing"[2] and with the downfall of the Phillistines before David: "And all the women came out from the cities of Israel to sing, and dance before Saul the King".[3]

We find religious dance in relation to the golden calf, according to the verse: "And it came to pass, as soon as he came near unto the camp, that he saw the calf and the dancing".[4] King David danced when he brought the Holy Ark to the City of David: "And David capered with all his might before G-d".[5] David felt such elation that he forgot he was the King, and Michal his wife disdained him in her heart, rebuking him: "Who revealed himself to-day in the eyes of the handmaids of his servants, as one of the vain fellows shamelessly exposing himself".[6] On festive days the young women of Israel would also dance: "Behold there is the feast of G-d in Shiloh […] and the daughters of Israel come out to dance".[7]

Our Sages said:

> Chassidim and public dignitaries would dance before them (before all the people gathered around the walls, and before the lights, so that all would see all; thus the Chassidim and public dignitaries would dance, that is, the greatest luminaries of the generation such as the members of the Great Assembly [Sanhedrin], the heads of Academies, and other wise men of Israel, but the general populace did not dance and sing, so that over-joyousness would not lead to lightheadedness. And all came to watch and listen). With torches of light in their hands, and while reciting songs and praises, the Levites with lyres and harps, cymbals and

---

1 Exodus 15:20
2 Judges 11:34
3 I Samuel 18:6
4 Exodus 32:19
5 II Samuel 6:14
6 II Samuel 6:20
7 Judges 21: 19, 21

trumpets, and musical instruments, recounting the fifteen steps, moving down from the general assembly of Israel to the assembly of women, correlating to the fifteen "Songs of Ascension" in the Psalms, which the Levites sang accompanied by instruments.[8]

The Talmud recounts how, on the 15th of Av and on Yom Kippur, the young women of Israel would come out into the vineyards and the countryside.[9] Of Rabbi Shimon ben Gamliel, it is said:

> When he rejoiced over the Ceremony of Drawing the Water, he would take eight lit torches in one hand, throw them into the air, then throw one and receive one, and none of them touched the other.[10]

Religious dance, noted Horodetzky, became rooted in the nation and integrated as a unique part of serving G-d: "They will praise His name with dance", and "Praise Him with timbrel and dancing" (Psalms 149:3, 150:4). On occasion, religious dance completed the religious service, and on other occasions, the dance per se was the service of G-d, like a thread connecting and holding the dancer until exhaustion. Religious ecstasy, which steadily increased as the dance progressed, brought the dancer to such deep inspiration [*hitpa'alut*] that he forgot the world entirely, rising ever higher in the heavenward flame.[11]

Concerning the 'end of days', the Talmud states:

> The Holy One, Blessed be He, will dance with the Tzaddikim, as he sits in the Garden of Eden.[12] And a thousands upon thousands of serving angels shall stand before them, holding lyres and harps and cymbals and all kinds of musical instruments, singing before them at their meal, and the Holy One, Blessed be He, Himself stands and dances at the meal, and the sun, the moon and the stars to His right and to His left dance before them with Him.[13]

2. The Importance of Dance in Chassidism

Music ameliorates the judgment, the source of blessing is in dance, dances directed for holy purposes; the ecstasy of the sacred dance can be equated to 'of a sweet savor to the Lord'.[14]

---

8 Uri Orenstein, *haNe'um vehaDrosh,* Bnei Brak 1965:146
9 b. Taanit, 26b
10 Sukkah 51a, 53a
11 Horodetzky, *haChassidut vehaChassidim,* Tel Aviv: 1951, pg.183-184
12 b. Taanit, 31a
13 Horodetzky, *haChassidut vehaChassidim,* Tel Aviv: 1951, pg.186, citing AlphaBeta d'Rabbi Akiva, in the *Otzar haMidrashim,* 417
14 Leviticus 1:9, as cited in Horodetzky, *haChassidut vehaChassidim,* pg. LIV

The above is how Rabbi Nahman of Bratzlav explained dance. He added that:

> If they only heard one explanation of Torah, with its song and dance, all else would be entirely nullified, that is, the whole world, even the animals and plants, and everything in the world, all would be nullified to the point of yearning, because of the immensely powerful pleasure.

"He himself would dance from time to time. This was his way", explained Rabbi Nathan his disciple: to dance with a melody of awakening and awe, and whoever did not witness one of his dances never witnessed goodness in his lifetime. And whoever was nearby must have felt the stirrings of true repentance for all his transgressions. The enormity of the arousal and ecstasy of all those standing there during these dances is indescribable.[15]

A Chassidic legend[16] relates the story of Rabbi Shabtai, a bookbinder, who lived during the time of the Besht. He was poor, and dejected: all his weeklong efforts did not yield sufficient to buy anything more for the Sabbath beyond bread and herring. But Rabbi Shabtai was so happy on the Sabbath that he would dance with great enthusiasm and joy. The Besht noticed his dancing from a distance, and said:

> By virtue of these dances, a child will be born that will enlighten all Israel; and the Tzaddik Reb Israel was born, known as 'The Tzaddik of Kozenice'.

Tales recall the dancing of Rabbi Levi Yitzhak (1740-1810) of Berditchev on *Simchat Torah*. He would hold the scroll with both his hands, flush to his heart, his eyes closed and his face as red as fire, the flame of Godliness. He danced and danced and his feet did not touch the ground, as though floating in the air in the synagogue, and the congregation stood at some distance, the awe of G-d having struck them. At that moment, the legend goes, the Upper Worlds lay silenced, and the serving angels ceased to recite songs to the Holy One, Blessed be He, and there was no greater joyous satisfaction in the Upper Worlds as during that dance of Rabbi Levi Yitzhak of Berditchev.[17]

The dances of the 'Zeideh of Shapoli' were also renowned. He would reach great joy and ecstasy in the service of his Creator. Every Friday after the *Kabbalat Shabbat* service he would begin to dance as his Chassidim sang; he would dance with such fervor and clapping that when Rabbi Avraham the Angel saw him, he

---

15 *Chayei Moharan*, Part 1: 19
16 Presented in Horodetzky, *haChassidut vehaChassidim*, pg. 191
17 Ibid

said: "These dances are more important to the Holy One, Blessed be He, than all his prayers".[18]

The custom of the Tzaddik, Rabbi Chaim of Kosov, was to dance every Sabbath eve with great ecstasy, until his face burned like a fire. It happened once that a bench fell on his leg, and the pain was so great that he ceased dancing. But not for long – only a few days later, he recommenced with the same enthusiasm, as though nothing at all had occurred. The Chassidim sought to stop him, as his leg was still not fully healed. He responded:

> Do you think I stopped dancing because my leg hurt? Not so! My leg hurt because I stopped dancing.[19]

Another anecdote relates to the *Baal haAvnei Nezer* of Sochotchov who, while reciting the *Hallel* and on reaching the verse "the mountains skipped like rams" (Psalms 114:4), would dance with such fervor that he floated in the air and only thereafter, would he touch the ground, and say, "this is dancing like rams".[20]

About the Tzaddik, Rabbi Naftali (1760-1827) of Ropczyce, it is said that his adherents danced in his courtyard on *Simhat Torah*. They danced with fervor, singing and chanting as was their custom, while their Rebbe watched from the open window that faced the courtyard. Suddenly he indicated with his hand that they should stop dancing, and when they did, the Tzaddik remained momentarily deep in thought, then said, "If a soldier falls in battle, must all the other soldiers flee? No! The war must still be fought! Dance!" So the Chassidim continued dancing. After the festival, it became known that at exactly the moment when the Rebbe had stopped his followers, the Rebbe of Owilnov, who was one of the Rabbi of Ropczyce's most accomplished Torah scholars, had passed away.[21]

What, in fact, is the latent power of dance? If we have so far discussed music as a way of serving G-d out of joy and as a way of nullifying sadness (see Chapter 2), when that joy manifests spiritually, the Chassid's soul becomes joyful. Here, however, dance is given a wider significance, in that while dancing, not only does the soul serve G-d but the body also serves Him, in the sense of "all my bones shall speak".[22] Thus, joy resides not only in the Chassid's soul and spirit, but in his whole being, including his body.

---

18 Ibid, pg. 191-192
19 S. Zevin, *Sippurei Chassidim*, Tel Aviv: 1985, For the Festivals, pg. 141
20 *beOhalei Tzaddikim,* Tales and Anecdotes on the Passover Haggadah, pg. 131
21 Ibid, pg. 185
22 Psalms 35:10. And in the *Nishmat Kol Chai* [the soul of every living thing] prayer recited every Sabbath,

Along the above lines, the swaying movements that manifest while praying can also be interpreted not as a way of concentrating in a more focused manner and preventing commonplace thoughts from intervening, but as another mode for drawing one's whole being into prayer. A person who sways while praying involves his whole body, and can be considered as 'dancing in his prayers', drawing his whole body into the joy of prayer, while his 'song' draws his soul into the prayer. In this way, the person praying becomes disconnected from the present world and entirely focused on serving G-d. This is the most perfect way to serve G-d. Horodetzky noted that "religious dance reached its peak when combined with singing and musical accompaniment in the Chassidism of the Besht". He further noted that "religious fervor to the point of self-nullification is one of the most important foundations of Chassidic doctrine".

"Shed and separate from the physical body and cleave with true fervor to the object of your devotion", explained Rabbi Jacob of Polonnoye, who was the Besht's most outstanding disciple. Only through such ecstasy can a person reach the level of 'the ascending soul'. From the lofty position of his spirit, he can make his way out of the material world and cling to G-d.

Horodetzky further notes that Chassidism found this kind of religious fervor in dance, combined with playing music and singing. Combining all three enabled them to serve G-d completely.[23]

The Talmud describes how Rabbi Akiva, when praying for himself, would start his prayers facing one direction, and later would be found facing another direction entirely, resulting from the many times he swayed and bowed.[24]

Idelsohn referred to the Kuzari, who formulated the question: "Why does the Jew sway when reading in Hebrew?" And the companion responds: "In order to awaken his natural warmth"; then continues: "For it is known that the body's movements are important to serving G-d, [distinguishing from] among all other nations, and religious dance developed from this". As already stated above in connection with King David, the Chassidim renewed the religious dance for the sake of arousing fervor, as well as the swaying body movements when praying.[25]

A particularly fine interpretation is offered by Rabbi Aharon (1736-1772) of Karlin: "Great is the power of the dance that lifts the person one *tefach* [a measurement of one hand-breadth] above the ground".[26] With this explanation, we are taught a new aspect of dance in addition to its meaning of "all my bones shall speak": here, there is a brief disconnection of the body from the ground, that is, a

---

23 Horodetzky, *haChassidut vehaChassidim*, pg. 188
24 b. Berachot 31a
25 Idelsohn, *haNegginah haChassidit*, pg. 7
26 Rabbi Aharon of Karelin, *Raz Simcha: Pitgamei Chassidim*, Jerusalem: 1989: 175

self-nullification, or nullification of the material, and an increasing closeness to the spiritual, to the Holy One, Blessed be He.

In the chapter *Interviews*, we find the explanation of Rabbi Yishaya Rattenburg of Jerusalem (the son of the Kassan Admor) on dance: while dancing, the dancer appears like a candle that is drawn upwards but nonetheless descends, which is likened to the soul being drawn upward while the physical body draws downward.

Rabbi Schneur Zalman of Liadi (1745-1813) described two people dancing together, distancing and coming closer to each other, which describes the relationship between a person and G-d. He explained:

> The joy of the Jewish people to G-d can be compared to dancing, where the two people dancing together distance from, and draw closer to, each other; the distance is the reason for drawing close. Just as it is not a real distancing, and is not internal and directed, but a way of dancing, so it is with the joy of the Jewish people in its form of distancing and drawing close. It is not a real distancing, G-d forbid, but bears the sense of drawing away in order to return.[27]

In an interview I conducted with the Chief Rabbi of Austria, Rabbi Chaim Eisenberg, he presented additional explanations for the importance of dancing on *Simchat Torah* (see full interview in appropriate chapter):

> There are various reasons for Chassidic dancing; for example on Simchat Torah, when dancing with the Torah scroll which is in the circle of dancers and designates the dance as being in honor of the completion of the year-long reading of Torah.
>
> Another explanation is that in such a dance, all dancers are equally distanced from the center of the circle; at the center of the circle is the Torah scroll which symbolizes the Holy One, Blessed be He; thus, no one should think he is closer to, or further away from, G-d than is anyone else.

3. Dancing before the Bride

It is well known that the Jewish sages were particular about gladdening the bride and groom, as is stated in the Talmud:[28]

> Whosoever enjoys the groom's [celebratory] meal and does not gladden him, negates five voices, as is said, 'the voice of joy and the voice of gladness, the voice of the bridegroom and the voice of the bride, the voice of them that say, 'Give thanks to the Lord of hosts'.'[29]

---

27 *Likkutei Devarim*, 86b, Section commencing: 'On the Eighth Day'; and see article by Yoram Yakobson, *Toratah shel haChassidut*, pg. 79
28 b. Berachot 6b
29 Jeremiah 33:11

The Germarra explains further:

> And if he gladdens him [the groom], he merits Torah, which was given in five voices, as is said: 'And it came to pass on the third day, when it was morning, that there were thunders and lightnings [...], and the voice of the *shofar* [ram's horn] etc.[30]

Rabbi Nahman bar Yitzhak said that "the person who brings gladness to the groom and bride is like a person who has rebuilt one of the ruins of Jerusalem".[31]

Dance gradually became increasingly important in the life of the Jewish people, to the point that the houses of Hillel and Shammai were divided over the issue of "how does dance before the bride?" Of Rabbi Yehudah bar Ilai it is said that he would take a sprig of myrtle and dance before the bride. Rabbi Shmuel bar R' Yitzhak would dance with three sprigs of myrtle, throwing one up while catching another.[32]

Bar Kapra was known to have said to the daughter of Rabbi Judah *haNassi* [the Prince]: "Tomorrow I shall drink wine when your father dances".[33] The book, *Chochmat Mano'ach* explains that this is why the phase is causative – *merakdin*, that is, causing to dance – rather than *rokdin*, that is, dancing; the obligation is not only that one must dance but one should cause others to join the dancing.[34]

Indeed, the Admors, despite differences of customs among them, were all very particular about dancing with the groom. The highlight was when the Admor himself danced before the bride. Dancing for the bride was known by various expressions, such as *Mitzvah Tanz*. This dance is already mentioned in the literature long before the advent of Chassidism.[35] The very first *Book of Customs*, which appeared in Venice in 1590, states: "In several communities, the mitzvah dance is danced by the men with the groom, and by the women with the bride".[36] Among Chassidim it was very important to uphold the teachings of both the House of Hillel and the House of Shammai, "How do we dance before the bride?".[37] This dance was conducted according to various customs: for example, the bride's father would dance first with the bride, followed by others of his family according to a certain order. Then the Rebbe would dance for a while, and finally, the groom himself would dance with her. This dance would be accompa-

---

30 Exodus 19: 16 and on.
31 b. Berachot 6b
32 b. Ketubot, 17a
33 b. Nedarim 51a
34 Booklet *Otzar heYediot*, Part 1, pg. 272
35 In-depth study on dance: Zvi Friedhaber, *Rikkudei Mitzvah: Toldoteihem, Tzuroteihen veRakdaneihem*, in *Duchan*, No.15, 5760 [2000]
36 Ibid, pg. 29, quoting Reb Isaac Tirnoya, Customs, Venice 5750 (1590), pg. 71
37 b. Ketubot, 16b

nied by "directions" given by the merrymaker, who would invite the dancers with various forms of jest and rhyming phrases. The merrymaker would employ his verbal and musical abilities on this occasion, and his activities themselves became an inseparable part of the dance.

An anecdote is related concerning Rabbi Mottele of Chernobyl (1770-1837), son of Rabbi Nachum 'the Great', the Maggid of Chernobyl (1730-1798). Rabbi Mottele would dance with the bride by holding one corner of a cloth serviette, and the bride holding another corner. His eyes were closed and his feet seemed to hover in the air, moving slowly in a circle. During such moments, he forgot reality and reached the level of self-nullification almost to the point of becoming "a real angel of G-d", as described by the Chassidim. He danced without ever stopping. Even when the bride, exhausted, could no longer continue and returned to her chair, Reb Mottele continued to dance, not sensing all that occurred around him. 'He is not of the world of judgment', said the Chassidim. The Tzaddikim of the generation said of him:

> Rabbi Mottele is the only one who has understood the hidden aspect of 'dancing before the bride', and if he had lived in the generation of the Houses of Hillel and Shammai, when the question arose, 'How should we dance before the bride?', he would have responded in his way. His dance before the bride was a dance before the *Shechinah*.[38]

Rabbi Shmelki of Sassov (1800-1869), son of Rabbi Moshe Leib of Sassov (1745-1807), held wedding festivities for his daughter's marriage. Guests at the wedding, on their return journey home, stopped to visit Rabbi Meir of Przemyshlan (1780-1850) who asked them to relate the special incident that occurred at the wedding. The visitors spoke and spoke, but the Rabbi was not satisfied with all he heard, and kept repeating his question, "What else happened there?" Finally they told him about the mitzvah dance: "While the groom danced with the bride, a tall man suddenly jumped into the circle of dancers, dressed like a bear, and danced a marvelous bear-dance. Everyone was amazed at the fascinating movements he made, and clapped. Suddenly he disappeared, as though he had never been there. And no one knew who he was". Rabbi Meir replied: "Yes, we do know. This was none other than our holy teacher, Reb Moshe Leib of Sassov, who descended from the Upper Heavens to gladden his descendants".[39]

Special melodies having immeasurable [spiritual] value are known to have been used when the Rebbe danced with the bride. Some Chassidim used the tune for

---

38 Horodetzky, haChassidut vehaChassidim, Chapter on Chassidic Music and Dance, pg.192
39 *Ohr haGanuz*, pg. 303-304

Eshet Chayil [A Woman of Valor: from Proverbs 31:10-31] which was customary for that particular Chassidic court.

There is a clear correlation between the Chassidic niggun and the Chassidic dance. The maturity of both are the result of hundreds of years of development. The Tzaddik usually had his own unique kind of niggun and dance, while that of his adherents was somewhat different. The two kinds of niggun and dance influence each other and are influenced by each other, but both share the same root, deeply embedded in the Upper Worlds. There is the single, great melody "from the world of the niggun" which encompasses all others, and there is also a state where niggunim unite, the fine, silent niggun of the Tzaddik merging with the rousing niggun of his adherents to form one mighty niggun of fervor and ecstasy, all for the sake of unifying G-d's Name with the *Shechinah*. There is also the concealed dance of the Tzaddik, with small, gentle movements of the feet, which mingles with the dances of the Chassidim, making the dance holy in honor of G-d.[40]

---

40 Horodetzky, haChassidut vehaChassidim, Chapter on Chassidic Music and Dance, pg.193

Chapter 5 – The Shabbat and Music

1. The Shabbat and Music

The Sabbath [*Shabbat*] is considered a day of rest. However, it is not a day of rest given to humanity for the sake of ceasing our weekday work and storing strength for the week to come. Shabbat has another significance, according to the verse: "And you called the Shabbat delight".[1] Shabbat is a day of light and joy, of festivity, a day in which the Jew receives inspiration [*neshama yetera,* lit. 'an extra soul'], a day which is entirely holiness and spirituality, and any material or physical act we perform on Shabbat receives different significance to that which it possesses during the regular weekdays. The meals we eat on Shabbat are not regular weekday meals but are sanctified in a special way as part of the uniqueness of Shabbat, through discussion of Torah and singing of songs around the Shabbat table. Singing on Shabbat is different in its glorious tones than the singing of weekdays, and receives a spiritual value. On Shabbat, the Jew is obligated to be happy, and all things which cause sorrow and gloom must be put aside, to be dealt with on weekdays. Thus, there is no mourning on Shabbat: mourning ceases an hour before Shabbat begins and resumes once Shabbat is over. For the same reason, the Sages determined that in the *Amidah* prayer of Shabbat, no pleas and requests are made of the kind said during the week. As the words of one of the Shabbat songs indicate, Shabbat is 'a kind of world to come'.

The Midrash refers to the verse, "For I have given you a good doctrine; do not forsake my Torah".[2] The Midrash[3] asks what is meant by 'do not forsake', and teaches:

> When the Torah was being given [on Mt. Sinai], the Holy One, Blessed be He, called to Israel and said to them: 'My children, I have good 'merchandise' in the world, and I am giving it to you forever more, if you will receive my Torah and guard it'. They answered and said, 'Sovereign of the universe, what kind of good merchandise shall you give us if we keep your Torah?' G-d replied, saying, 'The world to come'. Israel answered, saying, 'Sovereign of the universe, show us a sample of this world to come'. Then G-d answered them, saying,

---

1 Isaiah 58:13
2 Proverbs 4:2
3 *Midrash Otiot d'Rabbi Akiva haShalem,* Letter Aleph

'It is the Shabbat, which is one sixtieth of the [goodness of the] world to come, which is entirely [a state of] Shabbat, as is said: 'remember the Shabbat day'.[4]

The Midrash continues by asking: "How do we know that the world to come is wholly Shabbat?" And provides the response:

As is written: A Psalm, a Song for the Shabbat day.[5] 'Day' means the whole Shabbat: for Adam, on seeing the Shabbat, said words of praise to the Holy One, Blessed be He: 'A Psalm, a song for the Shabbat day, how good it is to thank the Lord and sing to Your Name, most high One.'[6] At that time the serving angels [*malachei hasharet*] descended in groups from the heavens, some holding lyres and [musical] pipes, while others held harps and cymbals, and other instruments of music, playing before Him, as is said: 'and sing to Your Name, most High One'.[7]

Regarding the verse, "because you did not serve the Lord your God with joyfulness'[8] Y. Yefet relates to the Chassidic court of Rabbi Bunim of Przysucha (1767-1827) and a particular Chassid who was pedantic, querulous and melancholy. He arrived in Przysucha one Saturday night, and related that he had experienced a problem on his way and was forced to spend the Shabbat somewhere along his journey. Rabbi Bunim said to him:

Shabbat brings guests together. When the New Month falls on Shabbat, the Shabbat receives her guest and gives it a reading of *Maftir* [Torah portion] and the *Mussaf* [additional] prayer. When a festival falls on Shabbat, the Shabbat gives it all the Torah readings and prayers. When *Yom Kippur* falls on Shabbat, the Shabbat also gives it her meals, and fasts together with it. But if *Tisha B'Av* falls on Shabbat, she gives it nothing, and postpones it to Sunday, as the Shabbat does not want to receive a melancholy guest, and it is better that such a guest arrives after Shabbat.[9]

Chassidism positioned Shabbat as the center of its Torah, social and public lifestyle. This led to the saying, "Whoever has not seen a Chassidic Shabbat has not seen a happy Shabbat in his life, nor felt higher spiritual uplifting".[10] Shabbat is not only the Creator's chosen day, but is also the day in which "all the *pnimiut* [internality] can be brought closer, and the self be nullified for G-d". Therefore, one should prepare for Shabbat during all the other days of the week, according to the *Ri"m* of Gur:

---

4 Exodus 20:8
5 Psalms 92:1
6 Ibid, 2
7 Ibid
8 Deuteronomy 28:47
9 See *Sefer Itturei Torah*, Tel Aviv: 1970, A. Y. Grinberg, Vol.6, pg. 168
10 Alfassi, *biSdeh haChassidut*, Tel Aviv: 1986, pg. 335

Just as one cannot arrive at the world to come without prior preparation in this world, so one cannot come to the Shabbat without prior ready-making. If one begins the Shabbat as one is, without any preparation or intentions, not only will such a person be unable to feel the light of Shabbat, but the Shabbat will reject him and drive him away. Thus, a Chassid should prepare daily for the holy Shabbat and from it, draw strength for all the coming days of the week.[11]

An example of this concept can also be found in the Talmud[12] which speaks of Shammai the Elder who, throughout his life, ate in honor of the Shabbat. When he saw a fine beast, he would say, 'that one is for Shabbat', but if he found an even better one, he would put the first aside and eat the better one for the sake of honoring the Shabbat. We learn also that the *Tannaim* prepared themselves for Shabbat during the weekdays.[13]

2. Welcoming the Shabbat

Receiving the Shabbat commences already while it is still daylight, and is conducted with glory and honor. In the times of the Talmudic sages, the Shabbat was received with poetic song and uplifting of the soul, as recorded:

> Rabbi Hanina would wrap himself [in his *tallit*- *prayer shawl*] and go out to greet the 'countenance' of Shabbat, and say: 'Come, let us go out towards the bride, Shabbat the queen'. Rabbi Yanai donned a special garment for the Shabbat eve, and said: 'Come, O bride; come, O bride'.[14]

Every Friday after midday, the Besht would pray the *Mincha* [afternoon] service with his disciples in a *minyan* and immediately afterwards, begin to welcome the Shabbat. When he was still newly revealed, he would go out to the fields in full daylight with his disciples to welcome the Shabbat. On one occasion during the summer while out in the field, the sheep had not yet returned from pasturing. The Besht and his disciples sang and gave thanks: "O come, let us sing to the Lord;

---

11 Ibid
12 b. Beitzah, 16a
13 The Maggid of Mezhirech, in his book *Maggid Devarav leYaakov*, Jerusalem: 1990, pg. 311 explains the dispute between the Houses of Hillel and Shammai in the narrative above. The House of Shammai made a mitzvah out of something accessible, while the House of Hillel raised the commonplace to the purity of sanctity. However, Shatz-Uffenheimer claims that the dispute reflects the later difference between traditional and Chassidic ways of serving G-d. With Shammai's approach, the accessible also became a mitzvah but Hillel raised the commonplace to the value of sacred; Shatz-Uffenheimer views this as already being a definition of Chassidic ways, later developed during the time of the Besht.
14 b. Shabbat 119a

let us shout for joy to the Rock of our salvation".[15] On hearing the prayers and song, the sheep stood up on their hind legs, their front legs raised high, looking like flames, and joined in welcoming the Shabbat.

It was also the Besht's custom to honor Shabbat by wearing white clothing, and enjoying Shabbat with his family over the songs and niggunim. The niggun for him was "a form of love and awe pouring forth from Above to Below, throughout all the lower levels".

On Friday evening he would make the *Kiddush* [blessing over the wine] with wonderful fervor, and sang songs and niggunim suited to the festive atmosphere of Shabbat. He sang with that same pleasant voice he used when working as an apprentice teacher, the voice to which the infants sang, bringing about the same great satisfaction in the Upper Worlds as the Levites had aroused when they sang in the Temple. The Besht's voice would immerse his listeners in a seeming spirit from heaven, imbuing them with a feeling of "serving G-d with joy".[16] In this way, the Besht reflected the soul's joy to the Shabbat.

There was no exaggeration to his statement that "anyone who had merited being among those who spent Shabbat with him, and ate at his table, received the elixir of life, for being near him was like a cure from all temptation, and also awakened holy and pure behavior in his home".[17]

The songs sung on Shabbat are alluded to in the letters of the word "Shabbat" which are initials for various phrases, some of which are: When bringing in the Shabbat, you shall sing; On the Shabbat day you shall sing poetically; When Shabbat has ended, you shall play [musical instruments]; Bring in Shabbat before its time; Let the Shabbat end late; When Shabbat is over, you shall eat.[18]

Idelsohn points out that the mystics sang profusely during Shabbat:

> For this purpose, the Ari would compose poetics and songs to honor the Shabbat, and he himself was accustomed to singing beautifully when welcoming the Shabbat, such as the poem *Lecha* Dodi, composed by his contemporary, Rabbi Shlomo Alkabetz. It is told of the Ari that once, on a Friday, close to the commencement of Shabbat, he and his disciples went out from the city of Tzefat [Safed] and began with: 'A Psalm of David: Ascribe to the Lord", then sang a song that welcomed the Shabbat, then the Psalm for the Shabbat day, and the song of Godly kingship, with beautiful melodies.

Indeed, from Tzefat, which was the center of mystical study and practice, the custom to sing profusely as a welcome to the Shabbat quickly spread, until musical

---

15 Psalms 95:1
16 Geshuri, article in *Machanayim*, 85, 5724 [1964] in his article on the Besht, citing *Beit Aharon* 21.
17 Ibid, citing *Ma'asiyot veMa'amarim Yekarim*
18 Ibid, citing Rabbi David Lida, the Ashkenaz Rabbi of Amsterdam, author of *Divrei David*

instruments began to be employed in the synagogue for this purpose. At the end of the 17th century it was customary in Italy to welcome the Shabbat with great joy and pleasant songs, and several communities welcomed the Shabbat with musical instruments, players and singers, and sorrow on Shabbat was forbidden.[19]

One of the loveliest and most famous Shabbat tunes is that for *Shalom Aleichem*. It is sung on returning home after completing the Friday night services in the synagogue. With the table covered in white cloth, the two *challah* breads placed on it, and the candles lit, every Jew sings "Welcome to you, angels of peace, angels on high". The Talmud refers to this:

> Two angels accompany each man as he returns from the synagogue to his home on Shabbat eve; one is good, one is evil. When he comes into his home and finds the table set, the candles lit, and his bed prepared, the good angel says, 'May it be Your will that he shall see another (the coming) Shabbat as this one', and the evil angel must say 'amen' despite itself. But if not, then the evil angel says, 'May it be Your will that he shall see another (the coming) Shabbat as this one', and the good angel must say 'amen' despite itself.[20]

This poetic song has been set to a wide variety of tunes throughout Jewish communities.

3. Shabbat Songs

The Hebrew word *zemirot,* used to refer to songs sung on Shabbat, is a plural form of the word for 'song', *zimrah*. Geshuri noted, however, that:

> *Zmirot* refers specifically to religious music rooted deeply in Judaism. Zmirot embody the spiritual delight of Shabbat, and only through them can the spiritual life of Shabbat be comprehended well. The *zimrah*, which had always been a powerful aspect of religious and cultural life, is considered both obligatory and a mitzvah at every festive meal. The zimrah arouses honest prayer and awe of G-d […] if a festive occasion cannot be thought of without it involving songs and singing, how much more apt is singing on religious Festivals. The *Haham Zunz* finds an allusion to singing on Festivals from the Midrash [homiletic interpretation] on the Song of Songs: 'When Israel eats and drinks, they praise and extol the Holy One, Blessed be He'.[21]

The Shabbat songs draw the Jew into a more elevated world than the one he inhabits during weekdays. On Shabbat, the power of the niggunim can be well felt.[22]

---

19 Idelsohn, *haNegginah haChassidit*, pg. 4
20 b. Shabbat, pg.119
21 Geshuri, article in *Machanayim*, 85, 5724 [1964] on Shabbat songs
22 A. Y. Rosental, *Kemotzeh Shalal Rav*, Jerusalem: 2004:171

Many minstrels composed songs of praise honoring Shabbat, which became common throughout the Jewish world, sung at the Shabbat evening meal, or during the Shabbat day meal, at the third Shabbat meal, or at the festive *Melaveh Malkah* [accompanying the queen] meal held after Shabbat had ended.

Many poets and authors from the non-Jewish world were impressed with the beauty and lyric atmosphere of Shabbat. The endeavored to describe the unique mood, holiness and purity with which the Jew – once the weekdays had ended, with their hard work and melancholy – celebrated his Shabbat, its beauty allowing all sorrow to be forgotten. They viewed the Jew observing his Shabbat as a person whose figure and radiant face was akin to that of kings or princes. Regarding the *zmirot,* they would say that no matter whether it was Shabbat eve or the Passover *Sedder*, Chanukah or Purim, when a Jew became immersed in the elevated spiritual mood, he sensed a feeling of exultation, and the clouds darkening the skies of his soul scattered.[23]

How did the custom of singing Shabbat songs develop? Avraham Rosental offers several sources for this practice:

1. Rabbi Yehuda heChassid writes, in *Sefer Chassidim*:
   It is the custom of Israel to recite praises and songs on Shabbat, as is written: 'And G-d blessed the Shabbat day'.[24] No-one understood what this blessing was, until Job uttered a curse (being the opposite of a blessing) which indicated that the opposite must be performed, as appearing in Job 3:7, 'Let no joyful voice enter'. Thus we understand that the Shabbat should be made joyful with songs and praises.
2. The Midrash (Song of Songs, Chapter 8) states:
   'My love has fled' – for Israel's way when they eat and drink is [to accompany it] with songs and praises'. And the Sages said (*Megillah* 12): 'The seventh day is Shabbat, when Israel eats and drinks and offers words of Torah and praises'.
3. The Zohar states (weekly portion of *Ekev*, 172):
   'The zmirot are considered one of the ten things that a person must include in the Shabbat meal'. This means, 'one must awaken song and joy at her table', for a new face has come.
4. Rosental refers to two sources: the *Mahar"il*, Rabbi Yaakov Halevi Molin of Magence (1365-1427) on Laws of the Shabbat, and Rabbi Yitzhak Barabi Moshe of Vienna (1180-1250), known by the name of his book, the *Ohr Zarua* (Part 2, section 95). Rosental noted that they waxed eloquent over the merits of the zmirot sung at the Shabbat meals, and especially those sung after

---

23 Geshuri, article in *Machanayim*, 85, 5724 [1964], on Zmirot Shabbat
24 Genesis 2:3

Shabbat ended, when they would sing songs that referred to the differentiation between Shabbat and the weekdays, and recite chants in this vein, and pray for speedy news of the Redemption.[25]

Geshuri, relating to this issue, noted the difficulty in determining when or where singing of zmirot first became customary. He quoted a note in an old book titled *Shtei Yadot* which indicates that the custom of singing zmirot derives from early Germany and Italy. However, this does not seem entirely correct. It is known that the Jewish community of Spain composed and sang Shabbat and Festival zmirot, and a tradition of musicians developed there who specialized in composing tunes for Shabbat and Festivals, many of which are still currently sung.

In short, we have no proven information concerning the source of zmirot, but several allusions refer to this tradition. Geshuri explored the issue further: on the verse, "And G-d ceased on the seventh day"[26] he quoted *Bereshit Rabbah,* Chapter 10 "G-d said, 'a new face has come here, let us chant songs'."[27]

Geshuri then referred to the interpretation in *Shocher Tov* on Psalm 92 which opens with "A Psalm. A song for the Shabbat day": when Shabbat commences, it is received with chants and songs. Quoting the *Ri"ff* (Tractate Berachot, section *Ein Omdim,:* 'Where it is stated that song is forbidden, this applies to things like songs of romantic love to extol vane beauty, which the Ishamalites are accustomed to calling Asha'r. But no-one of Israel is prevented from uttering words of song and praises extolling the virtuousness of the Holy One, Blessed be He".

Geshuri summarized by noting that:

Oneg Shabbat [the delight of Shabbat] is, then, one of the aspects worthy of honor. With the confidence appropriate to the spirit of an innocent people and its feelings, they declare (as cited in *Tikkunei Zohar,* section 6): "Whoever receives the Shabbat with joy and pleasure in this world, will find that his soul and spirit, when they leave his body, will be received in like manner in the world to come".

Similarly, regarding the verse, "On the seventh day, when the heart of the King was merry with wine", found in the Scroll of Esther,[28] the Mishnah asks, "And until the seventh day, his heart was not merry with wine?" The explanation given is that the seventh day was Shabbat, when Israel eats and drinks and includes Torah interpretations and recitals of praise.[29]

---

25 A. Y. Rosental, *Kemotzeh Shalal Rav*, on Grace after Meals, pg. 271
26 Genesis 2:2
27 Geshuri, article in *Machanayim*, 85, 5724 [1964], on Zmirot Shabbat
28 Esther 1:10
29 b. Megillah 12b

A meal in which songs and praises are voiced is called a *Se'udat Mitzvah*, because of the power of the songs which connect this physical meal to G-d, according to the explanation offered by Rabbi Nahman of Bratzlav.[30]

The importance of the *zmirot* sung on *Motzei Shabbat* [the evening when the Shabbat ends] is related to in the *Rashi Siddur* (prayerbook according to Rabbi Shlomo Yitzhak, 1040-1105), which cites Rabbi Yosef Tov Elem:

> Singing *zmirot* on *Motzei Shabbat* is a fine and suitable custom, similar to the King's subjects who accompany him with lyres, harps and with their voices; so does Israel accompany the departure of Shabbat the Queen with joy and songs.[31]

4. The Shabbat Table in the Admor's Court

The Admors customarily conducted the Shabbat meal together with the Chassidim. On Friday evenings, after synagogue prayers were completed and the Chassidim had eaten at home with their families, they would gather usually at the synagogue or the Rebbe's home, where the Rebbe would hold a Shabbat meal. They also gathered for the third meal, after the *Minchah* service on the Shabbat day.

If Shabbat with Chassidim was considered a kind of world to come, then Shabbat with the Tzaddikim was a kind of real world to come, as noted by Alfassi.[32] He described the situation as follows:

> Each Tzaddik according to his manner. Some eat all manner of foods at the Shabbat table, while others are satisfied with only wine and fruit. Some commence with *Shalom Aleichem* in a delicate and uplifting tune, while others commence with *Kiddush*. Some of the Chassidim sit crowded around the Tzaddik's table, and others crowd around him standing up in order to see his every move and learn from his ways.

Rabbi Hanoch-Henich of Alexander (1798-1870), who was second in line after the *Ri"m* of Gur (1799-1866), would say: "When the righteous Messiah comes, all will know the meaning of meals conducted by the Tzaddikim".

At table [*Tisch*], the Tzaddik and his adherents sang songs and niggunim designated for Shabbat, and the Tzaddik explained passages of the Torah from which courage and hope were drawn to cope with the coming weekdays. The concept of *shirayim* was basic to such a meal. The Tzaddik himself tended to eat very little, satisfying only minimal bodily needs, and he handed out the remainder [*she'arim,* in Hebrew, which became known as *shirayim*] to his Chassidim.

---

30 Retrieved on August 1, 2008 from www.kipa.co.il/jew/show.asp?id=3388
31 Siddur Rashi, Jerusalem: 1999: section 5134 pg. 267 line 17
32 S. Y. Alfassi, *biSdeh haChassidut*, pg. 341-342

The Sages also said: "Whoever does not partake of bread at his [the Tzaddik's] table has never seen a blessing in his lifetime".[33] The Chassidim receive the Tzaddik's *shirayim* and what is left of the meal is shared among them, as the Tzaddik's act of eating is altruistic, and the Chassidim would almost give up their souls to receive *shirayim* from the Tzaddik's hands.

The Kabbalah endows mystical importance to these *shirayim*, as food contains "elevation of the sparks". The Besht said:

> Why did the Holy One, Blessed be He, create man with the ability to become hungry and thirsty when He could have created a man able to live without food or drink? For it is said, 'their souls fainted in them'?[34] Therefore, G-d made man hungry for food and thirsty for drink, in order for him to uplift the sparks, that is, the souls that have fainted in [becoming] the food, which is the meaning of 'their souls fainted in them'.

The Chassidim viewed the *shirayim* as a meritorious 'charm' for filling them with heavenly awe, livelihood and good health. In some courts of Tzaddikim, a second table was set as soon as the first was complete. The second 'round' offered various delicacies in honor of the Shabbat. At this second setting, the Tzaddik would discuss issues with his Chassidim and relate Chassidic tales. The sense was one of "brethren seated together".[35] This second setting was usually lengthy, lasting until well into the night, and was one of the most beautiful periods of the whole holy Shabbat.

When I was a youth, I studied at Yeshivat Be'er Yaakov which was about an hour's walk from the city of Rishon leZion. My mentor, Rabbi Menahem Mendel Taub (1918-), the Admor of Kalev, established his center there, and constructed a very beautiful synagogue whose structure, furnishings and interior were produced based on various, interesting mystical revealed and concealed signs and purposes: for example, the number of electrical bulbs totaled 613 reflecting the same number of precepts, and formed the shape of the Torah scrolls. We, the Yeshivah students, would sometimes walk on Shabbat eve to Rishon leZion to enjoy the Shabbat table with our Rebbe. We were always received warmly there, so much so that he began conducting a 'second *Tisch*' especially for the Yeshivah students who walked all the way to Be'er Yaakov. He even called this "the lads' *Tisch*". At this second setting, he would often sing two songs that we particularly loved: the first was *Yah Ribbon Olam* [G-d, Sovereign of the Universe], from among the well known Shabbat *zmirot*, to a melody that the Rebbe himself, apparently, composed; and the second was a Hungarian song

---

33 b. Sandhedrin, 92:71
34 Psalms 107:5
35 Psalms 133:1

called "Solo Kokosh" (the rooster crows). The story goes that initially it was a non-Jewish shepherd's song, and the first Kalev Rebbe, Yitzhak Isaac Taub (1744-1821) 'acquired' it from the shepherd and removed the sparks: these sparks then became a sacred piece. The song tells of the exile and the longing of the rebuilt Temple. This song had particular grace and sweetness when sung by the Rebbe with his very beautiful voice.

The *Seudah Shlishit* [third meal of Shabbat] is considered wholly 'Chassidic' in nature. Before the advent of Chassidism, each person would eat this meal in his home with the family, while Chassidism set this to be the meal eaten at the *Beit Midrash* [house of study and prayer] among friends, with *zmirot,* niggunim, and extrapolations of Torah passages.

The *Seudah Shlishit* was not usually a grand meal, the custom being to provide only *challah* and herring. I remember that in Jerusalem, the custom was to eat a slice of *challah* smeared with olive oil, cloves of garlic and a slice of tomato, which was known as *sheeress.* The explanation could possibly be that Jerusalem was poverty stricken, and experienced shortages of foodstuffs, although the price of olive oil, garlic and vegetables was very low, and affordable by all. The word *sheeress* – so similar to *she'iriyot* [leftovers] – could also simply derive from the notion that what was eaten at the third meal were the items left after the two main meals of Shabbat. In order to avoid any unpleasantness to others of the community, this combination settled into becoming a known Jerusalem custom at *Seudah Shlishit.*

The third meal is connected to the forefather Jacob, who is considered the superior of the forefathers, and the main *Tikkun* [rectification] occurs during this meal. Some claim that the saying, "Better one hour of repentance and good deeds in this world than a whole life in the world to come"[36] refers to this third meal.[37]

Rabbi Eliezer Horowitz of Tarnogrod (1740-1806) stated in his book *No'am Megadim,* that for as long as Chassidim draw out the *Se'udah Shlishit,* those designated for Gehinnom are not judged, as all is still in a state of Shabbat. Indeed, the Rebbe and his adherents lengthened this meal as far as possible, distributing *shirayim* to the Chassidim.[38]

The Chassidim would also customarily spend the hours after Shabbat with the Tzaddik, joining him in the fourth meal known as *Melaveh Malkah,* a form of farewell from Shabbat. According to the Kabbalah, this meal is very important as the 'atlas' bone in the body is nurtured by this meal: the Zohar explains that when the Messiah arrives, the resurrection will occur through this bone.[39]

---

36 Pirkei Avot 4:22
37 In *biSdeh haChassidut,* pg. 342-343
38 Ibid
39 Zohar Part 2:28, see also *Eliyahu Rabbah* Section 300 subsection 3

For good reason, it became an established custom in the courts of the Tzaddikim to play music with great devotion as preparation to delving into Torah interpretations. This form of 'Torah preparation' became thoroughly entrenched, as can be seen from narratives in various anthologies (Ner Israel, pg. 279; Meir haChaim, Part 3). One such narrative relates that on the 2nd of Sivan 5731 [1971], the *Imrei Chaim* held a *Yahrzeit Tisch* [memorial anniversary meal] for the last time in his life, for his father, the *Ahavat Israel*. Before presenting his enlightenment on a passage of Torah, the *Imrei Chaim* sat deeply pondering, lost in thought, humming the melody of *Eloka Dileih* which he was accustomed to singing before teaching his interpretations. He sat this way for a long time, and finally requested that *Mayim Acharonim* be brought. When one of his Chassidim, Rabbi Chaim Naftali Adler, remarked, "What of your Torah discourse?", the Rebbe answered: "But I have already given it!".[40]

We can learn more of the importance bestowed on niggunim sung at the table of the Tzaddik from a narrative presented by Horodetzky (1871-1957) regarding his own experience:

> The niggun of a famous Tzaddik from the Ukraine, Rabbi Yaakov Yitzhak of Makarov, strongly influenced this writer. Some sixty years have passed, yet I remember things as though I had seen and heard them just yesterday. After the *Kabbalat Shabbat* [welcoming the Shabbat] service, the Tzaddik sat at the head of the table with his sons and grandsons to his left and right. Along both sides of the very long table sat the Chassidim, myself among them, while many others stood. We all watched everything, every small movement in the Rebbe's face, every small move. He sat a little bent over the table, his eyes closed. He sat, quiet: there were no words of Torah, nor any words of commonplace chatter. From time to time, only a faint sigh could be heard, but that sigh took hold and rolled about that great hall and without noticing, all the Chassidim began to sigh. And all the sighs joined together, into one great heartrending sound. Then the Tzaddik began to sing *zmirot* for Shabbat, with a pleasing voice, a voice that came from the depths of his heart. He sang a phrase and all the Chassidim repeated it after him, phrase after phrase, with the same niggun and the same intonation. This is what happened on the Shabbat eve, and again during the day at the second Shabbat meal. But the fervor and enchantment heightened at the *Seudah Shlishit*, held between *Mincha* and *Maariv* [afternoon, and evening, services]. The hall was filled to capacity, as the congregation of Chassidim knew that during this meal, "the *Shechinah* rested upon him": his ecstasy increasingly grew, and along with it, that of the Chassidim. It seemed as though night's darkness had suddenly appeared, to cover the world. The Tzaddik rose, prayed *Maariv* in that same place together with his adherents, and conducted the *Havdalah* ceremony [differentiation between Shabbat and weekday] and on taking the goblet of wine into his palm, sang the prayer known throughout the Jewish world: 'G-d of Abraham, Isaac and Jacob, guard Your people Israel from all evil.'

---

40 Rabbi Yosef Moshe Kahana, in *haMachaneh haCharedi* 20 Shvat 5767 [February 8, 2007], in the magazine *Korei Oneg*, pg. 8

Chapter 6 – Music in Mysticism

1. Mysticism (Kabbalah) and Chassidism

Kabbalah is the core, the internal spirituality of Judaism. It delves deep into Jewish content, into its mystical aspects. It does not seek to contradict Judaism, nor undermine it, but on the contrary, strengthens and supports it, fills it with vitality: Kabbalah and Judaism are one and the same thing. Kabbalah knows how to find the kernel of Judaism, rising higher than all practical applications, all secular narratives, and reveals the secrets and allusions, finding the spirituality within them.[1]

With the paragraph below, Yitzhak Alfassi opened his article on Kabbalah:

Kabbalah is an organic part of the Torah. The Torah is revealed to all, but its inner content is known only to few, thus it is known as "the concealed wisdom" and is relayed from one generation to the next, being received [*mekubal*] by the younger generation from the older.

This is such an important article, that I have chosen to quote further from it. Alfassi continued:

What we see in the Five Books of Moses as natural and straightforward in this physical world, the Kabbalah is able to show us at the level of the mystical. It rises above the simple narrative and shows us every entity's internality.[2]

Rabbi Yishaya Halevi Ish Horowitz (1565-1630), known as the *Shla"h*, summarizes the concept in one sentence: "The Torah is holy in its revealed form, but Holy of Holies in its concealed form".[3]

In the chapter discussing the connection between the mystical teachings of the Arizal and Chassidism, Alfassi claimed that Chassidism used Kabbalah as the basis of all its concepts, noting that:

Chassidism considered Kabbalah of utmost importance, both as a subject of study and as a way of fervently upholding its traditions, even though it allowed for the occasional contradiction. The official ideologue of the Chassidic movement and its first author, Rabbi Yaakov Yosef of Polonnoye (d. 1782), wrote: 'Just as a person possesses both body and soul, so the

---

1 Horodetzky, *haChassidut vehaChassidim*, pg. XI
2 *biSdeh haChassidut*, pg. 19
3 Horodetzky, haChassidut vehaChassidim, pg. XI

Torah possesses body and soul, and just as Adam was created first in physical form, and only thereafter 'He blew life force into his nostrils',[4] so we must learn first the body of Torah [text] and then learn about its concealed soul'.

Yet those who seek to study the concealed aspects prior to gaining proficiency with the scriptures and the Talmud must nonetheless be considered deserving of merit, as all the scriptures and Talmud are the totality of the body, belonging to all of Israel, in general; and thus, if an individual of the Jewish people, who is like one limb in that whole, seeks to learn one limb of the Torah, he is permitted to learn its inner aspects. It is the soul that directs that limb of his body.

Alfassi then quoted a section from *Yosher Divrei Emet*, authored by Rabbi Meshulam Feibish of Zabriza:

> The Gaon, Our Mighty and Holy Member of Israel, Our Splendor, Teacher and Rabbi, R' Israel baal Shem Tov of greatly blessed memory, the father of the Chassidim, who enlightened the world with opened gates of Torah wisdom, insight and knowledge, structured the foundations of Chassidism on the Holy Zohar and the interpretations of the Arizal, even though some cautioned him against such learning for its own sake, and emphasized that the focus is 'a matter of love of the Creator and awe of His Blessed Name'. It is impossible to explain to another what love in one's heart is, and this is the 'concealed' aspect [...] all the concealed aspects of the entire Zohar and writings of the Arizal are reliant upon fervor towards the Creator.[5]

In fact, Idelsohn also claimed: "As is well known, Chassidism is not an entirely new creation, a kind of 'ex nihilo', but is structured on the foundations of Kabbalah and mysticism, according to the form bestowed on it by the Ari, who drew on Kabbalistic sources in Israel that existed already before his own time. Clearly both approaches, the mystic and the realistic, have always run together like a silk thread throughout Jewish history".[6]

Alfassi further stated:

> All that was revealed to the Ari derives from the heavens above, from the Upper Worlds, which not all minds are capable of grasping; the Besht reached this elevated level, revealing the divine in this world.

As Rabbi Schneur Zalman of Liadi said:

> The doctrine of Kabbalah lifts the Jew to the heavens, the doctrine of Chassidism lowers the heavens to the Jew'.[7]

---

4   Genesis 2:7
5   *biSdeh haChassidut,* pg. 44
6   Idelsohn, *haNeginnah haChassidit,* pg. 1
7   *Pitgamei Chassidim,* pg. 99

Alfassi then continued:

> There is a fundamental difference between the approach of the Ari and that of the Besht in all aspects connected to serving G-d. In contrast to the self-mortification and pleading of the Ari, which exhausts the body, the Besht demanded that serving be through joy – 'weeping is very bad' – without fasting or self-torment, but through eating, drinking, and thereby serving G-d. And the *Baal haMaor vehaShemesh* (Rabbi Kalonymus Kalman Halevi Epstein – 1754-1823) would say that if another two luminaries had joined with him [the Besht], he would have nullified all fasts.

This approach on the Besht's part derives from his outlook that G-d must be served in all ways possible, for "in everything there are worlds, souls and Godliness". Concerning this, much has been ascribed to the Besht. I will present just one of the many issues ascribed to the Besht's Testament:

> The Blessed One wishes that he be served in all ways possible: sometimes a person, going along his way, stops to talk to someone, and then is unable to learn. One should cleave to G-d and perform Unifications. Further, when a person is on a journey and cannot pray and learn as he is accustomed, then He must be served in other ways. And that person should not allow himself to become upset, for the Blessed One is thus indicating that He should be served in all ways, sometimes like this and sometimes like that, which is why the opportunity has been given to you, on your way, to speak with this or that one, in order to serve Him in this manner.[8]

The implication of the above can be understood to show that despite the differences in the ways that G-d can be served, an exceedingly strong connection exists between Kabbalah and Chassidism, and that Kabbalah effected powerful influence on Chassidism from both the perspective of ideology and practical daily applications as far as forms of prayer, immersion in the *mikveh* [clothing on Shabbat, and so on, all of which elevate the sparks, the latter concept being focal to the doctrines of Chassidism.

2. The Importance of Music in Kabbalah

As noted above, because the main source of the Chassidic approach derives from Kabbalah, so does its music. Reverence for music in Chassidism becomes understood in light of the way it was perceived by the mystics, through whose perspectives we can appropriately comprehend other Chassidic writings.[9] One of the Tzaddikim is cited as likening the entire creation to a piano, where people are the

---

8 Ibid, pg. 47
9 Zvi Meir Rabinowitz as cited in Geshuri, *leDavid Mizmor*, pg. 156, in *haMusica baKabbalah*

players, and the wonderful notes of the tune spread throughout the world, completely filling it with infinite song and eternal singing.[10]

According to the Kabbalah, the origin of music is not in man himself but in the highest of worlds. All the tunes that people play are sparks derived from the song of the Upper Worlds. "Because the soul is carved from a Higher World", states one of the mystics, "and is accustomed to the melodies and singing of the serving angels, and the song of the Higher Spheres, when it takes its place in one's being and hears melody, it finds the satisfaction and enjoyment to which it had been accustomed while cleaving to its source in the pleasure of the Higher Spheres".[11]

Idelsohn, expressing his view of the importance of music in Kabbalah, noted:

> The Kabbalistic method of the Ari also considers music to be an important tool for uplifting and directing prayer. It is known that the Ari himself composed songs in Aramaic and urged his disciples to do likewise.

Idelsohn listed the most important among these: *Lecha Dodi* by Rabbi Shlomo Alkabetz (1500-1576), *Yah Ribbon Olam* and *Yedid Nefesh* by Rabbi Eleazar Azkari (1533-1600). Idelsohn, however, did note that "for quite some time prior to the Ari, music was considered extremely important in the literature of ethics and mystics". He presented a quote taken from *Sefer Charedim*:

> And if you can add nothing, seek out tunes, and when you pray, recite with tunes that you consider to be sweet and pleasant; with such tunes, recite your prayers, and say them with deliberateness, and your heart will follow the words of your mouth, etc.[12]

The Zohar also contains many references to the importance of music, as Idelsohn has pointed out. According to the Zohar, the whole world recites song, and all the host of the heavens plays music, and the Throne of Glory and even G-d himself sing: these are the four voices of music. Elsewhere, the Zohar states: "Everything that the Holy One, Blessed be He, created in this world sings praise and songs before Him, whether in the Upper or Lower Worlds". In another place, it is precise in referring to the pleasantness of voice, stating: "Whoever wishes to praise G-d with his voice, must have a pleasant voice, pleasant to the listener, and if his voice is not pleasant, he should not raise it".[13] The Zohar, on the verse, "Honor

---

10 Ibid
11 *Livnat haSapir*, on Kings 2, 3, 15
12 Idelsohn, *haNeginnah haChassidit*, pg. 2
13 Ibid, pg. 13

the Lord with your sustenance",[14] further states: "Through the joy of music gladden the heart, for the joy of the heart is like the music of all the world".[15]

Nonetheless, the singing of the Jewish people takes first preference, as is noted in the Midrash *Heichalot Rabbati*:

> When the serving angels seek to sing in divine worlds [...] the Holy One, Blessed be He, says to them: be silent until I can first listen and hear the voice of the songs and praises of Israel my child".

The Siddur Rav Amram explains:

> Come and see the praise of the Holy One, Blessed be He, who is fonder of Israel than thousands upon thousands and tens of thousands of serving angels, who serve and praise Him. Rabbi Simon said, 'G-d rises higher in his divine world when Israel enters their study houses and prayer houses and sings praise before their Creator'.[16]

The Zohar elaborates:

> When life is commenced with song, the Upper Worlds add the ability to know, to recognize, to reach what had not yet been reached.[17]

3. Excerpts from the Kabbalah relating to Music

Kabbalistic books are replete with references relating to the importance of music, but from the time that the Jewish world went into Exile, joy became forbidden according to Kabbalistic interpretations:

> In the time when Israel is not in the Holy Land, it is forbidden for a person to be joyful or to demonstrate joy.[18]

However, not only was joy in performing a mitzvah not forbidden, but was in itself a mitzvah, in that it was for the sake of the heavenly Name, arousing the individual to fervor and ecstasy to the extent of self-nullification. Such joy manifested its physical form in singing and music. The singing awakened desire and love between the Jew and the heavenly Father, "for the song causes devotion".[19]

---

14 Proverbs 3:9
15 Zohar on Yitro, 93a, as cited in Idelsohn, *Sefer haNiggunim*
16 Ibid
17 Zohar, Portion of Shemot, pg. 18b
18 Zohar Part III, 118a
19 Horodoetzky, *haChassidim vehaChassidut*, pg. 186, citing Rabbi Eliyahu DeVidas, *Reshit Chochma*, Section 'Ahava', para. 10; and Rabbi Y. Saruk, *Na'im Zmirot Israel* – Introduction

The verse, "When the morning stars sang together"[20] is explained by the Zohar as referring to the angels who sang before the Creator every night, during each of the three night watches: on each watch, each company sang its song, and in the final watch, which sees night turn into morning, all the stars and signs and angels, called "people of G-d", recite songs, as is said, "When the morning stars sang together".[21] When the morning commenced, all three watches stood and recited songs and praises to the Holy One, Blessed be He, and from these divine songs, King Solomon composed the 'Song of Songs', which included all matters of Torah and wisdom, power and might, what had been and what still would be, a song that the divine singers sang. There was no joy greater in any of the worlds than when the first Temple was constructed by Solomon. Then the divine and the earthly worlds commenced singing with the 'Song of Songs': "they sang the song of the Holy One, Blessed be He, every day", and the day on which this song became revealed to the world was perfect in all ways, and the *Shechinah* descended to the Earth and Solomon spoke with [the wisdom of] the holy spirit.[22]

The Zohar states that in the divine world, there is a place called "the chamber of music", which cannot be opened except through music; and from this chamber, the niggun spreads and extends through all worlds.[23] It further states: "The secret of melody is the sound of the *Shofar* which rises upwards: 'at that moment, all kinds of niggunim are awakened" – the niggun lies with the holy beings: "they clap with their wings to the tune facing each of the four directions"; and, "Torah was given with music, and the *Shechinah* resides in music". This is the secret of the holy melody that fills all worlds, "and Israel shed the exile through melody".[24]

In his book, Rabbi Israel Taub (1849-1921) of Modzitz presents a special discourse which quotes extensively from Kabbalistic works. For this reason, I have chosen to present parts of it in this chapter.[25]

In '*Ma'oz Tzur Yeshuati*' [lit. Mighty Rock of my Salvation] sung after kindling the Chanukah lights, we find the words, "People of insight established eight days for song and jubilation". Rabbi Taub notes that three seemingly unrelated issues are mentioned here: 'Men of insight' refers to the seven days of 'structuring' which correspond to the seven *Sefirot*, each relating to one of seven sanctified traits. 'Eight days' refers to the eight days of Chanukah. 'Established song and jubilation' refers to the melodies, and the wisdom [theory] of music. What, then,

20 Job 38:7
21 *Zohar Chadash*, 5b, 6a
22 Zohar Part 2, 18b; and see Horodetzky, *haChassidim vehaChassidut*, pg. 187
23 *Tikkunei Zohar*, Tikkuna 11, pg.26b
24 *Tikkunei Zohar*, Tikkuna 21 79b, 80a
25 *Divrei Israel*, New York 1967, weekly portion of Miketz, pg. 130-132

connects these three aspects? Rabbi Taub offers the following explanation: that the connection between 'men of insight' and 'eight days' is the festival of Chanukah which lasts for eight days, and is represented by the seven *Sefirot* for seven days of restructuring, together with their source, the *Sefirah* of *Binah*, totaling eight. But what, then, is the connection with 'for song and jubilation'?

Rabbi Taub responds to the above inquiry at length, but I wish to offer a more concise version of his explanation. It is known that nothing material exists in the world that does not have a spiritual root in the divine, especially the wisdom of music, whose roots are in holiness at the highest of levels. As we know, the service of the Levites in the Temple involved song, singing, and an unlimited number of musical instruments such as lyres, harps, and more, all using the wisdom of music, as is written in *Tikkunei haZohar* 11: "In divine worlds there is a temple that cannot be opened except by music, and King David came close to this temple through his music". Rabbi Israel continues by quoting from *Avodat haKodesh* (Section '*T'chelet*', Chapter 6): "Because the soul is carved from the divine, and accustomed to the melodies and songs of the serving angels and the Higher Spheres, when [the soul is] in the body and hears music, it finds the peaceful satisfaction and pleasure to which it had been accustomed when it cleaved to its source. From such ample pleasure and pleasantness, it is appropriate that it [the soul] be steeped in G-d's spirit, as it had originally been". Rabbi Taub then quotes the *Ye'arot haDvash* (Part 2, Section 7): "All the forms of wisdom are peripheral although they help explain our Torah, but we cannot speak of the wisdom of music, as it is the wisdom of song [...] How great is the power of this wisdom which all the divine angels and Higher Spheres play and sing in the proper order, the tones and the half tones, all rooted in the true wisdom". Rabbi Taub concludes that we understand, from the above, that the root of song's theory is exceedingly high.

As pointed out by Rabbi Taub, there is a well known section of Talmud: "The lyre of the Temple was seven-stringed,[26] as is said, '*Sova Smachot*'[27] [the fullness of joy]; do not say 'sova' but 'sheva' [seven], and the days of the Mashiach are eight-stringed, as is said, 'For the Leader, on the eighth',[28] and the World to Come is ten-stringed, as is said, 'With a ten-stringed instrument',[29] and also, 'With the ten-stringed psaltery, sing to Him'.[30] These phrases are interpreted to mean that one of the wonderful things that will exist in the times of the Mashiach is the eight-stringed lyre, which will be ten-stringed in the World to Come. It is difficult to understand

---

26 b. Arachin, 13b
27 Psalms 16:11
28 Ibid 12:1
29 Ibid 92:4
30 Ibid 33:2

the great wonder over these, as currently we have musical instruments with many strings, some having even more than ten strings, such as our modern harp. What, then, is so special about the eight or ten strings?

Rabbi Israel deals with the response to the above question at length, with a fascinating explanation on the theory of music. I shall try to summarize his words. Quoting the *Hon Ashir* interpretation on *Mishnayot*:

> It is known that music theory is constructed on seven tones which commence low and move higher. The next tone is a completely different note. It moves constantly upwards, to the seventh tone which is the highest of the tones, and each tone is entirely different from the others. The eighth tone, when reached, should also be different from the others being much higher than them, but in fact it is the same as the first tone which was lower than them all, and there is no difference between them except the octave. In other words, the eighth tone is one octave higher, while the lowest tone was a lower octave. Simply put, the eighth tone is the higher octave and the first tone is the lower octave. But there is no musical difference between them in the same way that a difference exists between the other seven notes. We see the same phenomenon when moving in reverse, that is, from the highest to the lowest tone: all the tones – from the eighth to the first – are different from each other, but the first and eighth are exactly the same, other than the eighth being in a lower octave. Thus, if two people play music together and one plays the first note while the other plays the second, their joint playing will be cacophonic to the ear rather than harmonious but if the two notes that they play are the first and eighth tones, it will be pleasing to listen to, as they share the same shade and are only differentiated by the octaves. For all music, there are no more than seven tones and no one has any idea how the eighth tone would sound, if such a one would exist.

Three conclusions are then suggested: 1) music theory is structured on seven 'steps' (tones) and that no more exist; 2) each of these seven tones are utterly different from each other, but the eighth, higher than the rest, is in actuality the same as the first; and 3) the highest tone of them all is the same as the lowest tone of all, and vice versa.

Rabbi Israel then referred to the Zohar on the verse, "The world is built on loving kindness"[31] – there are seven levels of holiness, commencing with loving kindness which is the highest, to love, awe, might and so on, up to the first level which is kingship [*Malchut*]. These seven levels are known as "people of insight" [*bnei binah*], and the eighth, highest level is known as "the level of insight" [*Binah*]. This level is of the same form and hue as the first one, that of kingship; [together, they] are like mother and daughter. These levels are called "tones", and can be understood in this world. But the eighth tone, known as "the great tone", from which all the lesser tones emanate, cannot be understood, as is said, "and the very great sound of the *Shofar*".[32] In other words, in this world it is

---

31 Psalms 89:3
32 Exodus 19:16

impossible to understand and grasp its essence, until the time of the Messiah, when we will be able to understand it, as is written, "And it shall be on that day, he will blow the great shofar", etc.[33]

Accordingly, we can now understand the Germarra relating to the lyre of eight strings which will exist in the Messianic period, compared to our current reality where no more than seven tones exist, corresponding to the seven days of creation and the seven attributes attainable in this world. Thus, when stating that in the Messianic period, there will be a musical instrument having eight strings, it is not the strings per se that is referred to, as instruments already exist having more than eight strings, such as the harp; thus, an eight-stringed instrument is no innovation. Rather, the strings relate to levels of which, currently, we are able to access seven vocal tones; but in the Messianic period, another, eighth tone, which cannot yet be grasped, will be added to this world. This is what King David referred to with "To the Conductor of the Eighth", that is, the eighth tone that will enter our sphere of comprehension in the future.

We can now understand the hymn, "people of insight established eight days for song and jubilation": 'people of insight' refers to the seven days of creation to which the seven tones correspond; 'eight days' refers to the eight days of Chanukah corresponding to the eight levels of insight, as is said, "The joyful mother of children"[34]; and 'established song and jubilation' refers to music's basic concepts, which currently are revealed as seven tonal levels but in the future, will contain an eighth, as is said, "To the Conductor of the Eighth".

Another brief discourse on the same topic presents Rabbi Taub's explication on the verse, "Take of the cuttings [*zimrat*] of the land"[35] quoting Rabbi Levi Yitzhak of Berditchev (1740-1810), author of *Kedushat Levi*, and his interpretation of the verse, "and with the songs of Your servant David" (taken from the *Baruch She'amar* prayer of the daily morning service). Music is structured in octaves, and the end of one octave is the commencement of the next, moving constantly higher, which is likened to climbing steps, one at a time. This is true also of love and awe of the Creator, which develops in steps which are referred to as 'high upon high'. In this vein, Rabbi Taub explains that 'the cuttings of the land' refers to musical theory. Similarly, Rashi interprets the verse, "and all sing to it for coming into this world" – this is what Jacob meant when he said to his sons, "Draw an allusion to the wisdom of serving G-d through the wisdom [theory] of music".[36]

---

33   Isaiah 27:13
34   Psalms 113:9
35   Genesis 43:11
36   *Divrei Israel*, weekly portion of Miketz, pg. 130-131

4. Use of Kabbalistic Writings as Texts for Melodies

The Sages who arranged the daily prayer orders also utilized Kabbalistic texts, integrating them into the prayers, as prayers are recited to a tune, whether that of the prayer itself or some special tune or melody, depending on the synagogue. These texts sourced in Kabbalah were also set to tunes by Chassidim, *baalei tefillah* [lay prayer leaders] or cantors. One of the most famous is the "Kegavna", a prayer inserted by the Chassidim into the evening service for Friday night, taken from the Zohar.[37] The melody for this prayer was written by the famous cantor, Pinhas Spektor, "Pintsik" (1872-1951). Nowadays there is hardly a prayer service among Chassidim where a professional cantor will not be requested to sing this work. Another melody was created by the cantor Shlomo Mendelson.

Another famous prayer is said when removing the Torah scroll from the ark. *Brich Shmei* is also from the Zohar.[38] This text was also set to music as part of the prayer service. Special melodies for it were written by cantors such as Yossele Rosenblatt (1882-1933), Mordechai Hershman (1888-1941), David Koussevitzky (1899-1966), D. M. Steinberg (1870-1941) and others.

Of course, we must also include Shabbat songs, some of which are Kabbalistic in origin as already noted in the section *Shabbat and Music*. These creations were written in Aramaic and include *Ya Ribbon Olam,* by Rabbi Israel Najara (1550-1625), or *Bnei Hechalei* by Rabbi Yitzhak Luria, the Ari (1534-1572) as well as songs in Hebrew.

5. Kabbalistic Composers

Many Kabbalists [mystics] were known for having composed songs with mystical content, setting them to tunes. As noted above, from his center in *Tzefat* [Safed] the Ari, of poetic and musical soul and influenced by his studies of Kabbalah, composed refrains for all the three meals of the Shabbat, being *Azamir Beshvachin, Asader liSe'udata*, and *Bnei Hechalei*. The Ari also encouraged his contemporaries and disciples to do likewise, and as a result, Rabbi Shlomo Alkabetz (1500-1576) composed the world renowned *Lecha Dodi*. Other mystics wrote poetry and songs in honor of Shabbat.

Rabbi Yehuda Ashlag (1885-1954) who wrote *haSulam*, a commentary on the Zohar, also composed songs and set them to music. Listening to these melodies, which were preserved by his son, Rabbi Baruch Shalom Ashlag (1907-1991), we

---

37 Zohar, on weekly section Terumah, 135a
38 Ibid, weekly section Vayakhel, 206a

can discern two types: the longing and desire for unity following distancing, and the love and joy on discovering the perfection of unity after having come closer. Both these states express the way that the Kabbalist unites with his Creator.

These melodies were composed in precise accordance with the spiritual laws on which the soul of the individual is structured. Because a connection exists between the human soul and the source of musical notes, they circumvent intellectual or affective knowledge and penetrate direct to the depths of the soul without obstruction.[39]

Rabbi Schneur Zalman of Liadi (1745-1813) is known to have composed ten melodies corresponding to the ten *Sefirot*. His famous tune, *Niggun haRav*, is based on the fundamental principle of 'the coupling of the Sefirot'.[40]

6. Tunes of Meron

Meron is a small township in the hills of the Galilee which became famous because of the *Tanna*, Rabbi Shimon bar Yochai [known by his initials as the "Rashbi", who is buried there. The Rashbi was one of Rabbi Akiva's most outstanding disciples and strongly opposed Roman activities in the land of Israel. He paid a high price for his views, having to hide in a cave for thirteen years together with his son, Rabbi Eleazar. According to tradition, it was during this period that he composed the Zohar

The anniversary of his death is *Lag Ba'Omer* [the 33rd day of the counting of the measures] and Israel's populace traditionally visits his grave on this date. A number of traditions are linked to this day. A boy who reaches the age of three is taken there for his first haircut, the 'op-shearen' in Yiddish, or "khalakeh". Some come to pray before the Rashbi, spilling their heart's inner secrets, asking that he speak well of them to the Creator of the Universe on this day, which is special to the Rashbi's soul. Others come to hear the *kleyzmers* play their music, which on this day has a unique sound. The tunes of Meron are the cradle in which Israeli kleyzmer music was born and develops. The clarinetist, Moussa Berlin (b. 1938) feels that the Meron repertoire, consolidated over tens, and perhaps hundreds, of years, has become synonymous with 'Meron music'. Moussa first came to Meron at the age of thirteen, and for the past fifty-plus years, he can be found playing the clarinet twice a year in Meron: on *Lag baOmer,* and on Adar 7, the anniversary of the passing of Moses. At Meron he plays together with other clarinetists, and their playing is like one great soul.

---

39 www.kabbalah.info/hekab/beginers_guide/music.htm
40 Meir Zvi Rabinowitz, as cited in Geshuri, *laChassidim Mizmor*, pg. 156, in the section, *haMusica baKabbalah*

There, by the gravesite, crowded with visitors from all sectors of society, it seems that time stands still. There are no disputes, there is a sense of being brethren, with wearers of black *kippot* [skullcaps] alongside those with brightly colored crocheted ones, men with Bucharian caps mingling with men in large, white Bratzlav headwear, some sporting an earring, alongside a child who is undergoing the *khalakeh* ceremony, borne on the shoulders of his *shtreimel*-wearing father, all together enjoying the wonderful music played by the kleyzmers, conducted by Moussa.

As the evening commences, the traditional bonfire is lit. Immediately afterwards, the kleyzmers begin playing the traditional tunes for this special day: *veAmartem koh leChai, bar Yochai Nimshachat Ashrecha, Amar Rabbi Akiva Ashreichem Israel,* and others. The public joins in with enthusiastic singing, dancing, led by a core group of celebrants who come every year. Over time, they developed a language comprehended only by themselves. "Niggun Sheffer", one calls out; the kleyzmers oblige and play the song most loved by Rabbi Chaim Sheffer, father of the famous Sheffer family from *Teveryah* [Tiberias]. "Niggun T'chiat haMetim" [Melody of the Rising of the Dead], someone else requests, and the company of kleyzmers changes its tune once again. Next is the 'bottle dance', the *debka*, and others, and the kleyzmers play long into the night.

The activity that Moussa Berlin always looks forward to is the march towards the nearby grave of the *Tanna*, Rabbi Yochanan haSandlar [the cobbler]. At about two in the morning, a veteran group of devotees gathers near the grave to conduct a *hitva'adut* [gathering of devotees with their spiritual leader]; the light from bonfires merges with the light of the moon reflected from above, and the atmosphere is uplifting. The tunes are mostly soulful, sourced in the heart, and the special mood leaves an impression that is not easily forgotten. During the day of Lag baOmer, Moussa returns to Rashbi's burial place, where he receives the children about to undergo khalakeh, with their families. Repeatedly he plays, for each and every young child, the tune for *Bar Yochai Nimshachat Ashrecha*, with the onlookers joining in the dance and song. "All year long I play at various events and occasions, at weddings and other festivities with enthusiasm, but from Lag baOmer on Meron, I draw my strength for the whole year", Moussa Berlin explains.[41]

Just who is Moussa Berlin? In an article edited by the journalist Zev Galili, for the *Makor Rishon* newspaper,[42] Professor Edwin Sarussi, Head of the Department for Research into Jewish Music, at the Hebrew University in Jerusalem, described him as "the senior kleyzmer". Galili added:

---

41 *http://www.aish.com/hsociety/society/Going_Up_to_Meron.asp*
42 23 May 2003

Researchers have spent decades following Moussa Berlin and his development. His melodies have been recorded, he has been interviewed, and in fact his compositions and personality constitute the basis for understanding the development of kleyzmer music typical to the land of Israel, a style of which he is the last torch-bearer.

Moshe Berlin – nicknamed 'Moussa' while doing his military service – was born in Tel Aviv in 1938. While studying, he became aware of the unique celebrations on Meron during Lag baOmer, and met the famous kleyzmer, Avraham Segal. In his final year of high school, Berlin joined a wind instrument orchestra run by the Elitzur Sports and Culture Organization. One day he came across an old, cracked clarinet there, which no one seemed to want. Berlin took the instrument and began practicing.

Mazor, in his book on kleyzmerim, referred to Avraham Segal as:

> The person who shaped the Eretz Israel [land of Israel] repertoire [...] is considered the most outstanding representative of kleyzmer in the land of Israel in the twentieth century. Segal drew his expertise direct from the generation of immigrants who shaped the local repertoire. Segal's contribution was important to its further development, and over time he became known as the leading kleyzmer at the Meron festivities, which was the central kleyzmer event in Israel for many years.[43]

In an interview I conducted with Mazor in Jerusalem, he noted that the encounter between Segal and Moussa Berlin created what could be called "the first Israeli kleyzmer", a result of Moussa's integration of contrasts: on one hand, Moussa is a typical Israeli whose ear follows trends beyond religious and ultra-orthodox society, yet on the other hand he continued Segal's lead and followed in his footsteps.

I asked Moussa what, in his opinion, is Jewish music. He responded:

> This is my philosophy. Not things I've read, but things I've come to realize from my work. Things I feel.
> In the 1970s, I reached a sort of plateau, saturation. From Avrum Segal I'd already absorbed everything I could, and I felt the need for change. During this period I encountered, for the first time ever, Giora Feidman's playing, which caused a turnabout in my own music.
> Giora is a fourth generation kleyzmer. His playing was like nothing I'd ever heard before. A friend from our synagogue organized a behind-the-scenes meeting between us at one of his performances. I told him that I wished to study with him. I wasn't an easy pupil, I had some incorrect playing habits and I needed to be forced into coping with technical levels. At the time, Feidman was at the outset of his climb to the apex of kleyzmer playing, and slowly the boundaries between the teacher's and the student's styles became blurred. I played my repertoire for him, as well as the old recordings. At first he rejected them, calling it "cat's mewling", but slowly he became more enticed. When I married some thirty years ago, he

---

43 Yaakov Mazor, *Moreshet haKleyzmerim beEretz Israel*, Jerusalem: 2000, Introduction, pg. 29

attended the wedding as a guest, and played together with Avrum Segal and other musicians. This was where he first encountered the experience and melodies of Meron.

Researchers date the beginning of kleyzmer music to the 17th and 18th centuries. I would date Jewish music a great deal earlier, to the time of the Temple. After the destruction of the first Temple, the Jewish players refused to continue making music. The poet of Psalm 137 says, 'On the willows, within, we hung our lyres'. The captors asked that they 'sing us a song of Zion'. What did the musicians answer? They do not give a direct response to the question, but say, 'How can we sing the Lord's song on foreign soil?' They don't say, 'How can we sing the songs of Zion'.

This is because music during Temple times was, first and foremost, a way to serve G-d. Once the people of Israel were exiled, they cast their decision on playing music. This was a decree that the Jewish public could not uphold, as the need to find musical expression is one of the most fundamental and natural to mankind. The Jew who sought to express himself musically without breaching the vow, 'If I forget you, Jerusalem, may my right hand forget its cunning'[44] found a way to do so. He developed a unique method. It's as though he said to himself, 'every time I play, I will recall the destruction'.

So if you ask me what Jewish music is, I'd say that it's a kind of music which, even when *freilich* [joyous] sounds somewhat sorrowful. Beneath the guise of joy you can hear the melancholy of 'I shall raise Jerusalem to my chief joy'.[45] Perhaps this was done subconsciously. Currently there are numerous non-Jewish bands [playing kleyzmer music] and I can tell in an instant if they are Jewish or not.

When I play, I think of how the public can feel uplifted through my music. I don't play if there's no purpose to the playing. So, I won't play in a concert hall where the only reason for doing so is to pleasure others. This is also why I don't play for any and every audience, nor do I play at home – there's no purpose to such playing.

I define the kleyzmer as a profession [from the world] of design. I move between joy and sorrow. I was once invited by a large company, to play at the memorial ceremony for the husband of one of the employees. I told them it's not appropriate, in my view. They replied, 'This is how we conduct our memorials: if you don't wish to play for us, we'll take the Cameri Quartet. We feel that your music is best suited to the family'. I deliberated over the issue the whole night, not sleeping, until I decided which pieces to choose. When I arrived there, I met a woman who had been with me in *Bnei Akiva* [youth group], and it turned out that she was the widow.

I chose a Modzitz tune; the *Tanya*, composed by Yossi Green and sung by Avraham Fried; and a soul melody. She sat before me and began to cry, and I didn't know if I'd be able to finish playing. This crying released something inside her.

[I asked]: What can make the music of non-Jews into something typically Jewish, when the sheet music appears practically identical? Moussa responded:

With the Jewish adaptation, the Rebbe would insert a *krechtz* [sigh] and a *kneitsh* [crinkle]. Not to mention the fact that I've heard of many instances where the Rebbe, after hearing tunes played by non-Jews, was able to discern that these were niggunim taken from the *Bet haMikdash* [the Temple].[46]

---

44 Psalms 137:5
45 Psalms 137:6
46 *http://www.makorrishon.co.il/article.php?id=868*

Chapter 7 – Musical Expression in Chassidic Courts

Even though opinion was unanimous as far as the importance of music in Chassidism as a manifestation of joy and nullification of sadness, and that it served as a significant component of the service of G-d, we find that the way it was expressed differs from one Chassidic group to another. The reason for this seems to be that following the passing of the Besht and his closest follower, the Maggid of Mezhirech, Chassidism splintered into sects, each led by an independent Tzaddik, as already mentioned in the chapter on Chassidism. Each sect's methods, and perhaps each one's location, influenced the musical style to which it adhered.

1. Modzitz Chassidism

Although the concept of music in Chassidism serving as part of service of G-d has been noted innumerable times, for the Modzitz sect, music actually constituted service of G-d. Yitzhak Alfassi noted:

> The Chassidic court most noted for music, and whose whole reality was based on it, is the dynasty of the Admors of Modzitz. They did not interpret the phrase, 'The world of music is close to the world of repentance' as was commonly accepted, but took it to mean that 'The world of music is repentance'.[1] Their whole being and their whole existence was one great melody, a melody to the Living G-d. While music held a position of importance in other Chassidic dynasties, Modzitz was the only court to understand the concept of 'Only through music is it possible to expect and merit Israel's redemption', and that 'The language of music is *Tzimtzum* [the contraction]; one melody can hold the power to express the contents of a cupboard filled with books.[2]

The founder of this dynasty was Rabbi Israel Taub (1849-1921); it was continued by his son, Rabbi Saul Yedidyah Eleazar (1882-1947). Rabbi Israel was a scion of the court of Kuzmir and its founder, Rabbi Ezekil of Kuzmir (1812-1856), who was R' Israel's grandfather. R' Ezekil was also very fond of music, absorbing this love of melody from his mentors: Rabbi Shmuel of Korov; and Rabbi Yaakov Yitzhak, known as the Seer of Lublin (1745-1815) and 'father' of all the Polish and Galician lines of Tzaddikim. It was known that Rabbi Ezekil of Kuzmir

---

1 *Imrei Saul,* Discourse 15, pg. 309
2 *biSdeh haChassidut,* pg. 500

would say that he does not feel the pleasure of Shabbat unless a new melody was composed in honor of Shabbat. His goal, as far as music was concerned, was solely to reveal the additional soul of a person, and raise those elevated sparks within each Jew. His fondness for Chassidic musicians became so well known that Kuzmir became a kind of miniature center for musical Chassidim.

Geshuri described the special visit of Rabbi Shlomo of Radomsk (1795-1866). R' Shlomo was known as a wonderful musician. Each *Shavuot* festival, he would visit a different Tzaddik:

> On one occasion he visited the Tzaddik of Kuzmir. Rabbi Emanuel of Pashdeborz, who himself was very fond of lively music and would often lead prayer services, asked the Tzaddik of Kuzmir to honor R' Shlomo by inviting him to lead the *Kabbalat Shabbat* prayers. The latter was so modest that he prayed in a very simple manner, until Rabbi Emanuel whispered to him, 'Here, it's the custom to sing the *Anim Zmirot*'. R' Shlomo then commenced singing *Anim Zmirot* with rousing enthusiasm, until the whole synagogue was filled with light. On the first day of *Shavuot*, the Tzaddik of Kuzmir again honored him by requesting that he recite the *Akdmaot*, being the central, poetic piece of the day, its content devoted to the giving of the Torah. Rabbi Shlomo agreed on the condition that chorists be sent to him, to be trained for prayer and song. The result was a group of eighty choristers who stood alongside him, among them the Tzaddik, Rabbi Shmuel Eliyahu, son of the Tzaddik of Kuzmir. When they all burst into song, with Rabbi Shlomo's voice above them all, it was as though the walls and windows resonated (*Niflaot Tiferet Shlomo,* section 120). The singing of the *Akdamot* together with the dancing of the Tzaddik of Radomsk were the talk of the whole town, and the immense scope of awakening caused by this singing led the Tzaddik of Kuzmir to pace the *Beit Midrash*, asking all the Chassidim, 'Did you ever see anything like it? Had you ever heard such a thing? Indeed, this was a festival of unforgettable song in Kuzmir'.[3]

Rabbi Israel, the grandson, absorbed his grandfather's love of music. While still a child, he would amaze his listeners with his musical creativity, and composed hundreds of melodies which made his name renowned worldwide.

In one of his discourses, Rabbi Israel noted:

> Great is the music that arouses to repentance, raises the person's soul, and brings the hearts of Israel to their Father in heaven.

Someone asked, "Is it possible that what books of ethics and awe cannot do, can music do?" The Tzaddik replied:

> I will relate a parable. To what is this similar? To a village boy who has a millstone, and on reaching the square, notices an alarm clock in the watchmaker's window, a clock with a pleasant ring that arouses a person from sleep. The villager wished to buy the clock, to wake him every morning. The watchmaker smirked, 'Why do you need an alarm clock? With your grinding, the wheels cause the worlds to shudder, and if they cannot awaken you, nothing

---

3 *Negginah veChassidut beVeuit Kuzmir uVnoteha*, pg. 38-39

will!'. The villager responded, 'Ah, it is the nature of the world that a person who has become accustomed to something which is constantly about him, no longer feels its presence. So even though all day and even during the night, I am in the vicinity of these great wheels, and their strong sound, I no longer feel them, and they no longer hold the ability to awaken me from my sleep. But the fine ring of this small clock is new to me, and will easily awaken me with its pleasantness'. So it is with music, too. Books on ethics and awe are always accessible to people and they have become familiar, so that they make no impression. But a new song contains the power to leave its mark, arousing people to pondering, repentance, and their return to good ways.[4]

Chassidim related that on one occasion, during his journeys through the forest, Rabbi Israel heard the voice of a shepherd singing. Immediately he requested the waggoner to stop and listen to the voice. Then he commanded that they continue. When the Chassidim asked for his explanation, he answered: "Do not wonder. When a person sings, he is confessing, and when a person confesses, one must listen. It makes no difference who is confessing; the main thing is that it is a person".[5]

His son and heir, Rabbi Saul Yedidyah Eleazar, possessed a dramatic, strong tenor and was a remarkable composer, producing literally hundreds of niggunim for every festival and occasion, setting verses or excerpts to song, creating new Shabbat *zmirot*, prayer tunes, and *Mitzva Tanz* melodies. His fame peaked while he was in Otboczek near Warsaw, when thousands of Jews, cantors and non-Jewish composers from everywhere in the world flocked, amazed at the Admor's prowess at producing niggunim with tens of motifs, without the assistance of sheet music.

With the onset of World War II, he fled to Vilna, where his appearance created a great stir and his music warmed even the distant-natured Lithuanians. Moshe Grossman, a Jewish author, noted in his book *In the Land of Enchanted Legends*:

The Modzitz music stroked me in motherly love, healed wounds, carried and transferred to another world.

His son Rabbi Shmuel Eliyahu (1906-1984), followed the Admor's footsteps, as did Rabbi Shmuel's son, Rabbi Israel Dan (1928-2006).

In fact, while writing these very lines, our Rebbe, Rabbi Israel Dan Taub returned to his Creator. May his memory be blessed.[6]

---

4   *Imrei Saul,* pg. 311, section 21
5   Kipnis, *laChassidim Mizmor*, pg. 33
6   *Negginah veChassidut beVeuit Kuzmir uVnoteha*, pg. 140-141

A saying on the importance of music to the Modzitz Chassidic court is ascribed to the first Modzitz Admor, Rabbi Israel Taub:

> We recite the blessing of *haBocher baTorah* [Who chooses the Torah] once a week, following the reading of the *Haftarah* [concluding readings]. However, we recite the blessing of *haBocher beShirei Zimrah* [Who chooses the poetry of song] daily, as part of the *Shacharit* [morning] service.[7]

It would be incorrect to say of Modzitz Chassidism that it has a particular style. In actuality, several styles of music are employed, as appropriate to the various prayers. March-style melodies are often used for the *Kaddish* prayers at the end of Shabbat and Festival services, or for the *Ein Kitzva* or the *Va'ye'etayu* that appear in the *Mussaf* services of the High Holy Days. For the first part of the *Lecha Dodi* refrains, written by Rabbi Shlomo Alkabetz, and parts of the Shabbat songs, the three-fourths waltz rhythm is used. Other famous niggunim employing a slow four fourths rhythm are known as *Mechalkel Chaim*. Slower melodies with the same rhythm became known as the *Ch'mol* niggunim after one of the High Holy Day prayers. Most were composed by Rabbi Shmuel Eliyahu Taub, grandson of the founder of Modzitz Chassidism, Rabbi Israel Taub.

The most predominant, typical and interesting aspect of Modzitz niggunim are the lengthy tunes which last for a full twenty minutes or longer. These became known as 'The First Opera', 'The Second Opera', and so on. Others were simply called after the texts used, such as the Shabbat song, *Yah Ribbon Olam*, and the niggunim for *Ana beKoach, Mim'komcha,* and so on.

One of the most famous melodies composed by Rabbi Israel was that for a Psalm, and known as "The Song for the Homeless". Another very popular tune is that for the *Ani Ma'amin* [I Believe] tenets: although this is not originally a Modzitz melody, it was adopted by the Rebbe and became famous as part of the lore around how he was saved from the transport to Treblinka. This will be related to further in the section on 'Legends and Narratives on Various Niggunim'. The longest and most famous niggun, however, in the Modzitz repertoire, is known as the *Ezkerah haGadol* [The Great Memorial]. It is countered by the *Ezkerah haKattan* [The Minor Memorial], said to have been composed in Berlin by the Admor Rabbi Israel while preparing for a medical operation (see: 'Legends and Narratives on Various Niggunim').

The Modzitz Chassidic niggunim were published in Geshuri's book, *Negginah veChassidut beVeit Kuzmir uVnoteha,* and in the *Tifferet Israel* booklet printed by Modzitz. Recently, a collection of niggunim composed by Rabbi Shmuel

---

7   From hearsay

Eliyahu appeared in a luxurious anthology titled *Mor uBesamim* [Myrrh and Fragrances] containing an introduction by Rabbi Israel Dan.

2. Chabad Chassidism

The word 'Chabad' is an acronym for *Chochma* [Wisdom], *Binah* [Insight] and *Da'at* [Knowledge]. Chabad Chassidism bases its views on the motto, 'The mind influences one's values'. This can be understood to mean that while serving G-d can be achieved through emotion, that alone is insufficient, and that emotion must be employed in conjunction with intellect, as the *Alter Rebbe* ['Oldest' – ie: first – Admor] pointed out: "Observe the world". In other words, one should not seek out the special, but serve G-d through the simplest of things, through Creation itself, through nature and objects, and learn in this way how to serve G-d. This approach contrasts with that of other Chassidic streams where emphasis was placed on emotion. Chabad's overall approach, therefore, was also applied to their views on music.[8]

Shmuel Zalmanov offered the following explanation:

> The niggunim of Chabad are in general different and unique, most being of a serious nature, intellectual, and their external style has a unique character, so that they are distinguishable from melodies of other Chassidic streams both in their internal as well as their external aspects. While, in general, the melodies of other Chassidic streams are light hearted and arouse joy and exhilaration, the niggunim of Chabad are generally weightier, with drawn out, moderate movements, rich with typical fine turns expressing the depth of thought and the soul's inner awakening.

Zalmanov then delves into greater detail, noting that:

> Among them are melodies of yearning, tunes of uplifting, niggunim of hope, joy and dance [...] Chabad music is entirely related to the inner aspects that rise from the depths of the heart to cause the soul to shudder. Their music has the power to refine and raise the person to a higher level.

Zalmanov summarizes:

> The central principle in Chabad niggunim is the 'feeling': it is structured entirely on the heart's emotion and the soul's devotion, thus does not require – as other niggunim do – any words or notes.[9]

---

8 From an interview with the Chabad representative in Vienna, Rabbi Aharon Katorza – see chapter titled "Interviews"
9 *Sefer haNiggunim*, Introduction, pg. 19-20

Among the most well known is the 'Four Babas' melody attributed to the first Chabad Admor, together with his equally famous tune for *Eli Ata veOdeka* [You are my G-d and I give thanks to you].

Rabbi Yosef Yitzhak Shneersohn (1880-1950) [the sixth Admor] noted that music was an opening, a gate through which one can reach the required state of existence.[10]

The *Tzemach Tzedek* (1789-1866) [the third Admor] was quoted as having explained a section of the Talmud Yerushalmi:

> When someone quotes another and mentions his source by name, it is as though that source stand there before him, in one's imagination; but when one plays the melody of another, the creator of the melody is there in reality.[11]

The Chassid Reb Hillel of Paritz was known to say:

> If one has no sense of music, one has no sense of Chassidism. Thus, whoever has a sense of music, has an even better sense of Chassidism. Chabad niggunim are the 'Mishnah' of music.[12]

Most Chabad niggunim have been published in the four parts of the *Sefer haNiggunim* [Book of Melodies] collated by Reb Shmuel Zalmanov. In 2000, the book was prepared for republication under the name *Niggunei Chabad*, of which two volumes have so far appeared in print.

3.   Bratzlav Chassidism

For this stream of Chassidism, music is the whole Torah, according to Rabbi Nahman, the founder of the Bratzlav [variously known as Breslov or Braslav] tradition. After his death, his adherents preferred not to position another Rabbi in his place. Rabbi Nahman wrote at length on music.

Horodetzky[13] noted that Chassidism found in the great-grandson of the Besht, Rabbi Nahman of Bratzlav, its strongest and most beautiful manifestation of dance, song and niggun. He loved these intensely, and could feel their beauty and grace to a degree which cannot be found among contemporaneous or later Tzaddikim of any stream of Chassidism. The following, quoting Rabbi Nahman, offers a view of his approach:

---

10   *http://chabad.info7bo7index.php?magazune=hat_&status=goto id&id=104*
11   Ibid
12   Shmuel Zalmanov, *Sefer haNiggunim*, pg. 30
13   *haChassidut vehaChassidim*, pg. 189

Know that every sphere of wisdom in the world has its own special melody, and is unique only to that sphere of wisdom; and from the melody, the wisdom is drawn, and even skepticism [denial of G-d] has its own unique melody; each and every sphere of wisdom, according to its aspects and levels, for each sphere has its own melody, belonging uniquely to it, and so forth, from level to level. Thus a sphere of wisdom loftier than another, will have a loftier melody, up to the point of Creation, which is the commencement of *Atzilut translator: this is worth explaining in a footnote, or special glossary, I feel* ok and higher [...] Belief also has its own melody, and the melody associated with belief is both unique to it and higher than that of all other kinds of knowledge, wisdom or belief in the world. In other words, [this refers to] belief in the *Ohr Ein Sof translator: see above re footnote, or special glossary,* ok which ensures the continuity of all worlds, its song being the highest of all melodies and songs in the world to which the spheres of wisdom and belief belong. And all the melodies of all these spheres of wisdom are drawn from that one which is uppermost of them all, as it is the melody that belongs to the belief in *Ohr Ein Sof* which is the highest of all [...] As far as the melody ascribed to [this] loftiest [level of] belief, no one can merit it other than the greatest Tzaddik of the generation. For he [such a Tzaddik] is likened to Moses, who was of the level of belief that contains the aspect of silence, the aspect of, 'Silence!, Thus the thought has arisen in me'[14], that is, it is of a higher level [even] than speech. This [refers] to [the song], *Az Yashir Moshe* [lit. Then Moses will sing]. For our sages have said,[15] 'The word *sang* was not used, but rather *will sing*, which is an allusion in the Torah to the resurrection of the dead, who in the future will sing, as all songs – from this world and the world to come – are [invested] in Moses, who represents the aspect of silence which merited a melody deriving from the highest [level of] belief of all, from where all melodies are derived. Thus, the music of the Tzaddik derives from this aspect of Moses, and through it, souls that fell into the skepticism of potential-filled space can rise, as their source derives from the uppermost belief, that is, the highest [level of] belief of all, and through this melody and belief, all skepticism becomes nullified, and all melodies become joined in this uppermost melody, being the source of all melodies.[16]

The power of the niggun, according to Rabbi Nahman, can bridge and connect two opposites:

For two things that are distanced from each other, such as opposites, can be connected through niggun.[17]

Thus we can understand that even a person greatly distanced from the Holy One, Blessed be He, can be aroused by music directed towards G-d, which reminds the person of his source in the world. And this is the principle of serving G-d through song and music.

---

14 b. Menchot, 29b
15 b. Sanhedrin, 91b
16 *Likkutei Moharan: Torah 64 Section 5*
17 *Likutei Halachot,* section *Nesiyat Kapayim*, Halacha 5 Clause 6

Chapter 8 – Composers and Lyricists

1. Tzaddikim and the Amud haTefillah

Many Tzaddikim would stand at the *Amud haTefillah* [prayer lectern] to lead [the congregation]. Some would do so every Shabbat, others only on Festivals, while yet others would lead their congregation in prayer only on the *Yamim Nora'im* [High Holy Days].

In *haNegginah haChassidit,* Idelsohn describes the various Admors who led prayers at the Amud haTefillah:

> Many of the greatest Tzaddikim were accustomed to singing when leading prayers, and the tales surrounding the prayers and melodies of the Besht are well known. His voice was very pleasant, and his singing rich with mighty emotions which influenced his listeners. He would lead prayers often, especially on the *Yamim Nora'im*, and was famous for his *Mussaf* services and his beautiful tunes. He was known as the prayer leader who excelled in his generation.[1]

The Maggid of Mezhirech, Rabbi Dov Ber (1704-1772), was also known to be blessed with a powerful yet pleasing voice, and heart rending singing that seemed carved from the flames of fire, enthused with great joy. It was his view that when prayers are uttered with great intent, the angels, the *seraphim*, and all other companies of the Upper Worlds also sing.[2] Rabbi Shneur Zalman of Liadi and Rabbi Levi Yitzhak of Berditchev, among others, were also known for their inspired prayer leading.

Seder haDorot heChadash contains a description of melodies composed by Rabbi Shalom Rokeach of Belz (1783-1855):

> Who can even begin to describe the great sanctity of his service [of G-d] when praying or reading from the Torah. All listeners felt how his spirit went forth and deliberated over repentance. And the most amazing aspect was that, although he could not play [music] and knew nothing whatsoever about music, his voice was sweeter than honey and nectar when he prayed or read the Torah. In this way, many souls of the Jewish people achieved full repentance, [finding refuge] beneath the wings of the *Shechinah*.

---

1 Geshuri, *laChassidim Mizmor*, pg. 23
2 Geshuri, *Niggunim uZmirot leShabbat*, in *Machanayim*, 85, 1964

The Maggid of Mezhirech, Rabbi Dov Ber, did not lead prayers even though he would lead the singing at Shabbat meals, as noted by Shlomo Maimon. Instead, he appointed a special *Shatz*, Rabbi Yehudah Leib Cohen of Annapoli:

> Whose voice was powerful [...] yet with the sweetness of his voice, he would mellow the decrees from on High. The Maggid would say that his voice is much loved in the Upper Worlds. He would also play music often when he prayed, and this so that between one note and the next, he could apply all the *kavanot* (*Beit Rebbi*, pg. 63).

Idelsohn notes that:

> Rabbi Azriel of Pilotzk, a disciple of the Maggid, was also known to be a splendid prayer leader, "because he prayed with his whole heart in a strong, pleasing voice, until he drew the hearts of all his listeners, preoccupied with the vanities of everyday life, to cling to the Creator of the Universe" (*Seder Dorot heChadash*). The Maggid's son, Reb Avraham, (1741-1776), known as 'the Angel', composed a melody that he would sing in order to awaken his soul. This melody passed to his son, Reb Shalom Shachna (1764-1808) who taught it to his son, Reb Israel of Ruzhyn (1797-1851). When the latter moved to Sadigora, he instituted the custom of singing this melody on Shabbat eve during the meal, enthusing the Chassidim. The melody has remained with the name 'The Ruzhyni Niggun' to this day.[3]

Rabbi Shmelki of Nicholsburg (1726-1778), who led prayers on Shabbat, Festivals and the *Yamim Nora'im*, would sing new niggunim that had never yet been heard. It was said that he had no idea of the exact tune he was singing, being so close to the Upper Worlds when he sang. One elderly man related that, in his youth, he sang with Rabbi Shmelki's choir. It was the custom to sing each prayer with its own melody, which the choir prepared and practiced in advance so that there would be no need to make decisions while praying, but the Rabbi often did not use those tunes, and instead sang entirely new ones.[4]

The statement that with his voice, he was able to mellow the judgments of the Upper World indicates, according to Yaakov Mazor, that the *Shatz* could operate in these higher spheres with his voice alone. Rabbi Nahman of Bratzlav also taught that the value and quality of voice are a condition for 'sweetening' judgments, when that voice is used for niggun and prayer.[5]

Rabbi Dov Ber,(1773-1827), the *Mittler Rebbe* [middle Admor] of Chabad, related to prayers conducted by his father, Shneur Zalman of Liadi: "He would sing, with all kinds of niggunim while praying".[6]

---

3   Idelsohn, haNegginah haChassidit, pg. 8
4   Martin Buber, *Ohr haGanuz*, pg. 173; see also *Sefer Ta'amei haMinhagim*, Chapter *Inyanei Tefillah*, pg. 53 section 108, remarks.
5   Yaakov Mazor, *Yuval*, Vol. 7, *Studies in Honor of Israel Adler*, pg. 40
6   *Sefer haNiggunim*, Introduction, pg. 14

In the Modzitz Chassidic court, the Rebbe would customarily lead prayers on the *Yamim Nora'im*, commencing with the first evening of *Slichot* [prayers requesting pardon], where he usually integrated some of his new melodies.

When the Chassidic leaders instituted a musical format to a prayer, integrating melodies was not just for their own sake as leaders of the congregation, but from a perception that saw music as influencing the Upper Worlds. Perhaps this is why there are so many songs for the *Yamim Nora'im* services, expressing the desire to beneficially influence the Upper Worlds, thereby allaying judgments.[7]

2. Rebbe-Composers

Who are the composers of Chassidic melodies? Certainly not individuals with advanced musical education, nor outstanding musicians, nor music researchers, nor componists who position one note after the next and create a song. The source of Chassidic music can be found in Chassidic elation and boundless devotion. Chassidic music is not forced. Its composer could be the simple, G-d fearing Jew who is unfamiliar with a section of basic *halacha* [law], and equally unknowledgeable on matters of rhythm and beat in music, but his heart feels and his soul sings, and both these – heart and soul – are greatly distanced from foreign influences.[8]

The settings of Chassidic melodies derive from various sources, but in many Chassidic streams, the Rebbe is the composer of tunes that remain associated with his court, while in others, a court composer is responsible for producing melodies. In most instances, however, we find both options, the Rebbe producing some tunes, and Chassidim from his court producing others. Chassidim other than the Rebbe who produce melodies are known as 'composers of the court'. The music they write is outstanding, and is considered as having received the Rebbe's blessing when the Rebbe himself integrates it among his own tunes at the *Tisch*.

Chassidic leaders, according to Zalmanov, viewed song and music as an important part of the Chassidic mode of living, and thus composed tunes themselves, or encouraged those of their adherents with musical abilities to compose tunes that would arouse the heart, or instill joy and merriment.[9]

Neither the court composers nor the Rebbes of Chassidic courts were familiar with musical scores and the melodies were not pondered around the table deeply

---

7   Ibid, pg. 44, quoting Rabbi Yishaya Meshulam Feish Rattenburg, son of the Kassan Admor, when I interviewed him.
8   M. Kipnis, as cited in Geshuri, *laChassidim Mizmor,* pg. 7
9   Shmuel Zalmanov, *Sefer haNiggunim*, pg. 19

and then written down, as professional composers are trained to do in conservatoria. Chassidic musicians would create their melodies while walking to the Tzaddik's home or the *Beit Midrash*, while involved in their business affairs, and all without ever penning them. Most tunes were integrated [into the repertoire] successfully.[10]

One fine example can be found in the Modzitz Chassidic court, where the Rebbe's talents not only manifested in his Torah discourses but his musical and compositional abilities. Many Modzitz tunes were composed by the Admors, whose melody-composing skills showed their brilliance in the most beautiful, and later most famous, tunes they produced, although several court composers' work was predominant in contributing to the treasure of Chassidic music.

The same is true for Chabad Chassidism. Almost all their melodies were composed by the Admors themselves.

3. Court Composers

Modzitz Chassidim

Among the famous composers in the Modzitz court are Rabbi Yudel Kopman Idelsohn "who was one of Rabbi Israel's most beloved composers, and whose melodies were the closest, from both the spiritual and musical aspects, to those of his Rebbe"[11]; Rabbi Yankel Radomer and Rabbi Azriel Fastag of Warsaw, "who composed many tunes to match their Rebbe's nature, and he would proudly note their excellence, singing the melodies at his table."[12]

Additional composers include Rabbi Shmuel Rozenbach (of blessed memory) and Rabbi Ben-Zion Shenker (may he live long) of Brooklyn.[13] The latter, in his capacity as both composer and musician, recorded most of the Modzitz songs on cassettes and discs, and also wrote and composed many works, some of which became sufficiently well known to join the repertoire of music in the Jewish world. Such pieces include the tune for *Eshet Chayil*, (Proverbs 31:10-31) sung on Shabbat eve, and the tune for *Mizmor leDavid* (Psalm 23) sung during the third meal of Shabbat.

A memory that remains etched in my mind to this day, occurred in 1967, immediately following the Six Day War. The Western Wall was freed by Israel's army. The first chance to reach the Wall was on the Festival of *Shavuot*. As a

---

10 Geshuri, *Negginah vaChassidut beVeit Kuzmir uVnoteha*, pg. 49
11 Ibid
12 Geshuri, *laChassidim Mizmor*, pg. 29
13 Geshur, *Negginah vaChassidut beVeit Kuzmir uVnoteha*, pg. 51

resident of Jerusalem, like so many others I, too, wished to be among the first to visit the place about which we had always heard so much in the stories told to us by our parents.

We remained awake the whole night, and at 4 a.m. we hurried towards the Wall, along with others who wished to pray there. Ben-Zion Shenker had come to Israel especially for this occasion, as had so many others. We walked through the Arab markets in the Muslim Quarter, entering through the Shechem Gate, and stopping every few meters to pass through the barricades set up by the Israel Defense Forces in order to assist in controlling the stream of people. Suddenly, Ben-Zion began to sing, "Great peace to those who love Your Torah, for they shall not stumble; may there be peace within your walls, and prosperity within your palaces" (text from Psalm 119:165 and 122:7). This song was composed in 'real time' and we all sang it all the way to the Wall. This song not only remained in my memory but became one of the most famous tunes in the Modzitz synagogue of Jerusalem.

Gur Chassidim

One of the most notable composers of the Gur Chassidic court was Rabbi Zalman Tutin of Polstok who had a pleasant, refined and clear voice which could reach notes higher than that of the average male. He played the violin and flute, and knew how to read musical notes well. He was one of the most frequent prayer leaders for the Admor, Rabbi Yitzhak Meir of Gur. Among his best known melodies are those for the *Akdamot*, and for *Heyeh im Pipiyot*. Another composer was the cantor, Rabbi Michl of Praga-Warsaw, an adherent of Rabbi Yitzhak Meir. Rabbi Michl's tunes were accepted very warmly by all the Admoric courts.[14]

A composer of our own times, and of great importance to the Gur Chassidic court, was Rabbi Yaakov Talmud. His tunes were especially famous in that they became well known beyond the Gur court, having been cut on records by the famous Gur cantor in New York, Reb David Werdiger, who also recorded many other Chassidic tunes such as those of the Melitz, Bobov and other courts. Cantor Werdiger's fame increased when his son Mordechai became a well known Chassidic singer, under the name, Mordechai ben-David [*Mordechai son of David*].

---

14 Geshuri, *laChassidim Mizmor*, pg. 28

Chabad Chassidim

Most of the niggunim sung by Chabad Chassidim were written by the Admoric leaders. As already noted, this can be seen in the publication of the *Sefer haNiggunim* containing most of the Chabad melodies.

It is difficult to find informative material on the main leaders of prayers in the Chabad court of Rabbi Shneur Zalman of Liadi, but it is known that the Rebbe greatly enjoyed listening to the Chassid, Reb Israel of Dobrovna, whose music the Admor found inspirational: for example, "And it came to pass, when the minstrel played, that the hand of the LORD came upon him".[15] This talent was inherited by Reb Israel's son, Reb Shlomo, who played the violin, mellowing the hearts of his listeners. His compositional abilities were impressive, and he composed many of the Chabad tunes which are still widely in use.

It is worth delving into the topic of Chassidic musicians by reading Geshuri's book, *laChassidim Mizmor*, particularly the chapter titled *Tzaddikim veChassidim beShiram veZimram*, where a great deal more detail is offered on these and other composers of various Chassidic courts, such as Rizin Zanz, Bratzlav, Chernobyl, and so on.

4. Singers and the Choir

Some Chassidic courts were able to allow themselves an accompanying choir. The choir's role, of course, was to sing during prayers, assisting the *Chazzan* [cantor] leading the service. Some of the choirs, however, composed new songs each year, especially before the *Yamim Nora'im* which was a wonderful opportunity to reveal them to a larger public. The choir, by being the first to sing these songs, assisted the congregation in learning the new melodies.

The Gur Chassidic court's choir comprised a conductor, male chorists and several children. Among the choir members were some who wrote new tunes for *Rosh Hashana* [New Year]. The songs were recorded for internal use only within the Gur Chassidic court. Each year, new tunes were composed, sung first on the *Yamim Nora'im* and thereafter on Shabbat or special occasions.

During prayers, the choir stood alongside the *Chazzan*. On reaching the appropriate point, the choir would burst into song. The *Chazzan* himself was, for the most, one of the choir members.

The Gur Chassidic court's other well known composers included Reb Arieh Goldknopf, who also conducted the choir; Reb Knopf, Reb Moshe Irenstein, and others.

15 II Kings 3:15

The Modzitz court did not always have a professional choir but the Rebbe's sons and several other musical Chassidim would listen to the new songs composed by the Rebbe, then assist him with publicizing the melodies by singing them when he led prayers – which he did unfailingly – every year on the *Yamim Nora'im*.

The Belz, Viznitz, and Bobov Chassidic courts trained adherents familiar with music, who then composed tunes or publicized the new tunes composed by the Rebbe. The songs were then recorded on cassettes and later on CDs which were sold to the general public.

5. Chassidic Chazzanim [Cantors]

Chassidic cantors could be the subject of a complete study in its own right. There were numerous cantors, some of whom became world famous. It has already been noted in the section on 'Music and the Formulation of Prayer' that most Chassidim were less comfortable with *chazzanim* and preferred lay prayer leaders, who could sing the prayer tunes and integrate special melodies into them when appropriate. It should not be forgotten that many of these 'leaders of prayer' were, in fact, the Admors themselves who were not interested in the status implied by the title of *Chazzan*. However, we cannot ignore the fact that among these 'leaders of prayer' were some who were nothing less than true *chazzanim*. [Although the following list could be longer,] among the most renowned, are Yerucham haKattan Bliendmann (1798-1891), Baruch Schorr (1823-1906), Nissan Spivak Belzer (1824-1906), Pinhas Minikovsky (1859-1924), and Avraham Ber Birnbaum (1865-1922).[16]

---

16 Geshuri, *laChassidim Mizmor*, pg. 29

Chapter 9 – Famous Niggunim: Legends and Examples

1. ha'Ezkerah (Niggun haYissurim) – Rabbi Israel Taub of Modzitz (1849-1921)

When referring to the longest and most famous of all Chassidic niggunim, Geshuri[1] wrote:

> From among the music playing Tzaddikim of the last [Chassidic] period in Poland, we can identify one of utmost ability, the Tzaddik Rabbi Israel Taub of Modzitz, [located] on the Vistula [River]. He became revealed through his niggunim, as a serious musical personality, with absolute control over his style, its characteristics and its unique development, as can be seen in his music. All his compositions greatly pleased his adherents, who accepted them with outstanding interest. Of the many niggunim that he composed and which manifested his creativity, the one that draws the greatest attention is the longest and most complex, replete with the senses of loftiness and glory, having a wonderful sense of flow, abundance and movement, and known as 'Niggun ha'Ezkerah'.

Concerning this same niggun, Schleifer[2] noted:

> This niggun is one of the longest of Chassidic niggunim, and the longest of those composed by Rabbi Israel of Modzitz (1849-1921), known as the 'Rebbe Sabba' [Grandfather Rebbe], founder of the Modzitz Chassidic dynasty. The niggun is called *ha'Ezkerah ha-Gadol* [the great] to differentiate it from *ha'Ezkerah haKattan* [the lesser], also composed by Rabbi Israel. It is additionally known as the niggun comprising the '32 babas' – that is, 32 motifs. It is structured around the first stanza of the liturgical poetic piece, *Ezkara Elokim ve'Ahameha*, written by the tenth century Italian liturgical poet, Amitai ben Sheftaya. This work is found in Ashkenazi prayerbooks for the *Yamim Nora'im*. It is recited in the *Shatz* prayer repetitions which constitute part of the *Ne'ilah* [closing service] for *Yom Kippur* [Day of Atonement]. The niggun, however, was not intended to be sung on Yom Kippur, being far too long, and due to many of the words being repeated: it was known that Rabbi Taub opposed repetition of words during actual prayer. Instead, its proper place was at the *Tisch* held by the Rebbe, especially in the period between *Rosh Hashana* [New Year] and Yom Kippur.

As pointed out earlier by Geshuri[3], up until that time niggunim of two or three refrains were the general rule and no niggun of serious length had yet been composed.

---

1 *Negginah veChassidut beVeit Kuzmir uVnoteha*, pg. 69
2 *An Anthology of Hassidic Music*, pg. 157-158
3 *Negginah veChassidut beVeit Kuzmir uVnoteha*, pg. 70

At the most, a niggun contained four refrains, a rarity in the Chassidic world. Only from the period of Rabbi Hayim Halberstam of Zanz (1797-1876) and Rabbi Ezekil of Kuzmir (1812-1856) did longer niggunim begin to appear as a result of artistic musical influences derived in Western culture. Geshuri claims, however, that "the initial innovators were not the Tzaddikim-Admors but Chassidim who played music, influenced by the West". Their music, Geshuri notes, shows a mix of Eastern and Western effects, in a kind of tug-o-war between the hard and soft scales frequently alternating as links in the long and varied musical piece. Geshuri further explains this as the reason for the awe in which the *Ezkerah* is held: created not by a 'musical Chassid' with knowledge or training in music, but by a 'musical Tzaddik', son of an outstanding musical Tzaddik, and grandson of a Tzaddik greatly admired for his musical prowess. In other words, the thread of music was entwined in the family's trusting hands, and passed from one generation to the next like a nurtured offspring.

Prior to the *Ezkerah*, other fairly lengthy niggunim were received with open arms by Rabbi Taub's Chassidim, but none made such a powerful impression as the *Ezkerah*, which represented a turning point in the Rabbi's niggunim and which came into being in a manner entirely different from that of all others: never before had it happened that a Tzaddik on his death bed focused all his thoughts on the creation of an expansive, enriched niggun. Geshuri provides greater detail on the length of the *Ezkerah*, but stresses:

> The length of his niggunim was not [a ploy] to fill up empty space (which is true of other musicians and their compositions). Rather, each section manifests a musical concept, and is a vital stage to the niggun's entirety. *Niggun ha'Ezkerah*, despite its length, is replete with ideas and each link could serve as the foundation for a serious of linked motifs. He [Rabbi Israel] could distinguish between vital or improvident length. For this reason, the value of the *Ezkerah* is so much greater than that of other, lengthy niggunim in Chassidism.

By way of example, Geshuri relates how Rabbi Israel, on hearing a niggun several times, had already assimilated it, and would also sing it at the three Shabbat meals, while shortening it or dropping unnecessary links. When his son asked why he did so, the Rabbi replied:

> I can recognize the wonderful links that derive from the composer's heartfelt emotion, and it is those that I sing, while the rest have little purpose other than to give the niggun length, thus have no benefit, so can be dropped.

Schleifer, when relating to the *Ezkerah haKattan*, wrote:[4]

> Regarding the circumstances under which this niggun was composed, the Modzitz Chassidim relate that the inspiration for it came to the Rebbe while awaiting an operation to amputate

---

4 *An Anthology of Hassidic Music,* pg. 157-158

his foot, in Berlin in 1913. According to the Modzitz Chassidic tradition, the Rebbe awakened during the operation, looked out through the window and saw Berlin's beauty, then recalled the verse, '[...] I see each city built on its hilltop, while the city of G-d [Jerusalem] is debased to the nethermost depths'.[5] The Rebbe was deeply concentrated on composing the niggun in order to distract himself from the operation, and the niggun integrates his own physical pain with his spiritual pain over the destruction of Jerusalem. However, it seems that from what Rabbi Israel told his adherents, he began thinking about this niggun some two years prior to his operation, after returning from Karlsbad, the *ha'Ezkerah haKattan* already clear in his mind.

Schleifer noted that Vinaver, author of the posthumously published *An Anthology of Chassidic Music*, by virtue of being very close to Rabbi Israel's son, Rabbi Yehiel Alter, enjoyed the privilege of hearing Rabbi Israel himself sing the niggun. This is how Vinaver described the niggun:

Ezkerah Elokim was very well known among Chassidim in Poland [...] I even heard its composer, Rabbi Israel of Modzitz sing it at a *Se'udah Shlishit* [third Shabbat meal] in Warsaw, where he lived during the First World War. I remember the special atmosphere in the darkening *Beit Midrash* where the Jewish men sat, staring, not daring to join in the singing. Only for certain sections did Rabbi Israel signal with his hand that we should join the singing, and even then, only a certain select few among the adherents were merited with being able to participate. One of Rabbi Israel's son, Rabbi Yehiel Alter, an excellent musician (with a precious, lyrical tenor) was permitted to assist his father in singing for as long as he wished.

Don Campbell, in *The Mozart Effect*, offers abundant examples as proof of the power of music to heal illness. He claims that in addition to healing, music's power can also assist medical treatment, and presents the case of the dentist, Dr. Verzel, who performed root canal treatment on a patient who was asked to play the guitar during the treatment. The patient 'moved to another world' and was completely relaxed, making the treatment very simple.[6]

In summary, I will quote from Geshuri[7] who offers a review of the niggun, *ha'Ezkerah haGadol*:

The niggun itself is fine, pleasant. The niggun flows easily, sometimes beating like a celebratory anthem, and other times seeping like a sad lament of the soul. One link thunders like a wave that lights up, rolling along full of life, splendid and pleasing, gladdening, clear; and the next link crumbles, drops down to the distant river. Link follows link, and before one melody has completely ended, its sounds still echoing, the next moves and thunders through the air, keeping [it] alive, continuing the treasury of colors, arousing new images, followed by more new images [...] and the niggun fills boundless space. Even wise people admit that with the

---

5 Amitai ben-Sheftaya, author of the liturgical poem appearing in the [Ashkienaz] *Ne'ilah* [closing] service of Yom Kippur.
6 *The Mozart Effect*, pg. 350
7 Negginah veChassidut beVeit Kuzmir uVnoteha, pg. 70

Ezkerah, an amazing composition was produced, founded on powerful material put together with the diligence of the bees, a composition that appeals to the mysteries of the soul and beats of the heart. And those notes! They find their exact target. This is the source of the mysterious aspect in songs composed by a Tzaddik, and the power that draws out his expression of it. It entices, from beginning to end, its listeners' desire to listen. He gave of the best generously.

Rabbi Meir Yehiel of Ostrowze (1851-1928) had a certain custom: whenever a Chassid came to visit who knew music, and especially a Modzitz Chassid, he would request that the *Ezkerah* be sung to him. Tears would fall from his eyes. After Rabbi Israel passed away, Rabbi Meir Yehiel said of him:

We can all be jealous of the Modzitz Rabbi, who left the world a precious legacy, his niggunim.

The Chassidim around him wondered at this, asking: "Rabbi, and your Torah [discourses], what of that?" Rabbi Meir, with his great humility, replied: "From my Torah, no one is awakened; but from the Modzitzer Rebbe's niggunim, every heart can be aroused to repentance".[8]

2. The Four Babas Niggun – The Alter Rebbe of Chabad (1745-1813)

Chabad's music appeared simultaneously with, and integrated within, the revelation of Chabad doctrines, around 1772-1773. The Alter Rebbe, founder of Chabad, possessed a very high level of both musical and poetic abilities, and composed ten niggunim, all of which were greatly admired by Chabad adherents.

His most well known niggun, the "Four Babas", is also known as "Rav's Niggun" or "The Alter Rebbe's Niggun". This niggun is wrapped in the fiery flames of holiness, its repeated motifs drawing closer to Godliness in a form that reflects the Chabad approach.[9]

This niggun contains great depth, and each movement is directed to a different lofty spiritual issue. Chabad Chassidim are careful about singing it and do so with great precision and attention, and only on specific occasions such as the three Pilgrimage festivals, Purim, Kislev 19th, Tammuz 12th, weddings, and so on.[10]

As already noted, the Admor Rabbi Shalom Dov-Ber, known as the *Rasha"b* (1861-1920)[11] explained that:

The Rebbe's niggun is directed to the four worlds, *Atzilut* [Emanation], *Bri'ah* [Creation], *Yetzirah* [Formation] and *Assiyah* [Action]. Each baba [motif] relates to one of the these four

---

8   *Imrei Saul*, pg. 311, Section 20
9   Shmuel Zalmanov, *Otzar haNiggunim,* Introduction, pg. 19
10 *Niggunei Chabad*, pgs. 4, 5, 6
11 Ibid

worlds. These four worlds in turn relate to the letters of the Tetragrammaton. The four letters of the Godly name shed their light on four of the levels of the soul: *Nefesh, Ruach, Neshama* and *Chaya*, which are found in each and every Jew. For this reason, it must be played with precision and care.

When this niggun is sung in a state of internal awakening, it is a most apt time for repentance and connection. When this niggun is played with pureness of heart, and following service through the *Tikkun Hatzot* [rectification and restoration], the reading of the *Shema* prior to sleep, and true prayer with deep effort, then one may merit personal salvation.

The Rebbe details the virtues of each separate motif:

It is obvious that the Rebbe composed this niggun while he was with the Maggid of Mezhirech; most of the Rebbe's niggunim are from that period. But it is also clear that the melodies, including that of the Four Babas, were refined only after he became 'Rebbe'.

Having completed what he wished to convey concerning the niggunim in general, the Admor then requested that the niggun be sung sedately: the first three motifs twice, and the fourth baba three times; this format to be played three times in succession, but on the third time, the final baba was to be sung ten times in succession, to lodge itself in all ten forces of the soul.

In Sefer haNiggunim,[12] we find:

When this niggun was sung, everyone stood in a state of great [spiritual] awakening, and each paid attention to see whether the Rebbe – our Alter Rebbe – stood alongside him.

Further on, the following appears:[13]

Some time later, our Alter Rebbe began to sing his well known niggun, repeating each baba twice, and the final, fourth baba several times; and when the Rebbe sang, everyone in the large *Beit Midrash* and the adjacent building connected to his thoughts, his powers and senses through the Rebbe's singing. Each and every baba, sung by the Rebbe, aroused a special part of the soul, and each one was raised to a higher position and state. Rabbi Yosef Kolbo and Rabbi Isser Kisas said that when the Rebbe sang, they could recall everything that had ever happened to them from the time of their earliest memory.

Rebbe Menachem Mendel, known as the *Tzemach Tzedek* (1789-1866), is also recorded as having related to the Four Babas niggun:[14]

When one relates an explanation, quoting the name of his source, it is as though that source stands there with him. My father and teacher, the *Moharash*, would say: 'When one

---

12 In *Likkutei Reshimot*, Section 2
13 Ibid, Section 14
14 Ibid, Section 43

sings the niggun of the Alter Rebbe, the Four Babas, then the time is ripe for repentance, as it is a time of Godly will, and even though there are different levels of Godly will at different times, they share one factor: G-d's will. My father the Rebbe began to sing the Alter Rebbe's Four Babas, and all accompanied him with great fervor and enthusiasm, deficient of external influences, each person withdrawn into himself, his past, present and future, and the great hall adopted the atmosphere of *Unetaneh Tokef*.

3. Niggun haMalachim (El Adon March) – Kozenice Chassidic Court

Rabbi Yitzhak Meir Alter, author of *Chidushei haRi"m* (1799-1866) related that in the year 5564 [1804], as a boy of no more than 5 years old, he was in Kozenice, where it was customary for the "Maggid haKadosh"[15] (1733-1815) to lead services on Shabbat. On reaching the liturgical poetic piece *El Adon*, those around him broke out in song, and the Maggid would recite the words. That particular Shabbat, on reaching the appropriate text, he himself began to sing a wonderful melody. Those praying with him did not recognize the tune and obviously could not assist him. At the end of the prayer, the Maggid noticed the wonder, and said:

> It is now some three years since Rabbi Shmuel Yosef Zbitkaver of Prague has passed away. After his death, several angels of destruction presented their prosecutions on his transgressions, but one interceding angel, created from the great commandment to save Jews from the sword and bring them to burial, raised its voice, and said: 'How is it possible that this commandment, of saving so many souls of our brethren Jews, does not determine the judgment? It is only fitting that he go immediately to Paradise'. Thus, a ruling was determined in the Court on High, that indeed he deserves an important place in Paradise for this *mitzvah*, but he could not immediately be brought there without his stains first being cleansed. And this cleansing took three years. Now, at this very moment, he was taken by the angles to his place in Heaven, and as they took him, they sang a wonderful, new song, which you just heard from me.

The various Admors of Koznits preserved this tradition faithfully, singing the sacred march on the *Yamim Nora'im* before reciting the *Keter* prayer. In the court of the Admor of Koznits the march was sung to the words for *Ein Kitzvah liShnotecha* recited on the *Yamin Nora'im*, according to the book, *beDarchei Varsha ha'Avelot*.[16]

---

15 Rabbi Israel Hopstein of Kozenice
16 *http://hydepark.hevre.co.il/hydepark/topic.asp?topic_id=1652135*

4. Yah Echsof – Rabbi Aharon of Karlin (1736-1772)

Geshuri described Rabbi Aharon ben Yaakov, known as Rabbi Aharon the Great of Karlin (1736-1772) as follows:

> He was one of the greatest composes of song that Chassidism gave to the Jewish world, and the founder of the Chassidic court of Karlin. He served his Creator with fervor through song and singing. Shabbat and song were, for him, synonymous, organically interconnected, inseparable, as Shabbat in its entirety is one endless song, a song of praise to the Creator of heaven, earth and all the hosts, in six days.[17]

Chassidim related that when Rabbi Aharon recited the Song of Songs with his special tune, on Friday afternoon prior to the Shabbat's commencement, the heavens above and all the Upper Worlds became silent, the serving angels ceased singing praises to the Holy One, Blessed be He, and all gathered around to listen to the Rabbi's sacred singing, so pleasant and sweet, taken straight from the chamber of music.

R' Aharon's singing, steeped in invigorated, sacred tones deriving in the world of truth and Jewish-religious spiritual awakening, served the gloriousness of Shabbat. He versified his song in great devotion, seeking the diffusion of materiality, as befits a day which is entirely holy. Devotion is the central and principle aspect of his song and is what provides the singing with its unique flavor and grace, both of which have the power to draw out and arouse love and awe in the heart of the listener.

Rabbi Aharon approached song quavering with holiness through the hymns of prayer, discovering in it a kind of life source which enables manifesting the hidden and mystic in the Jew's higher soul. His song not only laps pleasantly at the ear, but uplifts the heart and the soul: in Rabbi Aharon's singing, 'all my bones shall recite' the Shabbat's virtue, praise and majesty.

The niggun – *Yah Echsof No'am Shabbat* – was composed by Rabbi Aharon as a response to his deep yearning for Shabbat, and manifests his fervor for the sanctity of Shabbat. It is sung by Karlin Chassidim to this day. No other text became as beloved by Karlin Chassidim and Karlin's Chassidic offshoots as this, and it is considered the greatest of all the Shabbat melodies.

The niggunim composed for the sake of that particular liturgical poem are worthy of a separate section. The first of these derives from the golden era of that dynasty. Apparently composed by the first or second Rabbi Aharon, it is still sung by Karliner Chassidim to this day. They refer to it as "The Holy Niggun" due to an outstanding narrative. When the *Beit Aharon* [the name by which the

---

17 *Machanayim*, Journal 85, 1964. Article on R' Aharon of Karlin

Rebbe was known, based on the title of his book] visited his relative-by-marriage, Rabbi Israel of Ruzhyn (1797-1851), he saw that when this niggun was sung, the Riziner Rebbe's chair rose from the floor.

Another tune was composed by Rabbi Israel Perlov of Stolin (1868-1921) known as the *Yanuka*. The notes were recorded by Nehemia Vinaver and appear in *An Anthology of Chassidic Music*. According to Schleifer, it is possible that this tune, in fact, is not the original one but a separate melody of devotion, composed by Rabbi Israel Perlov, into which the words of *Yah Echsof* were integrated.

5. Ani Ma'amin – Rabbi Azriel David Fastag – Chassid Modzitz

"Who created the niggun for *Ani Ma'amin*?" This is the question, states Rabinowitz, that was asked by an American paper regarding that famous melody, to words which had always been sung with a slow, heart-rending and melancholy tune. The words of *Ani Ma'amin* were also recited by the Jews being transported to the Nazi gas chambers. Rabinowitz responds that the composer was Rabbi Azrial Fastag, a Chassid of the Modzitz Admor, Rabbi Saul Taub. When the Nazis transported Rabbi Azriel David Fastag, of Otvoczk, to Treblinka, he began to hum a tune which spread throughout the death train. Some of the Jews on that train with him miraculously managed to survive, and they ensured that the tune reached the Modzitzer Admor.[18] Rabinowitz adds:

> I had the privilege of hearing the Modzitzer Admor sing the *Ani Ma'amin* at Saratoga Springs, New York. People sat outside and inside, and from the eyes of us all, tears flowed on hearing this sorrowful melody.[19]

6. The Shepherd's Niggun – The Kalev Rebbe (1744-1821)

In Chapter 12, I relate to non-Jewish tunes adopted by Chassidim. This would include the famous narrative of the shepherd's melody, adapted by the Kalev Chassidim, as described by Schleifer:

> The shepherd's niggun is one of the most renowned melodies in the history of Chassidism. It is an example of the way Chassidim adopted melodies to redeem them of the impurity into which they had sunk.

---

18 See the detailed account of how the niggun was saved. Two Jews jumped from the train to Treblinka, after the composer promised part of his World to Come to anyone who brought his niggun to the Modzitz Rebbe. One of them survived and did so. P. Flasker, *Negginah veChassidut beVeit Kuzmir uVnoteha*, pg. 123.

19 As cited in Geshuri, *Negginah veChassidut beVeit Kuzmir uVnoteha*, pg. 33

Chassidic tradition relates that on one of the Kalev Rebbe's trips through the Ukrainian forests together with his Rabbi, Leib Sarah's (1730-1796) the Kalev Rebbe heard a shepherd at some distance, singing. He followed the voice, and found the shepherd sitting in the middle of the woods, singing a melancholy song to himself in Ukrainian, about the great forest that separates him from his love. Immediately the Rebbe sang the exact same tune, with Yiddish words that describe the Exile which separates him from the *Shechinah*. Having completed his own song, the Rebbe then asked the shepherd to sing the Ukrainian song once again, but the shepherd was unable to do so: he could not remember it. In fact, he had completely forgotten it. Filled with joy, the Rebbe cried out, 'I have purified the melody, and returned it to its holy station'.[20]

The original words to the song were:

Mountain, O Mountain
Bride, O Bride, how far you are
Mountain, O Mountain, quickly disappear
That I may reach my bride.

After adaptation, the words became:

Shechina, O *Shechina*, how far you are
Exile, O Exile, how huge you are
If only the Exile were small
Then the *Shechinah* would be close
If only I was brought forth from this Exile
We could then be together.

Avraham Korman investigated the sources of the non-Jewish melodies which reached the Kalev Admor. In his book, *ha'Aggadah uMashma'uta*, he relates also to "The Shepherd's Song" a little differently, and I feel it is worth being aware of this additional approach:

I will now present one of hundreds of Chassidic narratives, which speaks for itself. Rabbi Yitzhak Isaac Taub (who passed away on 7 Adar II, 5581 – 1821), the founder of the Kalev Admoric dynasty, was also renowned as being highly musical. His songs and compositions (their sources being Hungarian shepherds' melodies) are still sung by Chassidim to date. But how did he learn these non-Jewish songs? There was a wonderful man, known as Reb Leib Sarah's (Sarah's son); and Reb Yitzhak Isaac was the son of a very poor Rabbi's widow. As a child of eight, the latter was already required to shepherd the geese in order to receive a slice of bread. He wore torn, tattered clothes. Reb Leib learned of a 'high soul' [living] in a township somewhere in Hungary. Reb Leib appealed to the mother to hand her child over into his care, and [promised] that he would ensure the child's education and

---

20 *An Anthology of Chassidic Music,* pg. 212-213

needs. He took the child to Rebbe Reb Shmelkeh, the Rabbi of Nikelsburg, where the child did exceedingly well at his studies and became [a] great [Torah sage]. [later] He remembered the shepherd tunes from his childhood, and decided to redeem their holy aspects.

Korman claims that this narrative seems a little imaginary, nor is he certain of its veracity, other than the fact that Rabbi Yitzhak Isaac Taub, when young, was taught by Reb Shmelke. However, the fact that the core of the narrative appears in multiple sources indicates how famous it is.[21]

7. Niggun haMalachim – Rabbi Yaakov Yitzhak, Seer of Lublin (1745-1815) – la'El asher Shabbat mikol haMa'asim

The melody for *la'El asher Shabbat mikol haMa'asim* was composed by Rabbi Yehoshua ha'Aroch, great grandfather of the *Ba'al Hafla'a* and President of the Rabbinic Court in Tarnograd. It was sung almost every Shabbat eve at the table of the *Divrei Hayim* [Rabbi Hayim Halberstam]. The song was popularly called "Niggun haMalachim" [the angels' song] by the Chassidim. Tradition has it that one Shabbat evening, before saying the *Birkat haMazon* [Benediction after Meals], the Seer of Lublin fell into a deep state of devotion to the point of losing his soul; but on awakening some hours later, began singing *la'El asher Shabbat* with a completely new melody, as yet unheard by the Chassidim. The Seer related later that he learned this tune, while deeply meditated, from the angels who sang it before the Holy One, Blessed be He. Thereafter, the melody spread from one person to the next. The Holy Rabbi of Rafshitz then customarily sang this melody at his Shabbat table on Shabbat evenings, prior to *Birkat haMazon*. From Rafshitz it spread to Zanz where it was sung by the Rebbe there with great ardency. (Otzar Chaim).[22]

---

21 *ha'Aggadah uMashma'uta*, Introduction, pg. 39-40
22 *http://hydepark.hevre.co.il/hydepark/topic.asp?topic_id=1652135*

Chapter 10 – Adages referencing Chassidic Music

Adages are an important part of the study of Chassidism, and a short sentence can contain the ability to teach a whole concept. Many such phrases or sayings have become an integral part of Chassidic doctrine itself. For this reason, I felt it worthwhile to devote a special chapter to them.

1. Song

1. The tongue is the quill of the heart; the song is the quill of the soul.[1]
2. Song is like a parable, and its moral needs to be understood.[2]
3. Songs and refrains may be the works of those who are clever with words and phrases, but thereafter they were moistened well by the tears of Israel, to become *Selichot*.[3]
4. The same [format of] blessing used for the Torah is used for song and singing – *haBocher baTorah* and *haBocher beShirei Zimrah*; yet regarding [the blessing for] Torah, the word *eved* [servant] is used – *haBocher baTorah uveMoshe Avdo* [who chooses the Torah and Moses His servant], while for song and singing, the word *Melech* [King] is used – *haBocher beShirei Zimrah Melech...*[4]
5. We recite the *haBocher baTorah* blessing once each week, (during Shabbat prayers, following the *Haftarah* reading) yet we recite *haBocher beShirei Zimrah* daily (in the morning – *Shacharit* – prayer).[5]
6. For good reason, song and music hold the highest position in Chassidism. Through song, the Chassid rises to the Upper Worlds, reaches the wings of the *Shechinah* and the Throne of Glory, and merges with all that hovers above the natural world in which we live.[6]

---

1 Rabbi Schneur Zalman of Liadi, *Sefer haNiggunim*, pg. 21 (Introduction)
2 Rabbi Moshe of Kovrin, [cited by] Raz Simcha [in] *Pitgamei Chassidim*, pg. 123
3 Rabbi Levi Yitzhak of Berditchev, [cited by] Raz Simcha [in] *Pitgamei Chassidim*, pg. 123
4 *Imrei Saul*, pg. 305, Discourse 1.
5 Told to me, citing Rabbi Israel Taub
6 M. S. Geshuri, *haNiggun vehaRikud baChassidut*, pg. 18-19

א. שירה

1. הלשון – קולמוס הלב, השיר – קולמוס הנפש.[7]
2. שירה – בחינת משל, יש להבין את הנמשל.[8]
3. הפיוטים והפזמונים, הם מעשה ידיהם של בעלי לשון ומליצה. אבל אחר כך הורטבו יפה יפה בדמעותיהם של ישראל, ונעשו סליחות.[9]
4. אותה ברכה שמברכים על התורה מברכים על שירה וזימרה, הבוחר בתורה – הבוחר בשירי זימרה, ועוד יותר, אצל תורה כתוב "עבד" הבוחר בתורה ובמשה עבדו, ואילו אצל שירה וזימרה כתוב "מלך", הבוחר בשירי זימרה מלך.[10]
5. את ברכת "הבוחר בתורה" אומרים אנו פעם בשבוע, (בתפילת שבת, בברכות שלאחר אמירת ההפטרה) אך את ברכת "הבוחר בשירי זימרה" אומרים אנו כל יום (בברכת ישתבח הנאמרת בתפילת שחרית).[11]
6. לא בכדי תופסת השירה והנגינה מקום ראשון בחסידות. בשירה מתרומם החסיד לעולמות העליונים, מגיע עד לכנפי השכינה וכסא הכבוד, ומתמזג בכל המרחף מעל עולם הטבע שבו אנו נתונים.[12]

2. Niggun

1. Teardrops open gates, niggunim cause the walls to tumble.[13]
2. It is said that the chamber of music is next to the chamber of repentance. And I say, that the chamber of music is none other than the chamber of repentance.[14]
3. When I hear a niggun sung by a Jew, I can tell to what degree he is G-d fearing, and whether he is wise, or simple.[15] When I hear a person singing a melody, I can tell immediately how intelligent he is, and whether he is G-d fearing.[16]
4. Through the niggun it is possible to ascertain whether a person is steeped in belief in G-d.[17]
5. There is nothing in this world that does not have its own niggun, and even the skeptic [disbeliever in G-d] has his own special melody.[18]

---

7 רבי שניאור זלמן מלאדי, ספר הניגונים עמוד כ"א(מבוא)
8 רבי משה מקוברין, רז שמחה, פתגמי חסידים ע' 123
9 רבי לוי יצחק מברדיטשב, רז שמחה, פתגמי חסידים ע' 123
10 אמרי שאול עמוד שה מאמר א'
11 שמעתי בשם ר' ישראל טאוב,
12 מ.ש. גשורי, הניגון והריקוד בחסידות, עמוד י"ח-י"ט
13 Rabbi Nahman of Bratzlav, [cited by] Raz Simcha [in] *Pitgamei Chassidim,* pg. 137
14 Rabbi Israel Taub of Modzitz, *Negginah vaChassidut beVeit Kuzmir uVnoteha,* pg. 75, and Imrei Saul, pg. 309 Section 15.
15 Rabbi Israel Taub of Modzitz, *Imrei Saul,* pg. 316
16 Rabbi Israel Taub of Modzitz, *Negginah vaChassidut beVeit Kuzmir uVnoteha,* pg. 75
17 Rabbi Nahman of Bratzlav, [cited by] Raz Simcha [in] *Pitgamei Chassidim,* pg. 137

6. Some people's melodies do not originate from the chamber of music and song, but from the notes.[19]
7. Each lock has its own key, but the locksmith has a master key with which he can open all locks. That is the niggun.[20]
8. The niggun is the fastest way to access G-d's 'inner ear'.[21]
9. There are three levels of niggun: the 'simple' niggun which has neither words nor intent; the 'filled' niggun of the earliest Chassidim, which arouses repentance, contemplation, or love of one's fellowmen; and the 'directed' niggun which was composed or chosen by one of the Admors.[22]
10. The niggun has the power to rescue the person from even the deepest complications.[23]
11. When a narrative is related, a connection is made with the Rebbe's actions. When one repeats a Torah interpretation, a connection is made with the Rebbe's words. But when one sings his niggun, a connection is made with the Rebbe's thoughts.[24]
12. The secret of the niggun is not just the sounds that comprise the melody, but the silences and pauses, in the niggun.[25]
13. Each nation has its own melody, and none can play the melody of another; but Israel plays all the melodies together, in order to raise them to their origin.[26]
14. What is the difference between the niggunim for prayers, and the Chassidic niggun? The niggun used in prayer derives from directed purpose, while the Chassidic niggun brings that purpose [to fruition]; that is, awakening the heart.[27]
15. Music is the language of the soul, with its notes and derivaties; the language of soul is the *Tzimtzum* [contraction]; and what one niggun can express, cannot be expressed by thousands of words.[28]

---

18 Ibid
19 Rabbi Shalom Dov-Ber, [known as the] Moharsha"b, [as cited in] *Sefer haNiggunum*, Chapter titled *Likkutei Reshimot*, pg. 41
20 Ibid, pg. 41
21 Staiman, *Niggun*, Introduction, pg. xiv
22 *Otzar Pitgamei Chabad*, pg. 386, quoting *Likkutei Dibburim 3*, pg. 888
23 Ibid, pg. 385, quoting a discourse for 12th of Tammuz 5706, and *Sefer haNiggunum*, Chapter titled *Likkutei Reshimot*, pg. 41, section 90, citing the Moharsha"b
24 *Otzar Pitgamei Chabad*, pg. 301
25 Rabbi Israel Taub of Modzitz, Negginah vaChassidut beVeit Kuzmir uVnoteha, pg. 75
26 Rabbi Avraham of Sadegura, [as cited by] Y. Alfassi [in] *haChassidut veShivat Tzion*, pg. 168
27 *Sefer haNiggunim*, Chapter titled *Likkutei Reshimot*, pg. 38, citing the Moharash.
28 Rabbi Israel Taub of Modzitz, *Imrei Saul*, pg. 316

16. Those who compose melodies by combining notes do not produce real niggunim; they are not niggunim that are sourced in the heart.[29]
17. When [the efficacy of] the word ceases, the niggun speaks [instead].[30]
18. If one has a pleasant voice, and the Holy One, Blessed be He, is not given the opportunity to enjoy such a voice, it would have been better had that one not come into the world.[31]
19. The Torah is in niggun, the *Shechinah* resides in niggun, and Israel frees itself from the Exile through niggun.[32]
20. Rabbi Pinhas of Korzec customarily said: "Sovereign of the Universe, if only I knew how to sing, I would not leave You to reside in the Upper Worlds, but would perturb you with my singing until You came down to reside among us here".[33]
21. When playing music, the niggun itself speaks.[34]
22. There is no cry greater than that of silence.[35]
23. Whoever has no sense of music, has no sense of Chassidism.[36]

ב. ניגון

1. דמעות- פותחות שערים, זימרה – מפילה חומות.[37]
2. אומרים שהיכל הנגינה הוא על יד היכל התשובה. ואני אומר, שהיכל הנגינה בעצמו הוא היכל התשובה.[38]
3. כשאני שומע ניגון מתנגן מפיו של יהודי, יכול אני לקבוע עד היכן מגיעה יראת שמים שלו. ואם הוא חכם או טפש.[39] או: כשאני שומע ניגון מתנגן מפי האדם, אני מכיר בו מיד עד כמה הוא בר דעת, ואפילו אם הוא ירא שמים[40].
4. על ידי הניגון אדם ניכר, אם קיבל עול מלכות שמים.[41]
5. אין לך דבר בעולם שאין לו ניגון מיוחד, ואפילו האפיקורסות יש לה ניגון מיוחד.[42]

29 Ibid
30 I do not know the source of this adage but saw it used in Israel in advertisements for music.
31 *Sefer Chassidim,* Introduction in *Sefer heNegginah haChassidit,* Idelsohn, pg. 2
32 *Tikkunei Zohar.*
33 Martin Buber, *Ohr haGanuz,* pg. 128
34 *Sefer haNiggunim,* citing the Moharsha"b, pg. 39 Section 62
35 Citing the Rabbi of Kotzk; see interview with Saul Meizlish in the chapter on 'Interviews'
36 *Sefer haNiggun,* chapter titled *Likkutei Reshimot,* pg. 30
37 רבי נחמן מברסלב, רז שמחה, פתגמי חסידים ע' 137
38 רבי ישראל טאוב ממודז'יץ, נגינה וחסידות בבית קוזמיר ובנותיה עמוד 75, וכן, אמרי שאול עמוד ש"ט אות ט"ו
39 רבי ישראל טאוב ממודז'יץ, אמרי שאול עמוד שט"ז
40 רבי ישראל טאוב ממודז'יץ, נגינה וחסידות בבית קוזמיר ובנותיה עמוד 75
41 רבי נחמן מברסלב, רז שמחה, פתגמי חסידים ע' 137

6. ישנם כאלה אשר מנגינותיהם אינן מהיכל הנגינה והשירה – כי אם מן התווים.[43]
7. לכל מנעול יש מפתח משלו, אלא שלאומן יש מפתח כללי, שבו יכול הוא לפתוח את כל המנעולים, זהו הניגון.[44]
8. ניגון הוא הדרך המהירה ביותר להגיע לאוזן הפנימית של ה'.[45]
9. שלוש דרגות בניגון: ניגון "שוטה", שאינו אומר ואינו מכוון למאומה, ניגון "ממולא" ניגון של חסידים ראשונים, מעורר לתשובה, להתבוננות, או לאהבת רעים. וניגון "מכוון" היינו ניגון שחיבר או בחר אחד מן האדמו"רים.[46]
10. בכוחו של ניגון לחלץ את האדם אף מן הבוץ העמוק ביותר.[47]
11. כאשר מספרים סיפור-נעשית התקשרות במעשיו של הרבי, כאשר חוזרים על דבר תורה-ההתקשרות היא בדיבורו של הרבי וכאשר מנגנים ניגון-ההתקשרות היא במחשבתו של הרבי.[48]
12. סוד הנגינה הוא לא רק הצלילים המהווים את הניגון, אלא גם השתיקה והרווחים שבניגון.[49]
13. כל אומה יש לה ניגון משלה ואין אחת מנגנת בניגונה של חברתה, אבל ישראל מנגן כל הניגונים כאחד, כדי להעלותם לשורשם.[50]
14. מה ההבדל בין ניגון של תפילה לניגון חסידי? ניגון של תפילה בא מתוך הכוונה, ניגון חסידי מביא את הכוונה- התעוררות בלב[51]
15. נגינה היא שפת הנשמה, צלילים וניבים לה, שפת הנשמה היא הצימצום, את אשר יבטא ניגון אחד, אין תוכן בן אלפי מילים ביכולתו לבטאו.[52]
16. אלה היוצרים ניגונים מתוך תווים, אין נגינתם אמיתית, אין היא נגינה היוצאת מן הלב.[53]
17. במקום שהמילים נגמרות, המנגינה מדברת.[54]
18. מי שקולו נעים ואין הקב"ה נהנה מקולו ראוי לו שלא בא לעולם[55]
19. אורייתא בניגונא, שכינתא בניגונא, ישראל סלקין מגו גלותא בניגונא.- התורה בניגון, השכינה בניגון וישראל יוצאים מתוך הגלות בניגון.[56]
20. רבי פנחס מקוריץ היה אומר: ריבונו של עולם, אילו ידעתי לזמר, לא הייתי מניח אותך לדור בעליונים, אלא הייתי מציק לך בזימרתי עד שתרד ותדור עמנו כאן.[57]

---

42 רבי נחמן מברסלב, רז שמחה, פתגמי חסידים ע' 137
43 רבי חיים מצאנז, רז שמחה, פתגמי חסידים ע' 137
44 ר' שלום דובער, מוהרש"ב, ספר הניגונים, ליקוטי רשימות עמוד מ"א
45 Stauman, Niggun, Site xiv
46 אוצר פתגמי חב"ד עמוד 386 בשם ליקוטי דיבורים ג' עמוד 888
47 שם, עמוד 385 בשם שיחת יב תמוז תש"ו, וכן ספר הניגונים, ליקוטי רשימות עמוד מ"ב אות צ' בשם מוהרש"ב
48 אוצר פתגמי חב"ד עמוד 301
49 רבי ישראל טאוב ממודזיץ, נגינה וחסידות בבית קוזמיר ובנותיה עמוד 75
50 ר' אברהם מסדיגורה,י. אלפסי החסידות וישבת ציון עמוד 168
51 בשם מוהר"ש, ספר הניגונים, ליקוטי רשימות עמוד ל"ח
52 ר' ישראל טאוב ממודזיץ, אמרי שאול עמוד שט"ז
53 שם
54 לא ידוע לי מקורו של הפתגם אך ראיתיו בפירסומת על המוסיקה בישראל.
55 ספר חסידים, מובא בספר הנגינה החסידית, אידלזון עמוד 2
56 תיקוני זהר

21. כשמנגנים, הניגון עצמו מדבר.[58]
22. אין זעקה גדולה מן הדממה[59]
23. מי שאין לו חוש בנגינה, אין לו חוש בחסידות.[60]

3. Dance

1. Dancing before the Holy One, Blessed be He – are prayers.[61]
2. Every Sunday one should dance, either in thought or in actuality.[62]
3. Great is the power of dance, which can raise the person a *tefach* [handbreadth] above the ground.[63]
4. The angel Michael forms a crown from the shoes that slipped off the feet of Jews who danced on *Simchat Torah*.[64]

ג. ריקוד

1. הריקודים לפני הקדוש ברוך הוא – תפילות הם.[65]
2. צריך לרקוד כל יום ראשון, במחשבה או במעשה.[66]
3. גדול כוחה של הריקוד, שהוא מרומם את האדם טפח מעל גבי הקרקע.[67]
4. המלאך מיכאל עושה כתר, מסנדלים שנשרו מרגלי יהודים הרוקדים בשמחת תורה.

4. Joy and Sadness

1. Joy resides in the heart, but the heart cannot rejoice until it removes that which is warped from its heart.[68]
2. Joy is richness. No matter whether a person possesses money as plentifully as the grains of sand, if there is no joy in his heart, he can be called poor.[69]

---

57 מרטין בובר, או הגנוז עמוד 128
58 ספר הניגונים בשם מוהרש"ב עמוד ל"ט אות ס"ב
59 בשם הרבי מקוצק, ראה ראיון עם שאול מיזליש במדור ראיונות
60 ספר הניגונים, ליקוטי רשימות עמוד ל'
61 The Besht, [cited by] Simha Raz [in] *Pitgamei Chassidim*, pg. 175
62 Ibid, pg. 175
63 Rabbi Aharon of Karelin, [cited by] Simha Raz [in] *Pitgamei Chassidim*, pg. 175
64 The Besht, [cited by] Simha Raz [in] *Pitgamei Chassidim*, pg. 175
65 הבעש"ט, רז שמחה, פתגמי חסידים ע' 175
66 רבי נחמן מברסלב, רז שמחה, פתגמי חסידים ע' 175
67 רבי אהרון מקרלין, רז שמחה, פתגמי חסידים ע' 175
68 Rabbi Nahman of Bratzlav, [cited by] Simha Raz [in] *Pitgamei Chassidim*, pg. 179
69 Rabbi Tzadok haKohen of Lublin, [cited by] Simha Raz [in] *Pitgamei Chassidim*, pg. 179

3. Joy without consideration – becomes sheer wantonness.[70]
4. I'm afraid that even Israel's sinners are invited to the World to Come, for throughout their lives they are in a state of joy.[71]
5. He who lives in joy, fulfills the will of G-d.[72]
6. Joy holds an added virtue; if tears can open the gates, then joy removes those gates altogether, and destroys all partitions.[73]
7. The joy in performing a precept [*mitzvah*] or in singing negates the judgments and denunciations in both the spiritual and the material spheres.[74]
8. Joy is holiness, and sadness is the *Sitra Achra* [the 'other side'].[75]
9. The [evil] inclination seeks to defeat through the dimension of sorrow.[76]
10. In joy shall you go forth – in joy shall you leave your troubles behind.[77]
11. Melancholy is not a sin but the insanity that melancholy causes cannot be caused by any other sin.[78]
12. A Jew who does not step forward with joy at being Jewish is being ungrateful.[79]

ד. שמחה – עצבות

1. עיקר השמחה הוא בלב, ואי אפשר ללב לשמוח עד שיסיר עקמימות שבליבו.[80]
2. השמחה – עיקר העשירות, ירבה לו אדם כסף כחול ושמחת הלב אין לו – נקרא עני.[81]
3. שמחה בלא מחשבה – הוללות היא.[82]
4. חוששני שפושעי ישראל אף הם מזומנים לחיי העולם הבא, כיוון שכל ימיהם שרויים הם בשמחה.[83]
5. החי בשמחה – מקיים רצון הבורא.[84]
6. מידה יתירה יש לשמחה, ואם הדמעות פותחות את השערים, הרי השמחה מסירה אותם לגמרי והורסת את המחיצות[85]

---

70 Rabbi Dov Ber of Mezhirech, [cited by] Simha Raz [in] *Pitgamei Chassidim*, pg. 179
71 Rabbi Israel of Ruzhyn, [cited by] Simha Raz [in] *Pitgamei Chassidim*, pg. 179
72 The Besht, [cited by] Simha Raz [in] *Pitgamei Chassidim*, pg. 179
73 The Besht, [cited by] Y. L. Maimon [in] *Sarei haMe'ah*, pg. 62
74 *Otzar Pitgamei Chabad*, pg. 385, citing *Igrot haKodesh* by the Tzemach Tzedek, pg. 335
75 Rabbi Israel of Rizin, [cited by] Y. L. Alfassi [in] *haChassidut veShivat Tzion*, pg. 166
76 The Besht, *Tzava'at haRibsh*, as cited by Geshuri in *laChassidim Mizmor*, pg. 155, in the article titled *haMusica baKabbalah*, quoting Meir Zvi Rabinowitz
77 Rabbi Israel Yedidiya Eleazar Taub, *Imrei Saul*, pg. 312, Section 26
78 Rabbi Chanoch of ALexander, [cited in] Aharon Eshkoli, *Hachassidut bePolin*, Jerusalem: 1998:107
79 Ibid
80 רבי נחמן מברסלב, רז שמחה, פתגמי חסידים ע' 179
81 רבי צדוק הכהן מלובלין, רז שמחה, פתגמי חסידים ע' 179
82 רבי דב בר ממזריטש, רז שמחה, פתגמי חסידים ע' 179
83 רבי ישראל מרוזן, רז שמחה, פתגמי חסידים ע' 179
84 הבעש"ט, רז שמחה, פתגמי חסידים ע' 179

7. שמחה של מצוה ושיר, מבטלת את כל ה"דינים" והקטרוגים- ברוחניות ובגשמיות.[86]
8. השמחה היא קדושה, העצבות סיטרא אחרא.[87]
9. מכוונת היצר להפיל את האדם במידת העצבות.[88]
10. כי בשמחה תצאו – ע"י שמחה יוצאים מכל הצרות[89]
11. העצבות, אינה עברה, אומר רבי חנוך מאלכסנדר, אבל טמטום הלב שהעצבות מביאה, אין שום עברה יכולה להביא.[90]
12. יהודי שאינו מהלך בשמחה על כך שהוא יהודי, הרי הוא כפוי טובה.[91]

5. The Chassid and Chassidism

1. The Chassid lives in awe of the Heavens, while the *Mitnagid* [opponents of Chassidism] lives in awe of the *Shulchan Aruch*.[92]
2. The doctrine of *Kabbalah* raises the Jew to the Heavens, but the doctrine of Chassidism brings the Heavens down to the Jew.[93]
3. The Rebbe can position the ladder, but the Chassid must climb it himself.[94]
4. Kind David, of blessed memory, composed the Psalms. But what can I do? Recite the Psalms.[95]
5. A Chassid is someone who can fast while eating, and isolate himself [with G-d] while among other people.[96]
6. The Chassid must be like an infant: happy and crying. Happy – for being able to serve G-d; crying – over his transgressions.[97]
7. 'Chassid' is a combination of the letter *yud* with the word *chessed* [loving kindness]. This means that a Jew who deals with loving kindness [towards another] is a Chassid.[98]

---

85 הבעש"ט, י.ל. מימון, שרי המאה עמוד 62
86 אוצר פתגמי חב"ד עמוד 385 בשם אגרות קודש הצמח צדק' עמוד שלה
87 ר' ישראל מריזין, י. אלפסי החסידות ושיבת ציון עמוד 166
88 הבעש"ט "צוואת הריבש", מובא בספרו של גשורי "לחסידים מזמור" עמוד קנ"ה, במאמר "המוסיקה בקבלה" בשם רבינוביץ מאיר צבי
89 רבי שאול ידידה אלעזר טאוב, אמרי שאול, שי"ב אות כ"ו
90 אהרן אשכולי, החסידות בפולין, ירושלים 1998, עמוד 107
91 שם
92 Rabbi Menahem Mendel of Kotzk, [cited in] *Pitgamei Chassidim*, pg. 99; and in *Sarei haMe'ah*, Vol. 3, pg. 86 quoting in the name of Rabbi Pinhas of Korzec
93 Rabbi Schneur Zalman of Liadi, [cited in] *Pitgamei Chassidim*, pg. 99
94 Rabbi Yosef Izbicher, [cited in] *Pitgamei Chassidim*, pg. 101
95 Rabbi Uri of Sterlisk, [cited in] *Pitgamei Chassidim*, pg. 100
96 Rabbi Menahem Mendel of Warka, [cited in] *Pitgamei Chassidim*, pg. 98
97 The Seer of Lublin, [cited in] *Pitgamei Chassidim*, pg. 101
98 Rabbi Israel of Modzitz, [cited in] *Pitgamei Chassidim*, pg. 98

8. I found people dressed in tatters whose hearts were whole [closed], and I worked to change matters: to clothe them in whole garments and tear open their hearts.[99]
9. "With the merciful, show Your mercy [...] with the crooked, show Your subtlety" (Psalms 18: 26-27) means: in the company of a Chassid you will become a Chassid; but if you persist with evil, you will end up praying.[100]
10. If you believe that it is possible to spoil [something], then you must believe that it is possible to remedy [it].[101]
11. There are Chassidim who can point with their finger to the Heavens and say, "G-d is the G-d".[102]
12. Accept all that occurs to you in this world with love, and you will receive this world and the world to come.[103]
13. One who takes up no room, always finds room in every place (an adage on modesty).[104]
14. Where can G-d be found? Wherever He is allowed to enter.[105]
15. I cannot begin to imagine how the world would look without Chassidism.[106]
16. Chassidism is the poetry of Judaism, the Song of Songs of the Jewish soul.[107]
17. What is the difference between a wise person and the Rebbe? The wise one anticipates the future, but the Rebbe puts it into action in the present.[108]
18. A Chassid always asks himself, "Why?"[109]

ה. חסיד-חסידות

1. חסיד מורא שמים עליו, מתנגד, מורא שלחן ערוך עליו[110].
2. תורת הקבלה מעלה את היהודי לשמים, תורת החסידות מורידה את השמים אל היהודי[111].
3. הרבי מעמיד את הסולם, אולם לטפס על המדרגות – חייבים החסידים לעשות בעצמם[112].

---

99 Rabbi Menahem Mendel of Vitebsk, [cited in] *Pitgamei Chassidim*, pg. 101
100 Rabbi Meir of Przemyshlan, [cited in] *Pitgamei Chassidim*, pg. 99
101 Rabbi Nahman of Bratzlav, [cited in] *haChassidut veShivat Tzion*, pg. 122
102 Rabbi Menahem Mendel of Kotzk, [cited in] *Pitgamei Chassidim*, pg. 99
103 The Besht, [cited in] *Pitgamei Chassidim*, pg. 144
104 Rabbi Baruch of Storczyk [cited in] *Pitgamei Chassidim*, pg. 151
105 Rabbi Menahem Mendel of Kotzk, [cited in] *Pitgamei Chassidim*, pg. 14
106 Rabbi Eliezer Shach, [cited by] Natan Anshin in the weekly *laMishpacha*, pg. 18, March 31, 2005
107 M. S. Geshuri, *haNiggun vehaRikkud baChassidut*, pg. 18-19
108 *Otzar Pitgamei Chabad*, pg. 306
109 Rabbi Chanoch of Alexander, *beOhalei Tzaddikim: Sippurim uMa'amarim al Haggadah shel Pesach*, pg. 135
110 ר' מ"מ מקוצק, פתגמי חסידים, עמוד 99 ובספר שרי המאה (כרך שלישי עמוד 86) מביא זאת בשם רבי פנחס מקוריץ
111 ר' שניאור זלמן מליאדי, פתגמי חסידים, עמוד 99

4. דוד המלך ע"ה ידע לחבר תהלים, ומה אני יכול? יכול אני לומר תהלים[113].
5. חסיד – היודע לצום בשעת אכילה, ולהתבודד בהיותו בין אנשים[114].
6. חסיד צריך להיות כתינוק: שמח ובוכה, שמח-על כי עובד ה' הוא, בוכה- על חטאיו[115].
7. חסיד הוא צירוף של האות יו"ד עם תיבת חסד. לומר לך: שיהודי העושה חסד הריהו חסיד[116].
8. מצאתי אנשים הלבושים קרעים ולבותיהם שלמים, ועמלתי לשנות את פני הדברים: להלבישם מלבושים שלמים ולקרוע את לבותיהם[117].
9. עם חסיד תתחסד ועם עיקש תתפתל(תהלים י"ח, כ"ו), בחברת חסיד סופך ליהפך לחסיד, אך אם עיקש ריעך, סופך להתפתל[118].
10. אם מאמינים שאפשר לקלקל, צריך להאמין שאפשר לתקן[119].
11. ישנם חסידים המסוגלים להורות באצבע לשמים ולומר: "ה' הוא האלהים"[120].
12. קבל כל הבא עליך בעולם הזה באהבה, ויהיו לך עולם הזה ועולם הבא[121].
13. מי שאינו תופס מקום, יש לו תמיד מקום בכל מקום(על הענוה)[122].
14. היכן מצוי אלהים? במקום שנותנים לו להיכנס.[123]
15. אינני יכול לתאר לעצמי איך היה נראה העולם ללא החסידות[124]
16. החסידות היא הפיוט של היהדות, שיר השירים של הנשמה היהודית.[125]
17. מה בין חכם לרבי, החכם צופה את העתיד, הרבי עושה אותו[126]
18. חסיד שואל את עצמו תמיד: "מדוע"[127]

112 ר' יוסף מאיזביצי, פתגמי חסידים, עמוד 101
113 ר' אורי מסטרליסק , פתגמי חסידים, עמוד 100
114 ר' מ"מ מוורקה, פתגמי חסידים, עמוד 98
115 החוזה מלובלין, פתגמי חסידים, עמוד 98
116 ר' ישראל ממודזיץ, פתגמי חסידים, עמוד 98
117 ר' מ"מ מוויטבסק, פתגמי חסידים, עמוד 101
118 ר' מאיר מפרמישלן, פתגמי חסידים, עמוד 99
119 ר' נחמן מברסלב, החסידות ושיבת ציון עמוד 122
120 ר' מ"מ מקוצק, פתגמי חסידים, עמוד 99
121 הבעש"ט, פתגמי חסידים, עמוד 144
122 ר' ברוך מסטוטשק, פתגמי חסידים, עמוד 151
123 ר' מ"מ מקוצק, פתגמי חסידים, עמוד 14
124 הרב אליעזר שך, נתן אנשין בשבועון "למשפחה"מיום כ' אדר ב' 31.3.2005 עמוד 18
125 מ.ש. גשורי, הניגון והרקוד בחסידות, עמוד י"ח-י"ט
126 אוצר פתגמי חב"ד, עמוד 306
127 רבי חנוך מאלכסנדר, באהלי צדיקים, סיפורים ומאמרים על הגדה של פסח עמוד 135

Chapter 11 – The Chassidic Approach to non-Jewish Music

The Jewish [spiritual] leaders instigated numerous safeguards meant to distance Jews from the customs of their non-Jewish neighbors and prevent them from reaching a state where, G-d forbid, the non-Jewish religions would become appealing and lead Jews to adopt them. But what of non-Jewish songs? Does the same apprehension apply to non-Jewish music?

In fact, non-Jewish music presents two problems. Firstly, some pieces of music constitute a part of non-Jewish prayer rites, while others are songs describing the love between a man and woman. To use them as melodies for praising G-d does not seem quite right. Secondly, with non-Jewish songs, the fear that non-Jewish customs may seep into a Jew's behavior not only exists but becomes greater through the melodies, in that the souls of the singer or instrumentalist, the participants and the listeners become enthused, and could cause a sense of identification with a religion that is not their own.

Rabbi Yoel Surkis (1561-1640), who wrote the interpretive *Ba"ch* [Bayit Chadash] on the *Tur*, ruled in 1697 that there was no reason not to adopt a tune from a non-Jewish source and adapt it to synagogal use, provided it had not been integral to Christian ritual.[1]

What is the Chassidic view on this issue? Yaakov Mazor[2] writes:

> Among the shapers of Chassidic doctrine were those who tried to explain the phenomenon of acculturation in Chassidic music, providing it with the legitimacy of a religious command. Rabbi Nahman of Bratzlav (1771-1810), for example, merits non-Jewish music with the power of being able to draw G-d's attention to the suffering of His own people being tormented by the various ruling authorities, which would lead Him to saving his people. More typical is the outlook that points to the existence of sacred melodies in non-Jewish music, a result of the incessant struggle between Godly forces and those of the *Sitra Achra* [the 'other side']. These melodies fell, as it were, into the captivity of impure forces and awaited their redemption. In another version of this concept, it is not the melodies that await redemption but the hidden sparks contained within them. If we bear in mind that one of the roles incumbent on a Tzaddik is to redeem holy sparks and return them to the Higher Source, we can understand the keenness of Tzaddikim and their emissaries wherever they lived and throughout the generations, in seeking out tunes with an aura of sanctity. This explains the

---

1 Rabbi Yoel Surkis, Teshuvot Yeshanot: Laws of Prayer, Torah Scrolls, Synagogues and their Accoutrements, Response 27
2 haNiggun beFi haChassidim, pg. 8-9

multiplicity of foreign influences in Chassidic music, and the existence of a range of musical styles very different from each other. Indeed, for as many influences that exist in Chassidic music, there are just as many musical styles, from Polish and pseudo-French marches, to Austro-Hungarian waltzes, melodies and song from Romanian origins, Russian and Ukrainian folk songs, instrumental music in a mixed Roman-Balkan style, and dance songs of the Near East. To this, we can add lyrics deriving in non-Jewish folk songs, adopted by the Chassidim and which received new meanings of a Chassidic nature.

Idelsohn, in haNeginnah haChassidit, quotes Sefer Charedim:

[...] When one possesses a pleasant voice and sings foreign music, it spoils [him], for his voice's appeal was created to praise the Creator and not to be spoiled.[3]

Idelsohn later[4] relates to the phenomenon of non-Jewish music in Chassidism:

Most of the very pious Jews, also known as Tzaddikim, expressed their views concerning the value of music, and many invested effort in composing niggunim or gathering foreign melodies and rectifying them according to their own taste, that is, taking non-Jewish melodies and bringing them beneath the wings of the *Shechinah,* which was of utmost importance according to the views of several Tzaddikim.

Idelsohn then refers to the narrative of the Shepherd's song in the Kalov Chassidic court. This anecdote, referred to in Chapter 9, is referred to by Idelsohn in yet another form: where Rabbi Leib Sarah's was strolling in the forest, and saw a lad of eight, clothed in tatters, watching over a flock of geese. Rabbi Leib sensed that there was something lofty about the child's soul, which derived from the chambers of music and song. When he grew up, that child became none other than the famous musician Rabbi Yitzhak Isaac Taub of Kalev, Hungary (1744-1821), who later saved precious melodies from the shells [of impurity] and returned them to their sacred roots. Idelsohn continues with additional details on Rabbi Isaac of Kalev:

This Tzaddik was accustomed to traveling daily to the forest, where he would listen to sweet melodies sung by the shepherds. He would absorb those melodies, and draw them back into their sanctity, 'because all the melodies in the world are drawn from holiness, from a Higher Source, known as the Chamber of Music, but impurity knows no niggunim. Impurity known no joy, being the source of all sorrow'. Through Adam's sin, these niggunim fell into the realm of [impure] shells, being the *Sitra Achra,* [the 'other side'], containing holy sparks and also sparks of music. The Tzaddik of Kalev's actions, therefore, were aimed at returning these wandering sparks of music to their sacred place.

---

3   Idelsohn, *haNegginah haChassidit*, pg. 2
4   Ibid, pg. 8

Idelsohn adds:

The Tzaddik of Kalev not only redeemed the melodies, but even brought their lyrics back into the realm of sanctity. For example, he once heard a shepherd in the forest singing with broken heart, 'Mountain, O mountain, how huge you are; Bride, O bride, how far away you be'. The Tzaddik exchanged 'mountain' for Exile, and 'bride' for *Shechinah*. In this way, a sacred melody returned to its existence.

Shmuel Zalmanov notes that:

Occasionally the Chassidim would take various motifs from the shepherds' songs of yearning, songs from Volach and the Ukraine, being places through which the Besht and many of his Tzaddik disciples of concealed mystical abilities had passed during their periods of seclusion. After processing and refining these melodies, and uplifting the good sparks from within them, they became rectified, and known as Chassidic melodies. This is the reason for many of the Chassidic tunes being sung in the non-Jewish languages of their area in which they were rediscovered.[5]

Geshuri, on this issue, states:

The main aspect of the melody is the voice, and if that voice derives from impure origins, it is obligatory to uplift it, cleanse and sanctify it, until it is worthy of returning to the role for which it was created.[6]

Interestingly, the last Chabad Rebbe was not unequivocal in permitting the use of non-Jewish songs, and even went so far as to forbid it, in case of doubt. In responding to the question of whether it is permitted to make a recording of melodies for verses of the Torah (including Prophets and Writings) using melodies of non-Jewish nations, he advised:

One should receive the guidance of one of our own Chassidim, who is a teacher and learned on the issue, as to whether it is possible and worthwhile to permit them. Doubt them severely.[7]

Nonetheless, it is known that the Chabad Chassidic movement did adopt melodies found in non-Jewish spheres, the most well known being Napoleon's March and France's national anthem, 'La Marseillaise' which became the equally well known *ha'Aderet veha'Emunah leChai'yei haOlamim* [Glory and Belief of Eternal Existence].[8]

---

5   *Otzar haNiggunim*, Introduction, pg. 19
6   Geshuri, *laChassidim Mizmor*, pg. 14
7   *Sha'arei Halacha uMinhag*, Response 16, and read notes
8   From interview with Aharon Katorza, December 30, 2004

Just how did the French anthem enter the repertoire of Chabad niggunim? The last Chabad Rebbe studied at the Sorbonne, became familiar with the French and France's anthem which, apparently, he liked very much. When he left the Sorbonne and traveled to the USA, he took the melody with him. It was customary for the Rebbe to teach his adherents a new melody every *Simhat Torah*: he taught the anthem's tune to the words of *ha'Aderet veha'Emunah*. Since then, the melody and those words have become a tradition among Chabad Chassidim. Chabad also included certain melodies set to Russian or Polish words, testifying to the source of these niggunim, and the wish that Chassidim who spoke these languages would understand the texts.[9]

Mazor notes that the Viznits Chassidic repertoire also includes tunes which, according to their traditions, were redeemed by the Tzaddik, Rabbi Chaim Meir Hager (1888-1972) or redeemed at his request. The Tzaddik of Viznits explained redemption of these melodies with the verse, "Take of the cuttings [zimrat] of the land in your vessels and bring them as a gift to the man".[10] He read the verse as follows: "Take of the songs [zmirot] which have reached the earthly level, and present them as a gift to the Holy One, Blessed be He, by singing them on holy occasions".[11]

Mazor then refers to the Chassidim in Israel and two niggunim whose sources are indisputably Arabic. These melodies are sung on *Simhat Torah*. The narrative connected with one of them is remarkably similar to that of the shepherd's song which the Rebbe of Kalov redeemed, as described earlier; in this instance, however, the Tzaddik of Lalov, during his last visit to Israel before it declared independence, heard the tune from an Arab playing his flute as he sat in an alley on the way to the Western Wall.[12]

Rabbi Yishaya Rattenburg, son of the Kassan Rebbe, in the introduction to his *Zamru liShmo*, writes:

> Music and dance to gladden the Shabbat and Festivals and so on, was common among many of the Besht's disciples, and the latter's disciples, being considered holy work of great intent and unification, of such force that it could extinguish the soul [...] Among the Tzaddikim were those who sake non-Jewish tunes, and shepherds' tunes, and we cannot know how much effort they invested in their holy work of bringing them forth from their [impure] shells and defilement, yet other Tzaddikim were exceedingly cautious about not singing any melody whose source is unholy.[13]

---

9   Ibid
10 Genesis 43:13
11 Yaakov Mazor, *Yuval*, Vol. 7, *Mech'karim lichvod Israel Adler*, pg. 48
12 Ibid
13 *Zimru liShmo*, Jerusalem: 2000, Opening remarks, pg. 3

Many narratives refer to the Besht who wandered [from place to place] gathering the sparks of Jewish prayers, sparks that had become scattered throughout the non-Jewish lands. On one such journey, he encountered a shepherd who sat at the side of the road, playing his flute. Around him, the flock busied itself with feeding on grasses. What a wonderful melody! The Besht realized that this tune had the power to implement a great many rectifications. The melody was able to remove any impediment or obstacle and fill the world with song and singing. It was a melody drawn from the world of *Atzilut* [Emanation] and yearned to return there. "I will give you a worthy coin if you will repeat this wonderful melody again", the Besht offered the unkempt shepherd. "I don't feel like it", the lad answered in refusal. "And if I give you a coin of silver?", the Besht offered. "Ah, very well", agreed the shepherd, and played the melody again on his flute. "Now I will give you another coin if you will play it once more", the Besht continued. "For money, I will play it all day", happily responded the shepherd. He placed the flute at his mouth, but the melody was forgotten. He tried very hard to recall its notes, but simply found it impossible. He would never remember that melody again. The Besht hastily left the shepherd. "I have just fulfilled the *mitzvah* of releasing the imprisoned", the Besht told his followers. "The source of this niggun is ancient and extremely holy. It is a melody that was sung by the Levites in the Temple. When the Holy City of Jerusalem was besieged during the destruction of the Temple, the melody was trapped by the *Sitra Achra*, and has wandered ever since that time, from country to country and from one generation to the next, from one nation to another, awaiting its rectification. Now that I have freed it from its exile among the non-Jews, it is redeemed and can return to its pure source".[14]

The Besht was known frequently to say:

> Among the songs of the nations of the world it is also possible to find awe and love permeating from above to below, into all the lower levels.

---

14 Moshe Prager, *Rabbi Israel Baal Shem Tov*, Jerusalem: 1960, pg. 107-108

Chapter 12 – Musical Instruments used in Chassidic music

Rabbi Nahman of Bratzlav highly praised the ability to play a musical instrument, saying:

> When the prophet hears music from one who knows how to play it, then the spirit of prophecy fills him.[1]

Elsewhere, Geshuri quotes Rabbi Nahman:

> Listening to the sound of musical instruments played by one qualified to do so, and for the sake of Heaven, is a great merit and brings joy, to overcome the mind's [worrisome] thoughts, and merit perpetuity, and in addition, one can attain the spirit of prophecy and the spirit of sanctity and can allow his discourse to flow as water before G-d.[2]

It is not known whether specific instruments were favored by the Admors or Chassidim, but it is likely and presumable that the most popular included the violin, the flute and the clarinet. Among the Tzaddikim were some able to play the violin and in this way accompany the Chassidim who played music during Chanukkah.[3]

The Admors of the Kretchenif,[4] Nadvorna, Zotchke and Przemyshlan Chassidic courts can be counted among them. Others followed the custom of their fathers and played while the Chanukah lights were lit.[5]

Rabbi Yerachmiel Hopstein of Kozenice (1860-1909), grandson of the Maggid of Kozenice (1733-1815), learned to play both violin and oboe. Every *Motzei Shabbat* [Saturday night] he would visit the holy Maggid together with other Chassidim and play a familiar niggun for the song, *Eliyahu haNavi* [Elijah the Prophet]. On reaching *Hinei Anochi shole'ach lachem* [Behold, I am sending to you], Rabbi Yerachmiel would exchange the violin for the oboe, and continue to play.[6]

---

1 *Likkutei Moharan* 141, 54, 6
2 M. S. Geshuri, *Sefer haMo'adim*, Tel Aviv: 1963, Vol. 5, pg. 186; quoting *Ma'agalei Tzedek*, by Rabbi Mendel Ponitt of Munkatz
3 Ibid
4 See image in the Appendices of *http://www.nrg.co.il/online/11/ART1/025/771.html*
5 See images, as above
6 Yitzhak Alfassi, *Tzaddikim veChassidim*, pg. 171

Chapter 13 – Neo-Chassidic Movements

– **Rabbi Shlomo Carlebach**

Admittedly this book deals with the music of the classic Chassidic courts, but I feel it is impossible to ignore the unique phenomenon which occurred in our own times. This twentieth century phenomenon bears the title, "Rabbi Shlomo Carlebach".

Even if his approach was not always fully understood, or disputed, all agree that Shlomo Carlebach (1925-1994) is known for being unparalleled in the way he reached out to others. Through his special kind of music, interspersed with Chassidic stories, the joy he radiated and his love of Israel could be felt throughout his whole being by anyone who met him. Even if one had never met him previously, these traits in his personality led those in his vicinity to be immediately swept into the sense of belonging to his group and being truly a part of it. Perhaps Rabbi Shlomo Carlebach was not a Rebbe in the sense of the classic Chassidic Admors, but his chosen path allows the possibility of calling him Rebbe, just as all Chassidic Admors are known.

Moshe Stern, in an article in the newspaper *Makor Rishon*[1], details his biography:

> Shlomo Carlebach was born in Berlin on Tevet 18, 5685 (1925) as a twin brother to Eliyahu Chaim and son of Reb Naftali Carlebach and Pesia nee Cohen. By the time of his *Bar Mitzvah* [13 years old] he was considered a prodigy. In 1939 he arrived, together with his family, in New York. He studied in the "Torah veDa'at" Yeshiva and later became one of the first students of the Lakewood Yeshiva, New Jersey, headed by Rabbi Aharon Kottler, who described his student as 'the Rabbi Akiva Eiger of our times'. He was ordained as a Rabbi and studied also at Colombia University, an integration representative of his future approach. The atmosphere of the flower-children movement of the 1960s was not entirely foreign to him and certain aspects within it – spirituality, love of all and of course, music – melded well with his natural abilities.

On completing his studies with Rabbi Kottler in Lakewood, he became attached to the Lubavitch Rebbe and the Chabad Chassidic movement. Initially, he forged his path under close consultation with the Lubavitch Rebbe until certain differences of opinion arose between them on how best to draw fellow Jews closer to their roots. Thereafter, the Lubavitch Rebbe no longer agreed to be Carlebach's counsel, and their ways parted. Rabbi Carlebach also had close ties

---

1 September 29, 2004 – 14 Tishrei 5765

with the Modzitz Chassidic court: some recordings exist of Modzitz melodies performed by him. Certain Modzitz influences can also be felt in his compositions and his prayer formulations.

Rabbi Shlomo Carlebach's personality has been well studied. It seems that no one else's character has led to such divisions of opinion concerning his customs and ways. In an article in *Yediot Aharonot*, Ronit Tzach writes:

> This man, surrounded in his lifetime by expressions of enmity in equal measure as the expressions of admiration displayed by his Chassidim, became, in death, a spirituality authority that crosses all boundaries. The numbers of his Chassidim continues to expand, and annual festivals perpetuate him as a singer and a kind of modern Admor.[2]

It seems that during his lifetime, many did not realize just what he represented. Moshe Stern, in the article mentioned above, continues:

> So who, indeed, are you, Rabbi Shlomo Carlebach? A prodigal Tzaddik, a musical genius, perhaps a religious exegete, a hippie in religious-ultraorthodox garb? It all depends, of course, on who is making the observation, but it seems as though there was a bit of all these rolled into one. In any event, questions from the past are secondary in relation to the present, to what he represents now: his greatest strength was and remains chiefly his ability to be all-encompassing, a kind of prototype for felling the divides, for blurring the borders. This, it seems, is what the ears and souls of many in that younger generation latched onto, seeking as they did an escape path from the rigid categorizing enforced on them by the split reality of Israeli life. The American way of being is by nature more open and less stereotypical, and in an era of increased quandary and coping, the Carlebachian innovativeness, which preempted its own time, found comfortable padding for resurrection, as though invented in the here and now.

The clarinetist Moussa Berlin wrote:

> I had heard about Carlebach and was impressed by his playing when he arrived in Israel in the 1960s. We chased after him with a microphone wherever he went. Eventually a connection was made. In my opinion, Carlebach was not a great singer or instrumentalist. But the integration and interpretation that he gave to the verses or which he composed his songs was simply unique.
>
> Each time that Carlebach came to Israel, I would go to hear him play. It was difficult to attain any level of intimate connection with him, especially once he became a whole industry. I absorbed a great deal from him, and integrated his works into my repertoire. Initially the ultra-orthodox banned him, and when I played anything of his, they would ask that I stop. But slowly he became accepted. His *Mekimi meAfar Dahl* became a hit in the Yeshivas, without them even realizing it was one of his melodies. This happened to others of his tunes as well.
>
> Recently I played at a wedding. A request was made: when the groom covered the bride with the veil, could I play the *Ana beKo'ach*, by Rabbi Weiman? I asked the couple to sing

---

2   "7 Days" Magazine, February 4, 2005, pg. 34

the tune that they wanted me to play, and it turned out that it was a Carlebach song, without them even being aware of this.³

Because of you, Rabbi Shlomo, I love being Jewish; because of you I sing, and my whole album is dedicated to you. I learned what *Shabbat Kodesh* is, and what love is, I learned from you how to say thank you, and how to respect another as far as possible. Thank you for your beautiful, happy songs, and continue to watch over us from Above. How much you are missed by us now, more than ever; never cease influencing us and bringing us closer, and never cease loving us, despite everything.

Carlebach composed thousands of songs. Even he could not remember exactly how many they numbered. In an interview given to *Arutz 7*, an Israeli radio channel, he claimed to have composed over 4,000 or perhaps 5,000 songs, but only some 1,000 became particularly famous or well known. He never recorded the notes, and most of his works were sung from memory.⁴

In a eulogy written to commemorate ten years since his passing, Riki Roth described Carlebach:

Od Avinu Chai, Lecha Dodi, Essa Einai, and tens more of his niggunim are sung by all. The man who knew how to bring peace into this world with his joie de vivre, dancing and boundless love of Israel may have been recalled to the World to Come, but his songs continue to live.

Rabbi Israel of Modzitz was known to explain: "It is said that the world of music is close to the world of repentance, but I say that the world of music *is* the world of repentance". It seems that this statement became Carlebach's guiding light, always accompanied by his guitar, as he moved from city to city and from one country to the next, seeking out Jewish souls thirsty for their heritage, in non-Jewish lands. With his capacity for bringing Jews closer to their roots, his warmth and empathy, he succeeded in bringing hundreds if not thousands back to the Jewish lives, in no small measure through the power of his melodies. Brimming with vitality, he managed to become a cultural bridge between the secular, the traditional, and the religious Jew. His adherents present many reasons to agree with him, and just as many reasons not to, but never was a reason found not to love him. This was Carlebach, loved by G-d's creations and working to bring them closer to Torah.

Carlebach's performances drew huge audiences, and often, responding to requests, they would last until the small hours of the morning when an encore turned into a whole, new performance. On one occasion, when the clock hands had long since passed midnight, and most of the audience had left the hall, Rabbi

---

3   *http://www.makorrishon.co.il/article.php?id=868*
4   Moshe Stern, *Makor Rishon*, September 29, 2004 – 14 Tishrei 5765

Carlebach began to make his way backstage. An elderly Jew approached him, a Russian immigrant, and when the two looked at each other, they hugged and kissed each other, tears of joy streaming down their cheeks. They even recited the blessing over something new or renewed – *Shehechiyanu* – according to the *Shulchan Aruch*: "On seeing one's friend after a great many days, one is obligated to recite the blessing". Once they had exchanged a few words, Carlebach again stepped onto the stage, and began playing a moving niggun.

When Carlebach reached the end of the niggun, the old man gathered those left in the audience around him, and explained:

When Rabbi Carlebach was in Russia in the early 1970s, he conducted a *Rosh Chodesh* [New Moon] celebration in the Great Synagogue of Moscow. As soon as he began strumming his guitar, accompanying his tune with song, the hall began to fill with Jews. Thousands of bare headed men covered their heads with anything they could find, in order to sit respectfully in the House of G-d. for a moment, it seemed as though the synagogue had returned to its former life. Reb Shlomo sat in the center, and related teachings of the Sages, singing *Am Israel Chai* and *Israel B'tach baHashem* with us, tunes that the Iron Curtain had no inkling about but were well known to us. Most of those gathered there had no idea what the words meant, but the niggun was sufficient to allow them to sense the meaning. Many of them cried on that occasion.

It was time for Rabbi Carlebach to leave. But his heart was heavy at the idea – how could he just get up and go? From among his possessions, he took out his old *Siddur* [prayerbook], its pages coming apart, and began to give each of us one page, so that one person received something from *Mincha*, another from *Shacharit*, yet another from *Birkat haMazon*, and so on. 'So that you'll have something with Jewish value', he said. The pages from the *Siddur* were all handed out, and there were still hands open, awaiting and empty. What to do? He took his *Tefillin* and gave them to someone, removed his *Tallit Kattan* and placed it on another, removed his *kippah* and put it on someone's head, until, eventually, he stood there with nothing left to give. Just then I stood up, and cried out: 'Reb Shloimeleh, I learned in the *Chedder* until the age of five, but I have nothing left from the religion of my people. Give me something, too…

When Reb Carlebach heard this, he became very sad, but truly had nothing left to give away. He sat and thought, and after some moments, said to me: 'Know this, my brother, who I love, I have one more thing of Yiddishkeit with me – my heart, my heart which is all for the people of Israel. From there, comes the niggun *miMekomcha Malkeinu*, which we pray in all Diaspora synagogues; from there too, the tune for *Od Yishama* which is sung throughout all the Jewish communities in the world to bring joy to the bride and groom; and from my heart's chambers comes the song *haNeshama Lach*, in which G-d's creatures present their requests to their Creator during the *Yamim Nora'im*. My heart belongs to Yiddishkeit, to prayers and joy, to anticipation and redemption. I give it to you, and know that from now on, it is yours. If we ever meet, whatever you ask it to sing in your honor, it will be obligated to sing.

The old man ended his story:

Since then, I kept this promise in mind, and when I saw him, I asked him to settle his commitment.

When the old man was asked where he lives, he answered:

At the airport. Wherever Jewish youth needs me, that's where I am. And wherever I am, I always go to Jerusalem.

It is very interesting to note that prayer groups which adopted a Shabbat style of praying long since known as *Nussach Carlebach* popped up everywhere in recent years like mushrooms after a heavy rain; some conducted as a permanent *minyan*, while others are occasional, such as on the Shabbat when the new moon is blessed. Numerous organized "Carlebach Shabbat" weekends are held in hotels, advertised in the "Shabbat Carlebach" pamphlets that began being distributed last year.

Initially the phenomenon was peripheral, and just as with any change, it seeped into awareness slowly, with difficulty, until it found its place among the existing norms. Such difficulties are even more complex when the issue involves synagogues, the bastion of conservatism. Within just a few years, however, the number of *minyans* adopting the "Nussach Carlebach" with his songs, and in the more pedantic groups, his dancing, blossomed. Singing and dancing particularly typifies the *Kabbalat Shabbat* [receiving the Shabbat] service, starting with *Lechu veRanana*; then various sections of Psalms and especially the *Mizmor leDavid*, where the la-li-li niggun can be sung endlessly; and culminating with Carlebach's *Lecha Dodi*, which seems as though it has always been part of our lives. The melody for *miMekomcha* in the Shabbat morning service also became an inseparable part of that prayer, so much so that many of the Cantorial choirs currently active in Israel have included it in their repertoire.

It all began, apparently, in the Jewish Quarter of the Old City of Jerusalem, with the *Beit Shlomo* community, whose members pray every Shabbat at the Western Wall using a format that includes many of Carlebach's melodies. In Tzfat [Safed] the "Beirab" community adopted Carlebachian tunes, and the synagogue became a known and recognized center for prayers conducted according to Carlebach's melodies. Later, *Beit Yakar* in the Old Katamon area of Jerusalem adopted this style, especially since some of the community members were themselves Carlebach's students; then the *Lechu Neranenah* community of Raanana joined the movement. Currently there are tens more such communities, even in bourgeois Givat Shmuel, and not just for the younger generation!

A piquant anecdote describes the Carlebachian approach perfectly. A Jew who turned 70 last year visited his 50-something son-in-law, spending the Shabbat at the latter's home in Givat Shmuel haChadashah where he had recently moved. On Shabbat eve, the host took his guest to pray at the local Carlebach service, which had already achieved a noteworthy reputation, so much so that if one wishes to find even standing room on the outskirts of the prayer hall, one must arrive there early. The guest knew a thing or two about life: he had been born in Lodz, Poland, and experienced the Holocaust's horrors. After the service, he offered his opinion: "I have never been so moved by prayers. My grandfather had close ties with Chassidism, but nonetheless had never come across such a rousing and moving service in all his life as that of the "Carlebach Minyan" of Givat Shmuel.

"The whole of Rabbi Shlomo's life was devoted to giving, and everything he gave was spiritual. Even when he gave money, it was to charity", Yehuda Katz, his student for 23 years, told me. "He needed to know that everything he gave out would increase and strengthen eventually. I don't believe that in his lifetime, he allowed others to publicize him they way they do nowadays, when he no longer has any say in the matter". (From the abovementioned article by Moshe Stern).

The writer of these lines was also privileged to meet Rabbi Shlomo Carlebach several times, some thirty years ago in one of his appearances in Jerusalem, and eleven years ago when he visited Vienna where a film on his life was being recorded. From the very first moment that we met, he related to me with warmth and affection, as though we were acquainted for many years.

If I endeavor to describe Carlebach's greatness with brevity, I feel that the most apt term would be "simplicity". All his melodies were, in retrospect, so simple, yet they contained strong influencing forces. I presume that when he sang before a crowd, whether on Shabbat or in a concert, he did not prepare his voice as singers and cantors might, but simply picked up his guitar and began playing whatever song came to mind. However that song left his throat was not uppermost in his thoughts, a sure sign of his desire for simplicity and his natural behavior.

Chapter 14 – Interviews

This chapter presents the views of various people, ranging from Rabbis to Chassidim and Mitnagdim, academics and authors, on the topic of Chassidism and its music. All agreed to be interviewed of their own volition for the sake of the current study. The interviews are presented in alphabetic order.

1. Rabbi Aharon Catorza, Vienna[1]

Chabad's motto is, "Serve your G-d with joy". Music allows achieving this goal of serving G-d with joy. Chassidic music is meant to awaken us. Music also enables us to use our whole body in the service of G-d.

How would you define Chabad Chassidism?

Chabad is based on two important principles:

Firstly, serving G-d is not considered separate from the reality of this world but rather is a part of it. Chabad tends to use everything that exists in this world towards serving G-d in the best way possible, thus use of material accessories which exist in this world is not disqualified. An example could be broadcasting the Rebbe's discourses worldwide in real time, which requires a satellite connection, video receivers, and so on, these items being considered forbidden among other Chassidic groups.

Secondly, Chabad is an acronym for *Chochmah* [wisdom], *Binah* [insightfulness] and *Da'at* [knowledge]. Chabad's motto is "the mind influences meritorious attributes", that is, although we can serve G-d through emotion, that is insufficient, and emotion must derive from intellect, as the *Alter Rebbe* explained: we must also invest directed contemplation over even the seemingly simplest of things in the world, formed during Creation, such as trees, leaves and so forth, towards arousing our love and awe of G-d. By comparison, other Chassidic streams place greater emphasis on the emotional aspects.

---

[1] Rabbi Aharon Katorza is the Chabad emissary in Vienna. The interview was held in Vienna on 30 December 2004

How important is music in Chabad?

It is known that the Rebbe, Dov Ber, possessed exceptional musical sensitivity, but he asked G-d's to be merciful and take this ability from him, fearing that his love of music would harm his service of G-d. Towards the end of his life, he admitted that had his musical abilities remained with him, he would have been able to serve G-d far better.

I remember that every time the Lubavitcher Rebbe entered the *Beit Midrash* prior to prayers, and on leaving when they had ended, the Chassidim would break out in song, which the Rebbe would 'conduct' and encourage with his hand movements.

It is a Chabad custom that on any date of importance to Chabad Chassidism, such as the 19th of Kislev, being the day on which the *Alter Rebbe* was released from imprisonment, one special niggun for each Admor is sung. One such niggun is attributed to the *Tzemach Tzedek*, who himself sang it at his mother's gravesite (Niggun 32 in *Sefer haNiggunim*). When this niggun – related to outpouring of the soul – was played or sung, the Rebbe was seen crying in a heart rending manner, to the point that the Rabbanit requested that this niggun no longer be played.

The Rebbe explained that when a niggun belonging to a composer no longer alive is sung, that composer's soul is brought down into this world. The Chassidim added that with the Rebbe, this was no interpretation or imagination, but that they indeed saw that he was able to perceive the presence of such souls.

An interesting anecdote concerns Zalman Shazar, third President of Israel and a great supporter of Chabad Chassidism. Shazar wished to visit the Rebbe but the Israeli government agreed only on condition that the Rebbe come to him. In essence, the Rebbe agreed to this condition but decided to ask permission from his father-in-law, Rabbi Yosef Yitzhak Schneersohn. The Rebbe visited his father-in-law's grave and on returning, advised that he did not receive the sought after approval thus no choice was left for Shazar but to visit the Rebbe despite the government's non-agreement.

What is the difference between niggun and dance?

The Rebbe explains that dance expresses joy in the whole body, as well as the legs, and not just in the head and heart. An anecdote relates how the Besht wished to bless the new moon, as is customary at the commencement of each month, but the moon could not be seed. The Besht entered his room, and the Chassidism began to dance. Suddenly the moon appeared: the Besht explained that what he could not achieve with prayer, the Chassidism achieved with their dancing.

Who were the composers in the Chabad Chassidic court?

Some of the niggunim were composed by the Admors themselves, while others were composed by Chassidim or court composers who taught the tunes to the Admors. If they were acceptable, the Admors adopted them. The *Mitteler Rebbe* did not have a composer but instead, had an a-capella choir that composed and sang the tunes which have become part of the Chabad repertoire.

I love music but cannot decide which of the niggunim is my favorite. When I hear a niggun, however, I am almost always able to tell if it belongs to Chabad or another Chassidic stream. This is because, when I hear a niggun of another Chassidic group, I enjoy it very much but I feel that it only connects with my emotional aspects, whereas with a Chabad niggun, I feel it connects not only to the emotional level but drives me to becoming active.

What can you say about the "Marsellaise"?

For a number of years, the late Rebbe would customarily teach his Chassidim a new niggun on the eighth night of Sukkot, that is, on Shmini Atzeret. On one such occasion, he taught the Marsellaise to the words of *ha'Aderet veha'Emuna*, explaining that doing so returned the tune to its holy sources. The amazing thing was that some time later, the French government decided to change the words of the Marsellaise, which is France's national anthem, from words connected with war to words connected with peace.

2. Rabbi Chaim Eisenberg
Chief Rabbi of the Jewish community of Vienna, Austria[2]

What is Chassidism?

Chassidism is a unique movement in Judaism, which was initially opposed by all the Rabbis, especially the Vilna Gaon who placed a ban on it. Eventually, however, it came to be a fully recognized stream in Judaism which filled its followers with tremendous joy. Chassidim sought to create closeness between man and G-d, through prayer, and succeeded in gaining many adherents.

---

2   The interview was conducted in the Rabbi's offices in the Jewish Community Building, Vienna, 20 March 2005

Joy is the byword of Chassidim. Whereas Judaism generally sought to serve G-d through awe, the Chassidim primarily sought to receive love and joy, as is said: "Serve the Lord with joy and tremble in gladness (Psalms 2:11) – joy can be received when He is related to with respect.

In your opinion, to what degree is music important to Chassidism?

Music is extremely central to Chassidism, but not only in Chassidism. All the prayers we say are in a kind of tune generally termed 'nussach'. Chassidim used music far more widely, especially as wordless melodies, 'niggunim'. One particular Chassidic Rabbi used to say, "Words can bring us to one level, but the wordless niggun can raise us almost to G-d". Take, for example, niggunim of fervor, slow melodies, some of which are melancholy, some highly melodic: such as those sung on Shabbat afternoons at the 'third meal', as the day begins to darken and we are about to separate from Shabbat. The term 'dvekut' [fervor] derives from 'davek', meaning to come closer to G-d until we can cleave to Him.

This does not imply that when Chassidim are sad, they sing melancholy songs; it may be that for a short time, they are sad, but after several minutes of gravity, they once again attempt to return to a state of joy.

It is known that dance is very imp to Chassidism: how does it connect with music?

Chassidim are never entirely calm: when praying, they sway and 'dance', and dance and song simply belong together. A famous Yiddish song whose origins I can't remember – either Chassidic or Mitnagid sources – says: "When the Rebbe sings, all the Chassidim sing, and when the Rebbe dances, all the Chassidim dance". Dance is special. Not only does the dancer use his mouth but his whole body, as the verse says, "All my bones shall say" (Psalms 35:10).

Many interpretations relate to the importance of dance, such as during Simchat Torah when we dance with the Torah scrolls in a circle, indicating that the reading of Torah throughout the year has reached its conclusion. Another interpretation is that in the circle, each person is of equal distance from the center; the Torah is in the center, thus it is as though G-d Himself is in the center, which indicates that because we are all equidistant from the Torah, no one should think he is closer than the next person.

What is the importance of joy to Chassidism?

Judaism is, in fact, a very joyous religion. Some people think Judaism is a sad religion, as they come to synagogue mostly only for the memorial 'Yizkor' prayers on the *Yamin Nora'im*. *Yizkor* is indeed a sorrowful prayer in which we recall our deceased relatives, and thus is appropriately sad, but it certainly doesn't imply that all of Judaism is of this nature.

Of course there is a difference between a time of joy and a time of sorrow, but being sad is not a positive trait, and can lead to depression. When something occurs that saddens us, we can indeed allow ourselves to be sad while simultaneously accepting the situation as the will of G-d, usually called 'accepting with love'.

Among Chassidim, these aspects are more manifest. What is the source of sadness? Usually, it is sourced in a person's belief that either he did not receive what he deserves, or that he deserves far more. When this occurs, sadness surfaces, but the Chassid accepts any situation that envelops him, is satisfied with his lot in life, and this is connected with joy, as the verse states: "Who is rich? He who is satisfied with his lot" (Ethics of the Fathers 4:1).

It is commonly known that you enjoy music, and also like to sing. What, in your view, is the difference between Chassidic music and other Jewish music?

Indeed, I appreciate music which includes Cantorial, Chassidic and instrumental music. In each of the three forms, the Eastern European style can be found. Chassidic music includes melodies of a folk-song nature, but there are also abundant Cantorial pieces integrated into Chassidic music.

I am highly respectful of Chassidic music but it seems that lately, at weddings and other such occasions, music is played which is called Chassidic, although this is not entirely correct. The influence of the 'disco' and other moderns styles can be found which perhaps has a joyful effect and makes the dances successful, but it is not Chassidic music. On the other hand, I'm not such a purist as to think that everything must remain as it once was: once music was played with the violin and clarinet, and today completely different musical instruments are employed, although the original Chassidic music, including niggunim – some of which were composed by the Rebbes themselves – is, to my taste, far more authentic. Many cantors sing Chassidic niggunim, thereby expanding their repertoire for such times as these niggunim are appropriate.

Have you ever participated in a Chassidic 'Tisch', where the Rebbe eats the Shabbat meals together with his Chassidim?

On several occasions. I participated in a Chassidic Tisch, but nowadays the Tisch is well organized, whereas in the past it was far more spontaneous.

It's wonderful to join a Chassidic Tisch. First of all, being Shabbat, it is not permitted to use musical instruments. Additionally, at the Tisch, not only professional singers but everyone attending joins the singing, whether a person knows how to sing nicely or not, which gives rise to a sense of unity. The Rebbe himself 'conducts' the singing, indicating when to start a new song, and how long to sing it for. It's indeed a special atmosphere, very difficult to describe, the kind of thing one must experience for oneself.

When you hear a Chassidic niggun, can you identify to which Chassidic stream it belongs?

I believe that Chassidic music, like all music everywhere, is affected by external influences. It is said, for example, that Gur Chassidim adopted many marches of the Austrian military and therefore, composed numerous march-style niggunim. I don't know if that is true, but they are known for their marches.

The niggunim of the Modzist Chassidim are sweet melodies written by the Admors themselves, and are well known. There are also the 'court composers', that is, talented musicians who belong to a specific Chassidic group and became composers of Chassidic melodies, such as Reb Ben Zion Shenker of Modzitz, Reb Chaim Banet ben-Seret of Wiznitz, Reb Yaakov Talmud of Gur, and Reb Yirmiyah of Belz, among others.

What is your opinion of Rabbi Shlomo Carlebach: is it possible to refer to him as a Chassidic 'Rebbe', and relate to his followers as his 'Chassidim'?

Rabbi Shlomo Carlebach was an outstanding personality, descendant of a 'Yekkish' (German) family but his strong affinity with the Lubavitcher Rebbe drew him closer to Chassidic values. He was greatly learned in Torah, had a 'huge heart' and was a talented composer. In his concerts, he also integrated niggunim and Chassidic tales, a successful combination which enthused his audience, thus in certain aspects, he can indeed be considered as having the spirit of a Chassidic Rebbe.

I read an article which stated that Chassidic stories must be related very precisely, clearly indicated on whom the story is based, and exactly what occurred, which Carlebach also upheld very authentically. Carlebach's songs were not only for Chassidim but for any religious Jew, and he even sang for groups of non-Jews.

The Chassidic Song Festival conducted annually in Israel was, in the past, particularly successful in no small measure due to the many Carlebach songs which participated. Nonetheless, he went a little too far, as performers of his songs also included women, and the singing itself was far distanced from the Chassidic style.

What remains is a group of religious singers who are Chassidim, who are professional singers, some of whom are also composers, who sing at weddings and bar mitzvah celebrations: Carlebach is the 'father' of the singing style adopted by this group.

Did you have any personal experience of Shlomo Carlebach?

Yes, when Carlebach first came to Vienna, I was still a child but already owned his first record. It seems I was the first (Viennese) child with a Carlebach record: an American Rabbi visited my father and brought it with him as a gift, saying: "This is from a young Rabbi who sings beautifully". I listened to this record night and day, endlessly, and when Carlebach arrived, I knew all his songs from the recording. I sat in the front row at his concert, and sang all the songs out loud, and he was very surprised – who in Vienna could possibly already know his songs?

I'm sure there are hundreds and possibly even thousands of recordings of entire Carlebach performances where the audience joins him in the singing. After his performances, he would sit with a group of 'fans' and sing with them, and relate Chassidic stories to them until the early hours of the morning. This would all happen in some private home, and would sometimes last longer than the concert itself. This is also what occurred when Carlebach visited my home in the early 1990s, on a *Motzei Shabbat*. We had invited Carlebach to conduct the *Havdalah* service. He did – and it stretched on and on. He explained a verse, told some Chassidic stories, sang, to the point that the Havdalah candle, which normally would last for a period of several months, was almost completely used up.

At that Havdalah session, he composed his new tune for 'Hineh E'l Yeshuati'. I feel that the song had been 'ripening' in his mind for some time already, but there in our home, he completed it.

3. Mr. Israel Katzover, Jerusalem[3]

Can you offer a little background to your broadcasting activities?

For some sixteen years, I was the head producer of the Jewish and Chassidic music programs on "Kol Israel" [The Voice of Israel], the main radio channel of Israel. During that period, I not only produced these programs daily, with strong emphasis on special issues for occasions such as Festivals, weekends, Friday pre-Shabbat programs and *Motzei Shabbat* programs, but you could say that during this time, I changed the direction that these programs took, which strongly influenced the general approaches in Israel. When I joined the station at the end of the 1960s, most of the music played on the Israeli radio station related to Jewish content was *Chazzanut* [Cantorial] with occasional, more 'folksy' songs but no Chassidic music of those times was being played, nor were there Chassidic bands or singers. With regard to Sephardi music, Joe Amar was a budding singer at the time, and the odd other singer appeared but no young people. I had a feeling that a change was required, as the young people were not connecting to *Chazzanut*. In fact, from the 1940s to the 1960s – that period following the Holocaust – there were still sufficient people who related to Chazzanut warmly and who would travel great distances for a Cantorial concert. The younger generation, however, expected something else. I remember thinking to myself, how was I to change this? The first thing I did was look everywhere in the world, in the USA and even in Australia and South Africa, anywhere where there were Chassidic singers, and encourage them by giving their music a lot of air time in my programs. I remember receiving a letter from the American Cantorial Association claiming that I am about to 'kill' Chazzanut. Nonetheless, I didn't give up. Instead, I continued with the direction that I felt was right. I was also severely criticized by the produce of the Chazzanut program, Mr. Baruch Shein, who very forcefully requested that I do more to establish the Chazzanut program and stop producing my new program.

As part of my concept, I established the "Zmirot Hit Parade", the first Chassidic song program ever. It wasn't such an easy task!. On one hand, I had to battle with the Cantors and the Cantorial program's producer, while on the other hand

---

3   Mr. Israel Katzover is a journalist and author who, for many years, served as a senior producer for the radio station "Kol Israel", the chief radio broadcaster in the newly formed State of Israel; he was responsible for programs dealing with Chassidic music. During his employment there, he instituted the "Zmirot Parade" program which acted as the basis for his establishing a new style of programs that set the example for later such programs. Katzover was closely connected to the Chassidic Admors, composers and singers. The interview was held in his Jerusalem home on 1 June, 2005.

dealing with the management of Kol Israel who felt that the only hit parade should be for Hebrew songs.

I started the Chassidic hit parade program which ran weekly for sixteen straight years. It led to real change in attitudes towards Chassidic music. During that period, I was invited to the courts of various Admors, who thought that they might be assisted, through this program, in promoting the music of their Chassidic streams. I recall a meeting, for example, with several Belz Chassidim who said to me, "Look, in Gur, the composer Reb Yaakov Talmud produced several records with songs of Gur Chassidim, in Modzitz there's Reb Ben-Zion Shenker, who produced several songs that suited the Chazzanut program, so that sometimes one of his songs would close the program. And Chabad, of course, has its own records. But the Belz Chassidic court has none of this yet. Perhaps you can help us establish a choir and singers who are suitable for bringing Belz music to the public?"

Because I studied in the same class with the Belz Admor, and was well acquainted with him, the Chassidim asked me to approach the Rebbe and try to persuade him that Belz could also produce records with their niggunim.

Can you provide some more detail about your studies with the Belz Admor?

Of course. We studied in the same *chedder*. It wasn't any standard *chedder* but that of the Satmar Chassidim, in the Katamon neighborhood of Jerusalem. At that time his uncle served as the Rebbe of Belz, having been saved from the Holocaust and immigrating to Israel. They lived in Tel Aviv and every year, would spend half of that year in Jerusalem. They lived in the same house as we did. For years, this was the norm. Did he know, as a child, that he was destined to be Rebbe? Of course he did, yet he behaved like any regular child. Sometimes he was even quite mischievous. We became very closely acquainted. Sometimes, when he asked me to, I would accompany him on his trips overseas. So it happened that I came to him and convinced him that the Belz Chassidic court needs to establish a choir in order to publicize its niggunim. The Rebbe answered that he has no singers or others suited to taking on the job of organizing a choir. I answered that it would work out over time. He said, "I have no musicians able to do this". I replied, "I will find the musician" and I put him in touch with Moshe Moneh Rosenblum who, at that time, was at the commencement of his musical career. I brought Moneh to the Rebbe and after a brief conversation together, Moneh accepted the role and immediately busied himself with establishing the first Belz choir. He began testing children for the choir, interviewing at the Yeshiva, where he 'discovered' Yeremia and Breier and others who, over time, became the leading stars of Belz. Of course, after that, the Belz choir also received air time in my program. That was quickly followed by other Chassidic choirs such as Wiznitz, and other Chassidic courts. Nowadays, of course, it is impossible to think of a Chassidic court without its own choir, producing recordings and being played on radio stations.

To show you just how popular the "Zmirot Hit Parade" radio program became, I'll tell you another story. One day, a young Israeli Cantor living in South Africa came to the studio, and asked to record a song to be played in the Zmirot Hit Parade. It should be remembered that back in those days, it wasn't so easy to record; everything needed to be on tapes so making a recording was nowhere as easy as it is now. Of course we agreed, and everything went very well. Over time that cantor did very well, becoming famous – he is none other than Dudu Fisher. Avraham Fried of Chabad, and Mordechai ben David, the son of the Chassidic singer David Werdiger of Gur Chassidim, also appeared on the program.

There's no doubt that the program caused a revolution in all aspects of Chassidic music, especially since at that time, there was only one radio station in Israel, which devoted about four hours weekly to Chassidic music. Under such circumstances, all the public heard the program every week and knew all the new songs from the Chassidic courts. As a result, singers, groups and bands from all the layers of religious society approached us and requested – and received – an opportunity to appear in that program.

We're relating to current Chassidic musical trends, but what, in fact, is Chassidism, and what is the original Chassidic music?

I grew up in a Chassidic home and as I already related, studied in the Chassidic Satmer *chedder*. As a journalist, and through my work, I attended many Chassidic courts, and am very close with many of the Admors. I sense that Chassidic music is music that enters the soul. The music opens up moments of the sense of the soul's uplifting, and the heart can become exhilarated through the song alone, or by listening to others sing. The music speaks to the soul more than words do. Music in Chassidism is music with a soul, it expresses a unique atmosphere. It's hard to determine whether the music is authentic or not. We have to keep in mind that the Chassidim came from various places throughout Europe, and without a doubt they heard songs in those places, from the Ukraine and Hungary, from Poland and Russia, so obviously they absorbed something of the music of their origins, and a strange but beautiful combination developed between words from our texts, and music "from everywhere".

Chassidism is also something that makes us jump, want to dance, it expresses unity, one person with his hand on the next, forming a circle, with the Rebbe at the center and everyone else dancing around him. Many events are transformed by dancing, and the music sets the tone, creating the overall atmosphere.

Does music act as a special tool for Chassidim in their service of G-d?

Of course! Chassidic music holds several functions.

Firstly, it is used to accompany certain events. The Admors would conduct the *Tisch* which is in fact a kind of reception for their Chassidim, who for the most would come to the Admors court on Shabbat and Festivals. On such days, accompanying bands are not permitted. These gatherings included the Shabbat or Festival prayers, with the public joining in the singing. Therefore, various tunes and melodies were created and each prayer has its own special tune, the *Lecha Dodi* sung in a form that suits the G-d of the Universe, and so forth. Each prayer has its own rhythm and style.

Secondly, at the *Tisch*, which lasted for some hours, the Rebbe would give a Torah discourse. The Rebbe cannot talk for several hours non-stop, so the music gave the Rebbe a break, a rest, which the Rebbe needed in order to commence the next section of the discourse, and the niggunim sung were appropriate to the content of the Rebbe's interpretations. In this way, a beautiful and exquisite integration emerged between the Rebbe's words and the songs that were sung.

Thirdly, among the religious and Chassidic public were those with unique compositional and singing talents or beautiful voices. These people never had any openings to perform and make their voices heard – they would never, in principle, appear before a non-Jewish audience, but they could not easily appear before a Jewish gathering as most of the songs in their repertoire were related to prayer and thus did not suit the concert stage.

When I hear a song, I can ascertain its source. A song from Chabad is not at all like that of Modzitz, and so on. No Chassidic court's songs are like those of any other Chassidic group. Regarding the Modzitz court, it is known that the Admors, of the Taub family, composed the niggunim themselves. The Modzitz composers, such as Ben-Zion Shenker, whose home I visited frequently, followed their style.

Where do women fit into Chassidic music?

Women have no function in Chassidic music but in recent years various frameworks have developed where women sing for gatherings of women. By Jewish law, women are not allowed to make their singing voices heard for, in the presence of, men. Women who wished to express their vocal abilities in Chassidic frameworks, then, established choirs and bands which perform for women. currently there are women's choirs, bands, composers and even orchestras where musically talented women can perform at various functions for other women. It's still a fairly new but already established process and is innovative.

I like numerous songs from various Chassidic courts. I don't wish to go into detail, but I very much enjoy, in general, emotional songs. I always enjoyed the niggunim of Modzitz and Gur. I often attended the Gur *Beit Midrash* where I'd hear beautiful prayers from Reb Yaakov Talmud, who was a wonderful prayer leader during the time of the Rebbe, Reb Israel Alter, known as the *Beit Israel*. Reb Yaakov would conduct the Gur Chassidic choir. I even interviewed him in my radio program. He would of course conduct prayers in the Gur Chassidic style, but always added the new songs that he wrote. The soloist at the time was Leibl Goldknopf, who later became the conductor, and Knop Erenstein the father, and later his son. In the Belz Chassidic court there were Yirmiyah Daman, Breier, and the Fried family of Antwerp. One member of the Fried family would finance the records that they produced. The Viznitz Chassidic court had its own choir and beautiful songs, but it did not take off so strongly – perhaps the Rebbes did not encourage it sufficiently. Actually, in the smaller Chassidic courts, the idea took hold and developed well.

What in your view is the difference between a classical music concert, and a Chassidic music concert?

Classical music is always very beautiful but in Chassidic music I can feel soul – I feel that I belong more to the latter, it speaks to me more. I feel my Jewish roots, which I don't feel with classical music even though I enjoy it.

Would you prefer to listen to a Chazzan in the synagogue, or would u prefer a Chassidic synagogue?

I would prefer the Chassidic option, although I must say that currently, Cantors also have large choirs and integrate Chassidic melodies and niggunim into prayer.

What is your opinion regarding Shlomo Carlebach?

I was very friendly with him. Actually, in his lifetime, he wasn't considered to be an Admor – this occurred only after his death. He always appeared with his 'kibitzers', his fans, who went with him to every single performance in Israel. They weren't his official choir, but they sang and played with him at all his appearances. During his life, no one knew quite how to categorize him, and all kinds of sayings were attributed to him which were somewhat controversial in Chassidic circles. Only after his death his strength became recognized.

Currently in Israel there is a new Chassidic movement known as *Chabakuk* – this is a Hebrew acronym for a combination of **Ch**abad, **B**ratzlav, **K**ook and Carlebach. It is a Chassidic stream based on mixing alternative music with niggunim of Chabad, Bratzlav, Rabbi Kook, and Carlebach, a development of the "hill people". In a *Chabakuk* 'court', there is no leader, yet they are slowly expanding their influence, to which Carlebach strongly contributed. I think that if Carlebach were alive today, he would be the *Chabakuk* Rebbe.

In short, music became an integral part of Chassidism, and there is virtually no Chassidic group without its music, which serves as an indicator of how well the Chassidic stream is flourishing: the more interest and vitality there is, the more music is produced, and the more music that is produced, the more young people that Chassidic court draws into it, increasing its ranks.

4. Mr. Yaakov Mazor, Jerusalem
One of the greatest contemporary researchers of Jewish and Chassidic music.[4]

Rabbi Nahman of Bratzlav held the view that every Jew could reach the level of being able to pray by integrating prayer with niggun, towards serving G-d with greater fervor.

From conversations I held with Rabbi Shlomo Carlebach, and from following the course of his life, the way he led his congregation, and the manner in which he conducted the *Chuppah Kiddushin* [marriage ceremony], it is clear that he felt an obligation to strengthen faith among peripheral Jews even if that meant 'going down' to their level in order to bring them back to their religion. In this way, his actions emulate those of the Besht in the latter's own period. They are also appropriate to the perception of the role of the Tzaddik as this role consolidated itself among disciples of the Maggid of Mezhirech, and with Rabbi Nahman of Bratzlav. Clearly, Carlebach needed different tools in our generation to those required by the Besht in his generation.

---

4 Mr Yaakov Mazor, of the Jewish Music Research Center, Hebrew University, Jerusalem. Conversation held on 10 January 2005 in his Jerusalem home.

As a disciple of the Lubavitcher Rebbe, he was sent by the Rebbe himself to strengthen peripheral Jewish society, and draw these Jews closer to Judaism and Chassidism. When the Lubavitcher Rebbe learned that Carlebach's behavior, in the latter's outreach efforts, was not always appropriate to the expected behavior of a Chassid, he called him to a meeting and inquired about this aspect. Carlebach answered that this was his way of successfully reaching these Jews, in that he behaved as they did, and they therefore viewed him as one of them. This made it easier for him to influence them and bring them to *Teshuvah*. The Rebbe replied that he did not agree to this mode of behavior, and requested that Carlebach desist, and behave as is expected of him. Carlebach then responded that he cannot do that, and felt obligated to continue along the same lines as he had so far. At this point, the Rebbe indicated that their paths now separated, and that Carlebach no longer represented a Chabad *shaliach* [emissary] but represented only himself. Nonetheless, the Lubavitcher Rebbe blessed him that G-d should bring him success.

Do Chassidim have specific styles of niggun?

In general, we can say firstly that some Chassidic musicians claim the ability to identify a Chassidic dynasty according to the niggun being played. Secondly, as researchers, we have yet to find all the parameters that differentiate one dynastic style from another. However, we have found musical tendencies that characterize groups deriving from the same dynasty, as can be learned from our articles. Currently, Professor Andre Haidu and I continue to research these aspects. We hope to find the structures, modalities, meters and melodic motifs which typify each of the various styles.

With regard to fervor, can you relate to the phenomenon of "intonation"?

When certain Chassidic streams, such as Boyan and Chabad, sing together as a public, such as at the Rebbe's *Tisch* or conventions, there is a continual rise in intonation. Among Slonim Chassidim, intonation alters drastically, which does not normally occur when one sings alone at home – based on recordings of one of the leaders of Slonim Chassidism, who sang the niggunim with precise Western intonation with slight, occasional deviations. However, when the Chassidim sing as a public group, the changes in intonation can sometimes lead to a complete blurring of the tonality, and it then becomes difficult to identify even a single, whole phrase. This is because they change the intervals in the following manner:

in notes that rise, and especially those that ascend, the intervals become greater, while with notes that descend, the intervals lessen. When I inquired about this phenomenon, the Slonim Chassid was unable to offer any explanation. He did note, however, that the previous Slonim Rebbe did not like this shoddiness and attempted to change it by asking the musicians in the community to sing very loudly, thereby drawing the public into singing correctly, but the effort was unsuccessful. In this context, the Chassid with whom I spoke said that with regard to that particular phenomenon, the Slonim Rebbe did not permit singing of niggunim that did not originate in the Slonim Chassidic court; and when asked why he did not allow new niggunim to enter the repertoire, according to the verse, "Sing a new song to the Lord" (Pslams 149), the Rebbe joked that he had no need of new niggunim, because whenever he taught an old, original niggun, it 'returned' to him as a new, unfamiliar one.

In my view, the explanation for this phenomenon is that when a song is sung publicly with great fervor, the Chassidim enter a kind of trance state which manifests in extreme changes of intonation. It is also possible that not all the Chassidim change intonation, but a few do so with such intensiveness that they succeeded in drawing the rest of the public after them.

I remember a reception held for a bridegroom of the Slonim Chassidic court, where I recorded the event and the changes in intonation. I was able to pinpoint the place where the musicians led the changes while all those attending fell in line with them.

The composer, Yaakov Telchner, who lived in the second half of the 19th century and visited the Chassidic courts of Slonim, Karlin, and possibly also Chabad, may himself be the cause of the phenomenon of tunes that are shared by these three Chassidic streams.

What can you say about women's music?

Chassidic women do not have their own repertoire. They sing what the men sing. However, at some wealthy or large weddings, where the women were on one floor and the men on another, the women had their own band, such as at the wedding of the children of two Spinka Admors, in the 1970s. The *kleyzmers* played an entirely different range of music for the women, which included both the classic Chassidic repertoire, alongside waltzes and other music to which the women wished to dance. Music was also played that suited dancing in circles. Here I wish to point out that the women's circle dances are done to steps which are completely different to those of the Chassidim, and are instead far more similar to folk dances of Eastern European origin, as were danced in the pre-State period, and in the early 1950s in Israeli youth groups. These were apparently brought by the early Eastern European pioneers to Palestine. I also learned that the steps in women's dances are strongly influenced by Yemenite dancing. My conclusions were confirmed by a researcher of dance who accompanied me to various weddings, and observed women's dances. To date, no study has been conducted that explains the source of these steps and their development among women of Chassidic communities in recent generations, especially since dances of these kinds did not exist among women 25 years ago.

5.   Mr. Saul Meizlish, Kfar Saba, Israel[5]

What significance does Chassidism hold for you?

Chassidism is the only stream that saved the entire Jewish world, revealing the ability to serve G-d without necessarily being a Torah scholar of eminent brilliance, but able to serve G-d while working with the bellows, or at one's office desk, or at the lectern, without belonging to the great scholarly streams of Volozhin or Lithuania; it enabled serving G-d completely, and that is Chassidism's importance. Judaism was languishing yet craving for something new, which partly explains the success of the Shabbetaian movement, which offered Jews a manifestation of sorts of their Jewishness. On one hand, the Jew is an unwanted entity among his neighbors, being the exception to the norm, thus on the receiving end of pogroms and riots. On the other hand, many Jews in their own communities felt unrecognized and unimportant, respect and attention being given only to the great Torah scholars who sat all day studying in *Yeshivas* [rabbinic seminaries] in Lithuania and other centers. Suddenly, Chassidism comes along and says, "Look! You too, the simple person, are as equal as all Jews, if only you serve G-d with joy, and if you fill your life with joy and cling with fervor to G-d in your joy. If you devote yourself to upholding a Jewish life, then you are just as important as any other Jew; you are as important as any Torah scholar who fills himself with the Talmud and can quote verses, when you say a few Psalms or the Grace after Meals with directed intent".

---

5   Journalist, producer of radio and television programs, author, and editor of documentary features. The interview was held on 31 May 2005 at Apropo Café, Tel Aviv.

Chassidism viewed music as being so important that it became a part of its approach. What effect does music have, in fact, on Chassidism?

Rabbi Aharon of Karlin (1736-1772) said that the niggun makes us jump one *tefach* above the ground. Rabbi Meir of Przemyshlan (1780-1850) was known to say that the chamber of music and the chamber of repentance can be found together, and that if we open the door, we can pass through from this world to the next., and from the moment that we open the door and pass from the world of music to the world of repentance, we establish the Great Rectification. Regarding this, the Modzitzer Rebbe further explained that the Chamber of Music and the Chamber of Repentance are one and the same.

The niggun draws us into the greatest communal language in existence. The language of niggun can express everything. What commenced as the songs of the Levites in the Temple, played on musical instruments about which we still do not know all the details – such as the *'magrefah'* which is said to have had sixty thousand tones – developed later into the melodies for reading the Torah, then developed further into 'emotional' *Chazzanut* [Cantorial music] and then to 'intellectual' Chazzanut. Chassidism is the most supreme or transcendent expression of emotional experience integrated with logic and intellect.

Music is of utmost importance to Chassidism. It commences a person's everyday life, is found in annual events such as festivals and other occasions, is manifest on particular dates in a person's life such as the *Brit Milah* [circumcision] ceremony, Bar Mitzvah, marriage, and so forth. Even in death music manifests in Chassidism, such as with the anecdote concerning Reb Moshe Leib of Sassov (1745-1807) who arranged the marriage of two orphans – which is, incidentally, a great merit towards rescuing the community from crisis and plague – and during the marriage ceremony, heard the *kleyzmers* playing a special tune. He requested from his closest Chassidim that when he dies, he wishes this tune to be played while he is being buried. Some thirty years later, this group of *kleyzmers* were traveling through Europe when a terrible storm commenced and snow covered everything. They came to a junction where they should have turned left, but their horses pulled towards the right. The *kleyzmers* tried to redirect their horses but to no avail. The horses seemed to insist on turning right, and with little choice in the matter, the musicians accepted the situation, wondering what might eventuate. They found themselves, after a while, at the burial of Rabbi Moshe Leib, the street filled with mourners who came to offer their last respects. Then they remembered that this was the Admor who, thirty years earlier during the wedding of two orphans, requested that they play the same tune at his funeral. In an instant, they took up their musical instruments and played that niggun. It is said that no sadder yet simultaneously joyful niggun had ever been played as the niggun accompanying Rebbe Moshe Leib's funeral.

When you hear Chassidic music, how does it make you feel?

First of all, Chassidic music expands the heart; it allows overcoming all concerns, illnesses and crises of that day, and unites Man with G-d. With texts only, it is impossible to unite with the creation; that is only possible through niggun.

What is the wordless niggun?

In a niggun deficient of words, one in fact hears the silence. There are no syllables, nor limitations of words. We can quote the Rebbe of Kozk who stated that "there is no greater cry than silence". The wordless niggun crs the sense of both the broken heart, and the whole heart, concerning which the Rebbe of Kozk (1787-1859) also said, "There is no heart more whole than a broken heart, nor a ladder more crooked than a straight ladder". Perhaps the word 'ladder' here referred to the scale of notes which cannot remain straight; the wordless niggun hold the power to merge with nature, which is, obviously, of great importance in Chassidism.

When you hear a niggun, are you able to identify to which Chassidic stream it belongs?

These days, the niggunim have become intermingled and it's indeed difficult to designate them, but originally, each Chassidic group had its unique musical characteristics, such as the special marches of the Gur Chassidim, the lyric melodies of Modzitz, and in Chabad we find intellectual niggunim with an emotional aspect such as the famous "Four Babas" niggun and even the *Ufaratz'ta* niggun which fills us with the sense of togetherness. Karlin Chassidim are noted for their crying out: the story is told of a Ruzhyn Chassid who asked a Karlin Chassid why it was necessary to cry out so loudly, and was it possible to be more gentle? The Karliner answered, "When something hurts you, don't you cry out?"

Which niggun particularly speaks to you?

The niggun for *Yah Echsof,* of the Karlin Chassidic tradition, penetrates the heart, the whole of one's insides. I heard it recently in its source, in Karlin, Russia, where I shot a film on the Karlin Chassidic court celebrating fifteen years in Kiev.

    The world of music is a unique one, which opens the heart. An incident attributed to the Maggid of Kozenice relates how a child in a severe state of ill health was brought to him. The Maggid requested that ten thieves be brought to pray for the child. No one understood why he asked for thieves but the situation was critical, so his request was fulfilled. When the thieves arrived, the Maggid asked them to pray the *Mincha* [afternoon] service and recite certain Psalms. A short while later, the child rose, fully healed. There was great commotion in the city: people wondered how it could be possible that ten Tzaddikim were not called for instead. The Maggid explained: "When I saw the child, I saw that the gates of his life were locked. And who knows how to pick the lock of a gate? Only the thief's key". The niggun sometimes functions just like the thief's key.

6. Rabbi Yishaya Meshulam Feish Halevi Rattenburg, Jerusalem[6]
Son of the Kassan Admore, Rebbe Menahem Israel

How did the Kassan court originate?

Kassan is a branch of the Zhydachiv Chassidic court. Wiznitz Chassidim claim that they conduct prayers that follow the *nussach* of the famous musician, Reb Koppel Chassid, the father of the *Ahavat Shalom*. A family member asked the Admor known as *Imrei Chaim* if this was indeed true. The *Imrei Chaim* replied that even if it were true, many geneartions have passed since Reb Koppel Chassid composed his niggunim, and every musician adds his own touch to the music, so that almost certainly the *nussach* used currently is entirely different to the original.

My great-great-grandfather, the first Kassan Admor, was the grandson of Reb Zvi Hirsch of Zhydachiv and known as the author of *Ateret Zvi*. He was a disciple of the Admor, Rebbe Izik'l of Zhydachiv, and I am the grandson of both of them.

When the parents of the *Ateret Zvi* felt that it was time for them to leave this world, the Rabbanit told the Admor not to worry, that "Bamesilah Na'aleh" [We shall go up by the highway] which is an acronym for Berish, Moshe, Sender, Lippa and Hirsch, being the names of their five sons. In other words, there was nothing to be concerned over, as the merits of their five children speak for themselves.

---

6 The interview was held in his Jerusalem home on 11 January 2005. Rabbi Rattenburg authored *Zinru liShmo*, a selection of discourses from disciples of the Besht, and their later disciples, on joy, music and dance. His older brother inherited the Admoric position from their late father, although it is possible that in the future, he will become an independent Admor.

What can you say about women in Chassidism?

One of my grandmothers would behave as did the Admor. Her name was Sureh (ie: Sarah) Shlomzi, but she was known as the "The Przemyshlan Rebbetzin". She was the daughter of Reb Mendel of Zhydachiv, who himself was the son of Reb Yitzhak Izik. She lived in the *Me'ah She'arim* neighborhood of Jerusalem, and received the public in her home; she sat behind a curtain, and people would come to receive her blessing, ask advice, and she even gave Torah discourses. Towards the end of her life, she purchased a burial plot on the Mt. of Olives, and set up a tombstone, leaving only the dates yet to be engraved when she passed away on 29 Tishrei, 5707.

On one occasion the Spinka Admor, who was her grandson, and staying in her home, asked her how it happened that even though it is not permitted for a woman to learn Torah, she circumvented this prohibition? She answered him as follows: "I never learned Torah but my father, the Admor, would customarily rise every evening at midnight in order to learn. Among his daughters, a roster system was instituted to ensure that every night, one of us would stay up to awaken our father at the correct time; then we could go back to sleep. When it was my turn, instead of going back to bed, I would sit at the entrance to his room and listen to him learn, so that all my learning derives from hearing my father on my turn during that week".

When she passed away, a tenant rented the apartment. He came home from synagogue on the first Friday evening since moving in, and prepared to make *Kiddushi* [the blessing over the wine]. Suddenly the house filled up with mice – it was both intolerable and impossible to be rid of them. The tenant went to the Zvahil Rebbe (son of Reb Shlomo of Zvahil) who advised him: "Go back to your home and look for the source of the mice, then call out in that direction: 'The Rebbetzin no longer lives here' and they'll go away". This the tenant did, and so it was.

People would ask her to light a candle for them, in order to receive a blessing. It happened once that she lit a candle for a woman who had asked her for candles for Shabbat. A cat suddenly appeared and put the candle out. The Rebbetzin relit the candle, but the cat returned and put it out again. After this occurred several more times, the Rebbetzin requested that the woman come to her; she related the incident, and insisted that it would not be possible for a cat to do what it did repeatedly without some reason. When the Rebbetzin investigated more deeply, the woman finally told her that in the past, she had had a grandson who fell ill with typhus. In fear of becoming contaminated, the woman had closed the child up in the shed to die of his illness. "In that case", answered the Rebbetzin, "you in fact are a murderer and that is what the cat was trying to indicate to me. I am not willing to light a candle for a woman such as you".

My grandmother had a Torah scroll and *Tallit Kattan* in her home. It was tied to the doorknob, and when people came for a blessing, she would hold the Torah or the Tallit, but she never wore the latter.

She was a very unique person, and among her various roles, she took on the function of charity collector, traveling to various places to collect money for the needy. It is said that once, when she returned to her home, her husband asked the beadle to bring him a glass of wine. When the beadle sought an explanation, the Rabbi answered that when the Rebbetzin returns, the atmosphere inside the home is like that of *Motzei Shabbat*. This is based on the idea that Shabbat is the Malkah, the Queen, who is welcomed; and the Rabbi likened the Rebbetzin to the Queen.

What importance does music hold to the Kassan Chassidic court?

Prayer in the Kassan Chassidic court was always conducted with fervor. The first Admor, known as the *Bnei Shalishim*, Reb Yehosaf, was an extraoridnary prayer leader who had a special *nussach* especially in prayers such as the *Nishmat Kol Chai*. By the way, it was known that in Kassan the custom was not to recite the section of this prayer that says: "You listen to the outcry of the poor, You hear the screams of the destitute, and You save", where "outcry" in Hebrew is "shav'at", and "screams" in Hebrew is "tza'akat" forming the same initials as "Shabtai Zvi". The Admor customarily led the additional prayers on the *Yamim Nora'im* using his own *nussach* rather than that traditionally used by the Zhydachiv Chassidic court. My great-grandfather would lead the morning services on the *Yamim Nora'im*, but on one occasion, instead of singing a certain section in the traditional manner, he decided to sing in a more Cantorial form; the Admor turned to him and asked, "What's happened, have you become a Chazzan?"

Other sections of prayer were set to tunes composed by Reb Avraham Yitzhak of Horintz, and another of the composers was Rebbi Berish of Vyshaveh. The latter was known for the many tunes he composed for the Satmar Chassidic court, such as their melody for *Shalom Aleichem,* among others. Concerning Reb Berish, it is said that when he wished to compose a new niggun for Satmar, he would wrap himself in a *Tallit* like that of the Satmar Admor, in order to become inspired. When he composed for Wiznitz or any other Chassidic court, he would similarly dress in the garb typical to that Chassidic group before he commenced. Once he had completed composing the niggun, Reb Berish would announce his farewell from it in the following manner: "Niggun, niggun, I have completed writing you down in entirety, and as far as I am concerned, you are perfect, but I have no way of following up on your destiny in the future, and perhaps those listening will include changes – lengthening or shortening in parts – but know this: in my view, you are perfect just the way you are".

There was another composer in the Kassan Chassidic court – Reb Avraham Felverboim – who was both a *chazzan* and composer.

How did you reach the idea of writing a book on joy, music, and so on?

I was merited with the privilege of being the person to arrange the marriage for my oldest brother's daughter. My wife attended the wedding in the USA but it was not at all possible for me to attend. The closer the date of the marriage loomed, the more my conscience became disturbed. Eventually I decided that, to allay the unpleasantness I felt over this situation, I would write a special book on issues relating to brides and grooms which I would dedicate in honor of the marriage, and send to them. I began reviewing Chassidic books from which I had quoted over many years, and collated a special volume relating to aspects of marriage and music. I sent a sample copy to the wedding organizers and requested to know whether, in their opinion, the material was of a sufficiently high level; after all, this was to be my wedding gift. Their reply came quickly: "Not only is it excellent material but in our view, it is unique material that has never yet been delved into in an appropriate manner, and it is a shame that it should be published in a small booklet form". It was then that I decided to invest further and write everything I possibly could on music and then add an article on brides and grooms. I spent several years gathering a large quantity of material, which led to the book.

It is well known that Chassidim use several kinds of niggunim. One kind uses motifs that repeat in one of the following orders: verse A, verse B, verse C, verse B; or A – B – C; or A – B. I have seen explanations for this (I'm sorry that I can't remember the source of the explanation): the A – B – C – B form relates to the Tetragrammaton; the A – B – C form relates to the first three letters of the Tetragrammaton; and the A – B form relates to the Godly name comprised of the first two letters of the Tetragrammaton. In addition, when dancing, a person's appearance is like that of a candle, drawing upwards and then downwards, which is likened to the soul which is drawn upward while the physical body draws downwards.

A well known discourse by the *Baal haTanya* notes that the niggun is the quill of the soul, and indeed, there are two places in nature where I like to spend time – at the seaside, and in the forest. When I stand by the sea, and see the endless waves, I feel the urge to sing out loud, and feel no shame in doing this. The same is true of when I am in the forest.

I often lead prayers, and of course include Chassidic niggunim, nor do I have any problem with singing niggunim from other Chassidic courts, but when I repeat a phrase, I am careful about not singing it in exactly the same way as I did the first time. After all, why repeat the phrase if there is no change to it? Of course, prayers must be recited with the correct *nussach* and the tunes must be integrated with the words.

I recall an anecdote relating to my grandfather's uncle, Reb Mendele of Kalev, who lived in 'Nofker', a small townlet near Kalev. On a visit to the city, he led the prayers in the synagogue hall which was on the second storey. I do not know which *nussach* he used, but for the *Kedushah* in *Mussaf*, he recited the Chassidic *Keter*. At just that moment, the famous *Chazzan* Zvulun Zebl Kvartin passed by the synagogue and heard the prayer. After Shabbat, Kvartin mentioned to his close acquaintances that he wished to meet the *Chazzan* who prayed in that synagogue on Shabbat. The meeting was arranged; Kvartin was so enthused that, banging his hand down hard on the table, he said to Reb Mendele, "What a shame you became a Rebbe and not a *Chazzan!*". In a separate article, he quoted the Wiznitz Rebbe known as the *Ahavat Israel*, father of the *Imrei Chaim*, noting the *Ahavat Israel*'s teaching that one should never pass judgment on any niggun until one has heard it three times.

7. Professor Eliyahu Schleifer, Jerusalem[7]

What is your opinion of Chassidism?

To answer this question, allow me to preface with a little personal information. I come from a divided family, being a sixth generation Jerusalemite. My family on my father's side are .... and have lived in Jerusalem since 1830, while my mother's family came from Transylvania, Romania and are Wiznitz Chassidim.

Even though I was raised on the culture of the *Mitnagdim* (those who opposed Chassidism), I studied at the *Chazzanut* college, *Shirat Israel*, run by the famous Cantor, Zalman Rivlin who was a remarkable teacher. He accepted children to his school from the age of five years old. We also came every Shabbat afternoon to learn with him. Even though we were still very small children, we studied *Chazzanut*, notes and oratory. He devoted the first lessons to learning how to use the tuning fork. He would take the tuning fork in his hand, and show it to all the pupils. "In order to sing correctly, every *Chazzan* needs to know how

---

7   Professor Eliyahu Schleifer, Profssor of Sacral Music, Musicologist, Director of Cantorial Studies, Hebrew Union College – Jewish Institute of Religion. Member of Academy, Director of Jewish Music Research Center, Hebrew University, Jerusalem. The interview was conducted in the National Library, Hebrew University, Jerusalem on 12 January 2005.

to use this, because each of you must be cognizant of your own voice and its abilities", he would say.

At eight years old, we learned solfege, and how to present an explanation to an audience. We would stand on a chair in front of the stage (which was the table on which the Torah scrolls were read) and preach, and to this day I remember my first sermon, given at the age of eight. Chazzan Rivlin's prayers in the *Shirat Israel* synagogue in the Ruhama neighborhood of Jerusalem were accompanied by a choir that combined children and adults. By the age of eleven years old, I was conducting the choir.

He lived under very meager conditions, and no one knew how he earned his living. It was known that every year, when *Yom Kippur* ended, Mr. Katzalski, father of Efraim Katzir, who later became President of Israel, would give Rivlin two schillings: one being his Cantorial fee for the whole year, and the other for organizing the choir and teaching, so that no one should say that Rivlin taught for free!

He was an extraordinary person and an example to us all.

In my youth, I studied at the *Etz Chaim* Yeshiva, belonging to the *Mitnagdim*, who at the time claimed that Chassidim did not study sufficiently deeply. The Chassidic Yehsiva at the time was called *Chayei Olam* [Everlasting Life] but as children, we called it *Chayei Golem* [The Golem's Life].

This whole introduction serves only to clarify how distanced my childhood was from Chassidic doctrines. Despite my childhood, I must say that I love the Chassidic ways, I loved to attend a *Tisch* at the Gur Chassidic synagogue, or be with them on *Simchat Torah*, because I enjoyed their wonderful songs so much. I must admit, however, to two problems with the Chassidic world: their lack of accuracy – too many things are disorganized or imprecise, such as their Torah reading which is not always exact or where the Hebrew is not always correct. The second aspect is the phenomenon of crowding and swaying. They love to cram themselves into every social gathering, whether it's a *Tisch* or any other opportunity. My own private joke explains why they wear a silk *kapoteh* [long over-jacket] – so as not to stick to each other when they are crowded together.

Of course, the Chassidim are noted for some wonderful ideas, opening new horizons in Judaism, which was both brave and important. What is of utmost importance to them is the emotional aspect of their Jewishness, which in the *Litvish* world is a non-issue.

What is the importance of music to Chassidism?

It's not easy to give a brief answer, but in principle, Chassidism raised music to a very high level from both a conceptual ideological level and from the practical level. In fact, music was given a central position from the emotional perspective, but the Chassidim also view music as being connected to Kabbalah, with its Godly roots, thus music is considered sacred and must be redeemed from its lowly level and uplifted, just as Kabbalah relates to uplifting the sacred sparks.

Consequently, the Chassidim became more open to a variety of influences and their music is very rich. There is another point that should be given consideration: music is related to in the same way as the Oral Law, the latter being Torah which only Tzaddikim could understand and beyond the scope of the simpler people. Music was related to in this way too: writing down the notes was avoided as it was viewed as being necessary to keep it oral only. Not writing down the notes served an additional purpose: the Chassidim feared that it would then fall into the wrong hands.

Music is so important to Chassidism that the words of a prayer may be said somewhat perfunctorily, while the niggun is sung with great devoutness.

It is known that Chassidim would travel to their Rebbe to spend a Shabbat in his presence. When they returned, they would bring home the niggunim they heard there, and if they did not bring home a new melody, the feeling was almost as though the trip had been without purpose.

Support for the concept of music's weighty role can also be seen in the importance placed on the wordless niggun. It is known that the words of prayers hold special importance, and yet, despite this, the niggun is, for the most, wordless. Thus, we find the difference between 'true' Chassidim born into Chassidic families, and those who became Chassidim: the former contain within them a treasure trove of niggunim, as precision with the niggun is extremely important and imprecision is considered as destroying something at the level of the Upper Worlds. The Chassidim are very precise about singing the niggun exactly as the Rebbe composed and/or sang it, so much so that on occasion, arguments break out about just how the Rebbe sang one or another particular phrase. For this same reason, regarding the importance of music among Chassidim, we find more Cantors among Chassidim than among *Mitnagdim*.

Are there differences in the music of the various Chassidic courts?

Differences! Of course there are! If we compare, for example, the niggunim of Gur Chassidim to those of Bratzlav, the difference is enormous. The niggunim of Gur match their apparel: they dress and act as soldiers of the army of G-d, and their singing is that of a public with musicians and composers such as Yaakov Talmud, and later, Arieh Goldknopf. Their niggunim are complex. They are constructed from two to three motifs but there are also lengthy pieces constructed like a waltz or march, connecting one after the other like links in a necklace. These niggunim are sung with emotion but the main aspect is uniformity, like an army of Chassidim, as their clothing also portrays.

By contrast, the niggunim of Bratzlav allow a lot more freedom of singing, and while the Chassidim do sing together, the rhythms of their singing is more flexible, and they tend more to sing niggunim suited to the *Tisch* atmosphere, niggunim of devotion and so forth.

Another difference can be seen in the construction of the niggunim. A very predominant style centers around refrains in an A – B – C – B format. In other words, the niggun contains four refrains, three of which are different and one repeated. This form is common to most of the Chassidic courts, including Bratzlav, but I think that Gur Chassidim do not use this format in their niggunim. On the other hand, we should not forget the origins of both these Chassidic courts: Gur derives from Poland, and Bratzlav from the Ukraine. There is no doubt that the location had strong influence on the styles of their niggunim.

In some Chassidic courts, the Rebbe controls the niggunim, setting the tone and the rhythm, such as with Belz where the Rebbe makes a small movement with his hand, and the rhythm immediately alters. Many other such factors depend on the Rebbe's decision.

It was known that Rabbi Baruch Hager, the previous Viznitz Chassidic Rebbe, was very knowledgeable in the field of niggunim. When he established the Wiznitz Chassidic center in Bnei Brak, he ensured that niggunim were taught and played. He himself would often travel with his Yeshiva students, and teach them a niggun along the way. However, other Admors were less involved in the singing of niggunim.

It is also very common among Slonim Chassidim, for example, to sing one niggun repeatedly, many times in sequence over a lengthy time frame.

Which are your favorite niggunim?

I like niggunim that connect to fervor more than those meant for dancing.

Can styles be clearly pointed to in Chassidic music?

As a musicologist, it is difficult to determine any specific style, but I know that the Chassidim themselves are sensitive to differences and claim to be able to determine the Chassidic court to which a particular niggun belongs. In any event, they can most surely immediately identify the niggunim that are associated with their own Chassidic court.

In conclusion, I would like to present the explanation that Rabbi Rattenburg provides in his book, *Zimru liShmo*, regarding the style of niggun that we already mentioned, in the A – B – C – B format. Rabbi Rattenburg explains the verse, *Bnei binah y'mei shmonah* [Men of insight established eight days] from the Chanukah song *Ma'oz Tzur* [O Mighty Stronghold] sung after lighting the *Menorah*. Rabbi Rattenburg states that music possesses strong powers that influence the spirit, as the seven notes of an octave correspond to the seven lower *Sefirot*, thus each note contains special power, as does the soul which passes beneath the Throne of Glory, connecting to higher powers.

In the future, however, the eighth note will be played, which is what the Psalm refers to when it states, "To the Conductor of the Eighth". It referes to the eighth tone which will be revealed in the future. This relates to the third refrain in the niggun, which is at a very high level as far as 'religious ecstasy', being a level of fervor in which a human is unable to remain, thus we need to move down a level; but one should not go down to the level of refrain A, which is the point of commencement, thus we return to refrain B, which is the intermediary level. This is what is meant by 'serving G-d with materiality', that is, all our material, earthly service of G-d must aim for a higher level. This explanation proves that music has Godly origins, being in the *Sefira* of *Binah*.

8. Rabbi Moshe Shur, New York, USA[8]

What can you say about Rabbi Shlomo Carlebach's music?

Shlomo Carlebach never studied music in his life. His guitar playing, which was never particularly focused, was limited to no more than five or six chords which he used by taking advantage of the bridge. If you wanted to be accepted into his choir, there was no need of any entrance tests, nor even the most minimal knowledge of music, and you were immediately accepted. If so, what was the secret behind his international success?

His goal, which could even have been unconscious, was to bring his audience to realizing that each of us has a soul that holds increasingly higher levels of spirituality which can be reached through music.

Carlebach attained his purpose through a magical tool: repetition. Shlomo Carlebach customarily sang a song and repeated it sometimes twenty or thirty

---

8   Executive Director of Queens College Hillel, NYK, USA; member of Rabbi Shlomo Carlebach's choir from the end of the 1960s until Carlebach's death in 1996. The interview was conducted in Vienna at the Stefani Hotel on 11 July 2007

times in sequence. Through this kind of repetition, he led everyone participating to a state of amazing spiritual experience.

The classic example of such a song is *ha'Aderet vehaEmunah*, which is traditionally sung on *Simchat Torah*. It contains 22 alphabetic verses and when sung numerous times in sequence, the repeated letters, according to the Kabbalah, receive different meanings. When I was young, I sang this song with a thousand other youth; we sang it several times over, and it brought us to a very powerful level of fervor.

That's exactly what Shlomo Carlebach did – he repeated every song many times, until the participants entered a state of ecstasy.

Rabbi Aryeh Kaplan wrote a book exploring meditation in Judaism from the time of our forefather Abraham and up to current times. Other religions employ meditation, accessing it through a mantra; the Beatles used the phrase, "I get high with a little help from my friends", but we changed that to "We get high with a little help from Hashem!". The word "high" can be understood to be a unique uplifted discharge of the senses, which youth can access through external avenues such as alcohol or drug taking. With Shlomo Carlebach, we got "high" through music.

Shlomo was the product of Chabad. In Chassidic courts, the Rebbe traditionally conducts his *Tisch*, where he gives Torah discourses and ethical explanations, mingled with singing and a little liquor. With Shlomo, the liquor was substituted by the guitar, and the Chassidic stories he told were replete with ethics.

In the first book of Samuel, Chapters 9 and 10 relate how King Saul went to look for the mares that disappeared. Instead, he found a group of prophets, just as Samuel warned him: "And it shall come to pass, when you come to the city, that you shall meet a band of prophets coming down from the high place with a psaltery, and a timbrel, and a pipe, and a harp, before them; and they will be prophesying" (I Sam. 10:5). Then the verse asks: "'What is this that is come unto the son of Kish? Is Saul also among the prophets?" (ibid, 10:11). Saul was still quite young at the time, and apparently strongly influenced by the music and the prophets, and instead of returning with the mares, he returned as a prophet. Similarly, whoever attended one of Shlomo Carlebach's concerts returned home "high", which brought that person closer to her or his Jewishness.

I would call Shlomo Carlebach the Baal Shem Tov of the current generation, because the Besht was also strongly opposed in his own times.

Shlomo 'saved' many children from Chassidic families who did not want to follow in the footsteps of their Chassidic fathers, and thus became distanced from Judaism. They came to Shlomo, who exuded authenticity, and folksy simplicity, and he received each of them like a father, rekindling the spark of Jewishness in everyone who entered his home.

He never told anyone what to do. He never suggested to anyone to try and reach a specific sensation from the singing, he never asked people to keep *mitzvot* [religious precepts], never told them to keep Shabbat, but after singing with him, people began to do these things naturally, of their own accord.

He was a tremendous giver of charity, and gave away almost everything he owned. I myself was present when someone came to him asking for assistance, having lost all his money and on the spot, Shlomo gave away everything he had received for that evening's performance.

In my view, he was a Torah sage: it was not the music that motivated him, but Torah.

Chapter 15 – Appendices

1. The First Meeting between the Besht and Rabbi Yaacov Yosef

Following which the latter became the Besht's outstanding disciple:[1]
Narrative relevant to page 52

The glory of his Torah was always enclosed within the four cubits of Halacha [Jewish Law] and Talmud, his body and soul were mortified by fasts, abstentions and asceticism, and often he was sad, worried, tearfully fearful that he may not have upheld his obligations towards the Holy One, Blessed be He. Often, however, such sadness derived from a sense of depression and sometimes even despair. For this reason he could never experience joy in fulfilling the mitzvot [precepts]. I, on the other hand, was taught from infanthood in my father's home that "you must indeed be joyful". Jews should never despair even if they feel that they have reached the lowest place possible. Sadness and despair are indicators of spiritual deficiencies, of lack of confidence and faith in the living G-d, and the scope of his mercy. I hate, with the full force of hatred, that same sorrow which is completely – on both the inside and the outside – woeful, but I love the joy that derives from passion for G-d, joy which is important and dear to Him, because deep within, it encompasses woe and joins with spiritual signs that display aspiration, fervor, will, love, and the soul's craving. It is entirely filled with the secrets of what cannot be seen by human eyes, by intellect, nor even by vision or mental image, but can be seen by the soul's passion and the spirit's thirst for Godliness. I do not wish to lessen the value of tears, as the Sages have said (in Talmud Baba Metzia 59), "The gates of tears have not been locked". But joy bears double worth, and if teardrops open the gates, then joy eliminates them entirely, and eradicates all divisions [...] and believe me, the glory of his Torah after singing with the children, the pupils, always left me feeling great and special spiritual pleasure.

At such times, I would go out into the field and unite with my Creator, becoming purified through my yearning for my Maker, and there, in the expanse of the field, the power of *El Shaddai* became revealed to me. Silent and astounded, I would stand, gazing at the world of the Holy One, Blessed be He. My ears caught the spiritual sounds of the birds chirruping, and the bees humming, and it

---

[1] Rabbi Y. L. Maimon, *Sarei haMe'ah*, pg. 42-43

seemed as though the spirit of G-d bubbled in every living thing, in every plant and in every inanimate object. At such times, I would sense my great insignificance in comparison to the endless light of *Ein Sof*, and through an awakening from Above, my heart would warm, my soul would spill forth from within me, and from my mouth a well known song burst forth – (Kabbalistic song of praise – Yedid Nefesh, Stanza II): "Majestic, Beautiful, Radiance of the universe, my soul pines for your love. Please, O G-d, heal her now by showing her the pleasantness of Your radiance; then she will be strengthened and healed, and eternal gladness will be hers".[2]

But believe me, regarding the glory of his Torah, our Sages describe how (Talmud, Brachot 3): "A lyre was hung above King David's bed, and when midnight came, the northern wind [Heb. *Ru'ach Tzfonit*] would blow through it and play its strings". So, too, within me, there is a kind of concealed spirit [Heb. *Ru'ach Tzfunah*], so that when I wandered the hills and mountains, fields and vineyards, and viewed the expansiveness of G-d's creation, then that same northern wind (ie: concealed spirit) would blow through all 248 of my organs, and I would begin to play music within me, sing and recite songs to the G-d above, for all things being just so in His world. Of course, special sensitivity is needed for this, together with exceptional sentiment, with which not all people are blessed, but I have already drawn an allegory regarding this:

There was a man who played a very beautiful musical instrument. He played it with great sweetness and pleasantness, and those who heard it could not restrain themselves from feeling enjoyment from the enormity of sweetness and pleasure, which eventually led them to dancing, almost reaching the ceiling out of their tremendous pleasure, gladness and sweetness. Whoever drew closer to hear the musical instrument derived even greater pleasure, and would dance enthusiastically. It happened that a deaf person came by, unable to hear the wonderful sounds of the musical instrument, only able to see the ecstasy of the dancing people who appeared to him like madmen. To himself, the deaf man thought: "What causes such joy?" Indeed, if he had been clever, knowledgeable, and understanding, he would have realized what beauty was held in the sounds of the musical instrument and would have danced there too. (I heard these stories as a child from the elderly Chassidim,

---

2   According to Idelsohn, in *haNeginnah haChassidit*, pg. 1; quoting *Sefer haCharedim*, Chapter 7, which states: "One of the most precious modes of awakening ecstatic affinity derives from the 'lover' singing 'A Song of Companionship'." See also, Schleifer, *Anthology of Chassidic Music*, pg. 44: "This beautiful hymn was written by Rabbi Eleazar Azikri (or, Azikari), author of *Sefer haCharedim*, of the circle of mystics in Tzefat [Safed] in the 16th century. This hymn came to be accepted by the Chassidim as the opening of prayers for Shabbat eve, and it is also customarily sung as part of the Shabbat songs.

who said that the Besht related these words to Reb Yaakov Yosef regarding the merits of song and melody. I also found these stories among the works of Reb Moshe Chaim Efraim, quoting his elder, the Besht, in *Degel Machaneh Efraim*, on the Torah portion of *Yitro*, and I copied them exactly as they were recorded).

The Besht's adages on song and singing, on the joy that, deep inside, derives from the deepest dolefulness, on the Godly spirit that sparks in every living creature, every plant and inanimate object, set Rabbi Yaakov Yosef to pondering, and his thoughts became entangled in his sharp mind as though plunged into clouds of fog. It seemed as though the Besht's enthused remarks caused all of Reb Yaakov Yosef's emotions to dissolve. Such an effervescing began to occur in Reb Yaakov Yosef's soul, that he himself had no notion of its content and scope. He felt as if some higher spirit had taken hold of the fringes of his mind. New ideas, which he had previously never considered, rose in his heart and inspired him. Those things which he had heard were admittedly, or at least in his view, strange and gave cause to wonder, but during that conversation, Rabbi Yaakov Yosef had focused all the powers of his attention on scrutinizing the Besht's face. He saw that the Besht's eyes filled with a unique kind of tranquility, acquired from deep thought and from uplifting of the soul above common daily occurrences. He saw that a beam of light shone on his face like a wondrous heavenly flame which seemed to emanate from the Uppermost Light.

2. The Besht's Role as Kindergarten Teacher's Assistant

In which he integrated music in his work with the children.[3]
Narrative relevant to page 57.

During his youth, it became necessary for Rabbi Israel to ensure his own livelihood. He became an assistant to the kindergarten teacher. He fulfilled his role whole-heartedly. He was required to bring the infants to the study house or the synagogue and teach them when to say *AmenYeheh Shmei Rabbah, Kedushah,* and *Amen,* again, in a pleasant voice. This simplest of acts served as Reb Israel's first step in publicizing *Chassidut,* for in his heart, he declared: I will not preach at first to these young children, tiny infants of the world, but I will prepare them to be pious according to my perceptions. They bear no doubts, only wonderment and belief. Their love is whole, their awe is whole, and their hearts are their focal point – only G-d can measure the innocence of their hearts.

---

3 M. S. Geshuri, Machanayim, Vol. 46, 5720 – 1960, Chapter on The Besht – Assistant kindergarten teacher in Galicia

Reb Israel began caring for the children, their souls cleaving to his because of the tremendous love he poured into them. It was the kind of love that had been plundered from him in his own childhood when orphaned; and from which he understood that every person is like an orphan in need of the love of a father and mother. He performed his work as assistant kindergarten teacher with great joy and willingness, with faith and affection, mingled with traditional songs. When they sang in antiphonal responses, the gentle, lovely sounds coming from the mouths of these babes held the power to cause the threads of one's soul to tremble, and light the holy sparks in one's heart.

Like little waves lapping against the steadfast rock, the young children milled about him. And he – sometimes looked but did not see, sometimes saw but did not look. The homes of the children's parents were his makeshift refuge. The children would rise early, and come home late, only to spend as much time with their Rebbe as they could. The children would go with him to the synagogue, filled with love, and like him, they would close their eyes during the prayers; they would dance as he did, enthused, not noticing those who mocked them; they would call out '*Amen Yeheh Shmeh Rabbah*' as though crying out for help, singing out the words that the congregation would normally read in passing; they did not allow the *chazzan* to skim by them and end prayers quickly. The children seemed to be a part of Reb Israel, and he a part of them, and all together were like one whole entity. The joint singing of the children and the assistant kindergarten teacher could be heard not only in the classroom or the synagogue, but in the public spaces, in the streets and in the market. The children passed through the streets on their way to the synagogue, their mouths spilling songs of religious content. Whenever Reb Israel walked with the infants to the synagogue, he would sing with them in such a pleasant voice and with such great desire that it could be heard at great distances.

As they moved within the courtyard of the synagogue, their song was like prayer, his adult voice mingling with their young, clear, fresh voices, and the voices together seemed to be paving their way through the distances, borne on high.

Reb Israel and the infants passed through the dissonant jumble of the market and its trading, where Jews with heads hung low, burdened by the weight of their *mitzvot* and concerns over their livelihood, cleansed and sanctified their thoughts before commencing their prayers.

Here, then, was a congregations of babes led by one adult, who sang as they did, as loud as can be. On occasion, a crowd of people would make their way over to see this parade and listen to the sounds of their religious songs. Then the people's hearts were aroused with emotion and awe, with honor for the Heavens.

Others, however, viewed this action as deviant from the traditional norms, and slowly began to make their protests known to the community's benefactors.

Then the parents came and removed their children from that *chedder*, but to no avail: the children refused to accept such a decision, and although they were sent elsewhere, the children crept away, returning to 'their' *chedder*.

At the same time, there were some who told of wonders: of a child who was ill, and Reb Israel wrote the child's name into his own hand-written *Siddur*, and the child healed. Another person related that he had sat alone in the adjacent *chedder* and had heard Reb Israel arguing, speaking his words out loud, and someone responding; if anyone doubted it, the children silenced that person.

In his childhood, Reb Israel himself would flee from the *chedder* to the forest. Now he led his pupils to the forest, where they gathered medicinal plants. They found a snake: Reb Israel killed it, and afterwards, the children stoned it. Reb Israel explained to them that snakes live not only in nature, but also in humans, and must be eradicated. He would bring the children to the spring, to the pool and to the dark caves, where they would pray; he would appear to the children as though first fading, then becoming powerful, speaking in light and darkness to G-d, the souls in the trees, and the waters.

When the mothers came to take their infants home, they would hear words of Torah from him which seemed to have come direct from Sinai; then the parents simply were unable to refuse the children's wishes. The children were mesmerized by the Rebbe's singing in the courtyard, which many people heard; and on hearing it, they recognized the deep love of G-d it contained. Many were the people who blessed these children; many eyes filled with tears as these people smiled on seeing them, whispering: "From the mouths of babes and suckling infants You have established strength" and they likened this singing to that of the Levites in the Temple. The author of the Besht's biography testifies that "the Besht's service [of G-d] rose on High, and G-d's contentment was like His contentment from the songs sung by the Levites in the Temple".

Reb Israel continued implementing his ideals, and over time the children's singing and the content of their songs heard by the community had tremendous influence among Jewish neighborhoods. It appears that this public display of singing with the infants was none other than the starting point from which the application of music became fundamental to Chassidism, for with his voice and those of the infants, the gates [of Heaven] opened, and their sounds poured forth through the sinews and veins to the very heart and the mind, the waves of song were borne on the wings of the wind (spirit), and mingled with the thousands of voices of song floating in the air, and the impression received was as though the whole world sang along with them.

These children eventually became faithful, pious Chassidim, loyal to their assistant kindergarten teacher's path, who themselves later attracted many followers.

3. **Legends and Tales**

*(i) The Diamond – For Chabad's Day of Redemption
19th Kislev*[4]

On the morning of that day, the 19th of Kislev, 5559 (1798) the *Alter Rebbe*, Rabbi Shneur Zalman, was able as always to distinguish between light and darkness even though, in his cell, it was nonetheless dark and gloomy. He wrapped himself in his *Tallit* and *Tefillin*, directed his heart and soul towards Jerusalem, and prayed with great fervor, begging for the redemption of Israel. After his prayers, he prepared the portion of buckwheat that comprised his breakfast, and while doing so, the tune known as "Four Babas" entered his heart, and his lips shaped the verse, "Redeem my soul in peace".[5]

At that moment, a beam of light entered his cell as the door opened. Accompanied by his entourage, the prosecutor entered, the release form in his hand.

The Alter Rebbe departed. Many of the guards bent their heads to receive the Rebbe's blessing as he passed by. He reached the gates and stepped out into the street. He did not know where to go. Petersburg was a large city, and the Jews residing there behaved as people do in cities, enclosed in their homes. It was impossible to know which home held Jewish residents, and which did not. The Rebbe decided to examine the doorposts and in this way, identify Jewish residences by the *mezuzah* on the doorway.

The Chassidim who had spent great sums of money in order to secure the Rebbe's release, which they knew would occur close to the 19th of Kislev, stood ready to greet him, tables of food prepared for the Alter Rebbe in thanksgiving. However, the *Mitnagdim* who had informed on the Rebbe to the authorities, claiming that the monies he collected to send to the poor of Israel were instead being directed to the Sultan to increase his military powers in preparation for war against the Czar, were also certain that the Rebbe's fate would be clinched on this date. In fact, they were certain that the decision would be the most severe possible. They, too, prepared tables laden with the choicest foods to celebrate their success in defeating what they viewed as 'the evil cult' of Chassidism.

The Alter Rebbe, exhausted from his imprisonment, slowly made his way down the street checking doorposts. On seeing a mezuzah, he understood that it belonged to a Jewish home. Inside sat a Jew recently returned from Lithuania, who traded in meat and had, over time, become the supplier for the barracks in the city of Petersburg. He was affiliated with the *Mitnagdim* although he was not

---

4 David Cohen, *Thirty Six Legends,* Ramat Gan, pg. 101-104
5 Psalms 55:19

learned in Torah. He only knew that instead of saying *Na'aritzcha veNakdish'cha* in the *Kedusha* of *Mussaf* on Shabbat, the members of this Chassidic 'cult' recited *Keter yitnu lecha*, which greatly angered the Vilna Gaon. The meat supplier, through his contacts with the authorities, knew that on the 19th of Kislev an exceedingly severe judgment would be passed on the hated Rabbi's fate. He had prepared a celebratory repast for his friends and acquaintances who would join him to show their thanks for the decree on the Rebbe who incited against tradition.

There was a knock on the door. The businessman opened it, to find a Jew with his *Tallit* and *Tefillin* held under his arm, his face pale, his beard unruly, and his eyes deep. The businessman asked who he was; the Rebbe, with great modesty, answered that his name was Shneur Zalman and he had just been released from prison.

"Are you *Rabbi* Shneur Zalman?", the Mitnagid cried out, his face burning with anger while nonetheless trying to appear as though receiving his guest, having invited him to sit and having already served him tea. While the Rebbe sat, stretching his limbs, the man went quickly to his kitchen and brought back a sheet of paper, a quill and inkwell, but in his other hand he held an axe. He handed the writing materials to the Rebbe, saying, "You have been saved from the non-Jews, but you will not be saved by me. Write this down, and sign it: that Jews should say *Na'aritzcha veNakdish'cha* rather than *Keter* in the *Kedusha* of *Mussaf*!", and the man stood there brandishing his axe. The Rebbe's face was white and weary, but his eyes sparkled with joy. He looked upwards, and said, "Master of the Universe, see this, how Your Jews, even if they are simple folk, are devoted and faithful to You, and because this Jew thinks that *Na'aritzcha* surpasses *Keter*, he is prepared and ready to harm me". The Jew heard the Rebbe's words and his heart was softened by regret. While he stood there trembling, enthused Chassidim burst into his home, having heard from the prison guards that the Rebbe had been set free, and having presumed that he had entered this particular home, being the closest Jewish home to the prison. They found the Rebbe seated, his face pale, but in his eyes there were tears of joy, even though the householder stood trembling beside him. The axe fell from the householder's hand.

"What is happening here?", asked the Chassidim, and the Rebbe responded, "This Jew fulfilled the *mitzvah* of welcoming guests when I arrived here; but he thinks that for the Mussaf Kedusha, *Na'aritzcha* surpasses *Keter*". The Chassidim burst into laughter, and one turned to the businessman to tell him this anecdote:

> A King was about to be crowned. The court wished to place a very precious diamond in the crown. What did they do? They gathered all the diamonds in the country, and sat two experts down, equipping them with magnifying glasses, and positioning a Cossack to guard not only the diamonds but also the experts. The two experts sat turning the diamonds over, searching for the best one in the pile, and eventually found a small stone. They discussed

whether it was the best, the prettiest, and so forth. The Cossack, on the other hand, saw a large diamond sparkling brightly, and wondered to himself what kind of experts these were, focused on such a small diamond; how could they not see the great, beautiful one? He approached them and made his thoughts known. The experts laughed and explained to the Cossack that his might in eating and drinking may be great, but what could he possibly know of diamonds?

The Chassid continued, explaining to the businessman: "This anecdote parallels both of the experts, the Vilna Gaon and our Alter Rebbe, who debate what must be said in the *Kedusha*. The Gaon says that it should be *Na'aritzcha*, and our Rebbe says that it should be *Keter*, and who are we, the simplest of people, to interfere in such deep matters?"

The *Mitnagid* then fell at the Rebbe's feet, and asked his forgiveness, and invited the Chassidim to his table. As they sat celebrating, the Alter Rebbe said: "King David, may he rest in peace, was joyful and thanked the Holy One, Blessed be He, for redeeming his soul, for it is not the body that is tormented but the soul, and the cause of the King's joy was that his redemption was peaceful".

Then, to encourage the Chassidim to maintain peace among all Jews, he began to sing a niggun. The Chassidim joined in with great fervor, and the Mitnagdim who meanwhile came to the businessman's home to celebrate the judgment with him, saw the Rebbe, saw his eyes brimming with love and mercy, and heard the niggun, which penetrated their hearts and awakened their regret and repentance, and they, too, became great Chassidim.

The Chabad Chassidim set the 19th of Kislev, the date on which their Rebbe was freed, as a day of celebration. Among their customs at the celebratory anniversary meal they hold is to eat buckwheat in memory of the breakfast eaten by the Alter Rebbe in prison, to sing the Rebbe's niggun, and to dance enthusiastically.

(ii) The Holy Thief – A Life Story[6]

Inspired by the Besht, Rabbi Shlomo Carlebach also told stories of holy thieves. He told about Moisheleh the thief who, every time he stole, would go to the Besht. The latter would bless him, and the police would then forget about Moisheleh.

After the Besht passed away, the thief was expelled in shame from the Beit Midrash. He threw himself on the Besht's grave, crying bitterly in complaint: "Everyone else was a Rebbe only for Tzaddikim but only you agreed to be the Rebbe of thieves, too".

6   *http://www.hazofe.co.il/web/katava6.asp?Modul=24&id=25593&Word=&gilayon= 2077*

That night, the Besht appeared to him in a dream and told the thief that from then on, his grandson, the *Degel Machaneh Efraim*, would become his patron. If his grandson was at all doubtful, Moisheleh should confirm the Besht's directive by explaining the Torah portion of the week in accordance with the manner it is learned in Paradise, and which the Besht would teach him in this dream. And so it was. The police left the thief alone following the Tzaddik's prayer. But Moisheleh, having tasted true Torah study, did not go back to thieving, for his soul sought Torah, and he became a great and well known scholar.

(iii) The Flute[7]

In the times of the Rav (known as the Besht), a Chassid lived in a village greatly distanced from the Jewish community. The Chassid led an honest and faithful existence, believing in G-d, and conducting his life charitably. Every year in the month of Elul he would come to town, where a place was kept for him in the Rav's Beit Midrash. This man had an only son whose heart seemed closed and whose soul seemed not to want to learn, nor could the boy read the alphabet. He was just like so many other farmers of villages, living without Torah; he would care for the cattle and shepherd the flock, as the villagers did, and he would play the flute as they did. His father bore this fate quietly. He did not badger his Rebbe with requests to change his son's heart and fill it with a new spirit, yet he could not understand G-d's ways, or why he was given such a son.

When the boy turned thirteen, the father decided to take his son with him to the city to pray there, and educate him a little. However, the son wandered all day among the markets and streets, and the father was barely able to bring him home. The father prayed to G-d to open the youth's heart, and give him the spark of a Jew, so that his offspring would not be considered a withered plant, useless and shameful to the community and its people.

The day of Yom Kippur came. On that day, every year, all the Jews gathered, young and old, wealthy and poor, to pour their hearts out in the house of G-d, before the One on High, and seek forgiveness for all their sins and transgressions, for a person's misdemeanors are many! The ministering angels stood to the right of each person, while the evil angels fought with them. A clash of worlds! The battle of the generations! And on that great and terrible day, the battle renewed with full force. There was immense fury at that time in the world, for sin had overcome good, and the power of the prosecutors was strongest.

---

7   Michah Yosef ben Gurion, *Aggadot Am*, Leipzig: 1928, pg. 118-119

In vain, the leader of the prayers went from world to world, seeking mercy for his people. Wherever he turned, the enemy had already arrived. He called for Elijah the Prophet, but could not find him. He called for Ahiya the Shilonite, his teacher, but he was not there. Then he approached the Chamber of the Messiah, but it was shut. He stood at the lectern, his eyes like those of a dead man. For hours he stood, not moving, and fear and horror fell upon the faces of those gathered to pray, so that they prayed with holy awe, unable to make their voices heard on seeing their Rebbe standing as rigid as a palm tree. "Angels on high, open the gates before this oppressed and tormented people which begs for its soul", but the gates did not open. Satan himself guarded them that day, the great metal key in his hand.

The villager boy stood all day in the corner alongside his father, watching the lips of the people moving, whispering words he could not understand which were written on pages, all black lines and dots. The people around him cried. They sobbed quietly, and a great swell of emotion grasped the boy, an emotion he had never yet felt in all his life, so painful that it seemed to be clasping his throat and strangling him.

Being a shepherd, he would, in G-d's own courtyard – that is, Nature –have struck up a melody with his flute, a song of expansive lands, with the sun at its zenith in the heavens; or a song that spoke of the day's end; or perhaps a song for the beginning of Autumn; or for when he lay alone beneath the endless skies. As he stood there among the people from whom sadness flowed, he, too, wished to pour his heart out. He wanted to feel his flute in his hands and play it.

The boy's father saw him searching and asked, "What have you got there?" The boy answered, "My flute!". The father was alarmed, and said, "Do not touch it, for today it is forbidden". The boy, however, did not understand his father's intent, and took out the flute, but his father did not let him play, grasping the boy's hand with a cloth, for the flute is unholy on such a day and should not be touched, according to Torah and the Sages. In this way, the *Mussaf* and *Mincha* prayers were chanted and completed.

On reaching the closing *Ne'ilah* prayer, the Rebbe remained wrapped in his *Tallit* and white garments without moving, and the hearts of the congregants seemed defeated before the Godly Judge, the One on High. As night fell, indicating that the gates would be locked even before they had opened on that awesome day, the boy could no longer hold back his tempestuous emotion. The strength of his arm overcame that of his father, and he put his flute to his lips, and played a tremendous blast. The congregation was scared. The people turned to look at him, seeking the source of this sound, so strange to a house of prayer on the Day of Atonement. The father struggled with his son, but the Besht lifted his *Tallit* over him, signaling with his hand that the boy should be admired, and the color returned to the Besht's face.

A heavy weight was lifted off Creation. The sound of the flute rose to the highest heavens, and it was a time of good will against which Satan could not remain upright. All the gates and prayers of the Jewish people of that year, and the previous year, and all the years until then, assembled before the Throne of Glory of the Merciful Father, who hears the murmurs of every mouth, and the message was heard: "I have forgiven according to Your word!". The congregations of Jews everywhere breathed with relief.

(iv) The Se'udah Shlishit Meal at the Rebbe[8]

Impressions recorded by Mr. Y. Kipnis on his participation at the Seudah Shlishit with the Rebbe, Rabbi Saul Yedidyah Eleazar of Modzitz.

The lanes of Otwock that led to the home of the Modzitz Rebbe were filled with people. So many people, of so many kinds! Jews with Shabbat clothes and fur hats, Jews with beards and *payot* (side curls), Chassidim and young male students, the future grooms, the disciples of Germarra, walking shoulder to shoulder, filling the whole width of the street. The community benefactors made their way there, hands clasped behind their backs; young people made their way there, in short clothes and shaven faces. Walking. Everyone was walking to the Modzitz Rebbe for the Seudah Shlishit meal, to hear niggunim, to hear his voice sing the melodies he composed, and with which he filled his table with glory.

The Modzitz Rebbe was a direct continuation of the golden chain of Modzitz Chassidism founded on negginah, commencing with the grandfather, Reb Israel of Modzitz, who composed the shepherd's niggun, *Mizmor leDavid*, and the *Niggun for the Homeless*, composed when the Jews were forced to leave their homes prior to the first World War.

A known story relates to the Modzitz Rebbe and the niggun of yearning, the *Ezkera*, composed in Berlin while the surgeon, Professor Israels, amputated his foot. Chassidim sing this niggun, drawing on it as a an endless source of spiritual uplifting.

In Otwock, Rebbe Saul Yedidyah Eleazar continued to intertwine service of G-d in his niggunim. He 'conducted' the singing at his *Tisch* with songs that he composed for prayers. These songs were sung not only by Modzitz Chassidim but also by the Chassidim of other courts as well.

---

8   M. S. Geshuri, *Negginah veChassidut beVeit Kuzmir uVnoteha*, pg. 61-65

The 'Grandfather Rebbe' of Modzitz, it is said, would hum his niggunim – a humming filled with sanctity. Reb Saul sung them in a wonderful voice, thereby becoming known as an inspiring leader of prayers to whom all came to listen.

When I entered the Rebbe's home, I felt as though transported to another world. In all the surrounding houses, lights already shone. Shabbat was already over, and only the Rebbe's home remained veiled in a curtain of darkness where hundreds of shadowy forms moved, bumping into the walls of the Rebbe's Beit Midrash.

"Ssshhhhhh", people outside whispered, "ssshhhh, be quiet!". And through the open windows and doors of the Beit Midrash a wonderful voice could be heard, a tenor, spilling in lyric tones: *Bnei Hechaleh Dich'sifin*. What an exotic *nussach*, and what yearnings, trembling on the horizons in the twilight of Shabbat. It was the Wolyn form of *Bnei Hechaleh* that was so heart-moving. Its hues were so Jewish, and so Disapora. The Modzitz style ignited the imagination far more, just as somewhere, among the mountains of the east, someone created a hymn to the Creator, as though 'finding' it on his flute, and finding it filled with longing. *Yehon hacah...* hundreds of Chassidim joined the singing of this fiery niggun, until the atmosphere felt charged, as though the air, the house, the very trees and the Beit Midrash moved too, and were moved by this atmosphere. With each motif of the niggun, the atmosphere became more electric, as did the wonderment, the souls warming with Chassidic fervor, with Chassidic ecstasy.

"This is the Rebbe's new niggun, just recently composed", I hear the Chassidim seated at an outdoor table, whispering. If this indeed is the creation of the Rebbe – so I think to myself – then he is truly a great composer, one of the very few with such abilities in the field of Chassidic music, as music involves both song and words, and this is far better than the melodies we hear at Habimah![9]

"Ssshhh, the Rebbe is discoursing on a point in Torah". I try to get my head through the doorway; perhaps I will catch something... to no avail. The heat produced by these hundreds of Chassidim crowded together like one entity thrusts me back outside.

Next, the Rebbe declares: *Yedid Nefesh Av haRachaman*. Instantly, the mood alters. What a tremendous difference in character and essence there is between the niggun for *Bnei Hechaleh* and that for *Yedid Nefesh*! Ecstasy gives way to impressive improvisation and antiphony. A Chazzan and singers. The Rebbe sings, and the Chassidim sing along. When the Rebbe alters the scale, the Chassidim alter their accompaniment accordingly. This is the kind of music we hear late at night on Radio Budapest. As though the violin 'loses' control. All the other instruments follow suit. One thinks – oh, this is the finale. But then another

---

9   Habimah is the National Theater of Israel, in Tel Aviv

round of melancholy notes spills forth, immeasurable, endless. For a moment, the sanctity aroused by the initial niggun seems to wane when suddenly, from within the darkness, comes the Rebbe's singing, as though playing a musical instrument: *Mizmor leDavid*. It leaves an impression: the first niggun is allegro moderato; the next niggun, the *Yedid Nefesh*, is an adagio; and now, the *Mizmor leDavid* in scherzo; a symphony at the Seudah Shlishit! The soul dips in a sea of grace, of satisfaction, of religious humor, the sounds those of a cantata.

Following the *Mizmor leDavid*, a choir of Chassidim sing, in perfect unison, the *Yetzaveh Tzur Chasdo*. Only the Chassidim sing, while the Rebbe joins by humming. After that, the hall shudders at the niggun that follows, the *Ezkera*, sung to the words of *Baruch El Elyon*, and in the darkness, one can palpably feel the deep admiration felt by Jews in their eighties, standing gathered outside – inside there is no room at all – and with saddened faces, they absorb the sounds of the niggun composed by the Rebbe's grandfather. Next to me stands such a man, completely 'Ashkenazi' and aristocratic; his admiration is memorable: "Ah, ah, ah", he sighs, "*that* is a niggun, a pleasure to hear".

Finally, the Rebbe commences a series of niggunim that indicate our departure from Shabbat. Included were a special niggun for *Ki Eshmera Shabbat*, and another for *Shabbat Hayom*. It seemed as though trumpets and flutes, and even drums, and all the other wind and percussion instruments, played to the departing *Seudah Shlishit*. How powerful the force of the Chassidim whose mouths imitated musical instruments. Seven niggunim were sung by the Rebbe with his Chassidim: for the seven planets and for the seven days of the week. When the Rebbe finally entered his own private study to recite the Grace after Meals, the Chassidim began singing even more strongly and with greater fervor: *Shir haMa'a lot*. Their voices were forceful, purposeful and fresh, as though, just this very moment, they had begun singing!

Walking. Walking. Jews in Shabbat clothes and fur hats, in skullcaps, Chassidic Jews, rows and rows of Torah disciples, young Chassidic students, the generation of bridegrooms, apprentices, all marching along with light step, Jewish benefactors, young Jews in modern clothes and shaven faces. From where do all these servants of G-d come? Walking. From the Modzitz Rebbe, from the *Seudah Shlishit*, from hearing the niggunim, feeling replete with the melodies of the Modzitz Rebbe.

I walk through the deep sands too, and do not know how to describe how I feel. I am simultaneously amazed and disappointed. I heard a world filled with music, wonderful Chassidic motifs, tones filled with religious ecstasy, I heard universal music, musical complexities, free melodies, melodies of departure – like a typical military march, with its oompah-pah from the accompanying trumpet. If you wish, these could have been tunes from the period of Bellini and Rossini. If you wish, when the rhythm stops, one can identify excellent jazz.

To myself, I wonder: if the Rebbe is blessed with the memory of genius, and is able, without any knowledge of notes, to compose such complex niggunim and remember them all, can all the music that I just heard be considered the original outcome of the environment? Independent Chassidic-religious music? One thing is for certain: that the music of Modzitz, the melodies and the impressions, is a Polish-Chassidic layer of folklore.

(v) The Soul of the Musician

At midnight, a voice penetrated the room where the Maggid of Kozenice sat, weeping: "Holy Jew, be compassionate to the miserable soul which for these past ten years, has wandered the world of desolation".

"Who are you?", the Maggid asked, "and what did you do with your earthly life?"

"I was a musician", the voice replied, "and I sinned as all wandering musicians sin".

"Who sent you, then, to me?"

Then the voice sighed. "I played music at the Rebbe's wedding, and the Rebbe praised me, and wished to listen to more, and more, and I played one niggun after another, wishing to be looked upon favorably".

"And do you still recall the niggun you played while I was led to the wedding canopy?", questioned the Maggid.

The voice sang the niggun.

"This coming Shabbat, your redemption will come", declared the Maggid.

On the Shabbat eve immediately following this conversation, the Maggid sang the *Lecha Dodi* with a melody that no one had ever yet heard, and which the singers in the synagogue simply could not memorize.[10]

(vi) The World of Music

"The Jew" – the *Kadosh* of Psishcha (Przysucha) saw, in the form of a vision, that the illness suffered by the Maggid of Kozenice was worsening and that the danger of death hovered nearby. Immediately he commanded two of his adherents, who were wonderful singers and knowledgeable in music, to travel to Kozenice and bring Reb Israel's soul back with their niggunim. Waiting no more than a scant moment, they set off without delay, arriving at the Maggid's synagogue as

---

10 *Ohr haGanuz*, pg. 255

Shabbat commenced. Fulfilling their instructions, they received the Shabbat with songs and melodies. When their voices filled the room in which Reb Israel lay, he listened attentively, and his face shone with light. His breathing became more regular, his brow cooled, and his hands, which had been clenched against the spasms, rested easily on the blanket covering him. Finally, he opened his eyes, looking around as though awaking from slumber, and said: "The Holy Sage saw that I had passed through all the worlds. The only one I had not visited was the world of music. This is why he sent me these two emissaries, to bring me back through that world".[11]

---

11 Ibid, pg. 257

Epilogue

To conclude this section, I wish to quote from an article by Dr. S. Z. Cahana, *El haRina v'el haTefillah*, which appears in the introduction to *Kol Israel*, authored by Cantor Shlomo Ravitz, and edited by M. S. Geshuri.

The world of the Holy One, Blessed be He, is like a sea of song, bursting forth from every single corner, commencing with the wheels of the heavens and to the deepest depths. All sings and all praises the Creator of the world, each one with its own verses of song, as is written in the *Perek Shirah* [Chapter of Song] (where each entity sings: the inanimate sings its song, the day and night sing their song, the plants sing theirs and the animals sing theirs, and so forth). The Torah itself is a song of the world, as is alluded to in the precept of writing a Torah scroll, found in the verse relating to song: "And now, write this song for yourselves"[1] and all the great Sages of Israel, commencing with Adam and up to our very day, all recited songs. When Adam was created, he began [his life] by reciting song[2]; Moshe sang his song, "So Moses will sing"[3]; Miriam sang, "And Miriam responded, 'Sing to the Lord for He is highly exalted; He has hurled the horse and rider into the sea'"[4]; the Prophetess Devorah sang, "And Devorah sang, and Barak son of Avinoam"[5]; Channah also sang, "And Channah prayed, and said: my heart exults in the Lord [...] because I rejoice in Your salvation"[6]; and King David poured his heart out to G-d through song[7]. This refers chiefly to his refreshing book known as Psalms, which contains songs and praises, chants and prayers, confessions and the inner workings of the hearts. Following King David's example, his son Solomon, the wisest man of all time, composed the Shir haShirim [Song of Songs], and following the footsteps of both these, the Levites, Prophets and Sages of each generation to the present filled and continue to fill the world with song, and whosoever recites song in this world will merit singing in the world to come.[8,9]

1 Deuteronomy 31:19
2 The Midrash Bereshit Rabbah 22:13 relates to the verse, *Mizmor shir leyom haShabbat* [A song sung for the Shabbat day] stating that this is the song sung by Adam, forgotten by the generations immediately following him, but renewed by Moshe in Adam's name.
3 Exodus 15:1
4 Exodus 15:21
5 Judges 5:1
6 I Samuel 2:1; and the *Rada"k* notes that this song refers to the kings of other nations compared to the people of Israel.
7 Also: And David spoke these words of song...: II Samuel 22:1
8 b. Sanhedrin 91
9 Quoted from *Kol Israel*, Tel Aviv: 1964, pg. 17

Sheet Music and Manuscripts

*The Jewish National & University Library Jerusalem, Mus 4 C 20(a)
Original manuscript from haNeginah haChassidit (Chassidic Music) by Avraham Zvi
Idelson (who also composed Hatikva, Israel's national anthem.*

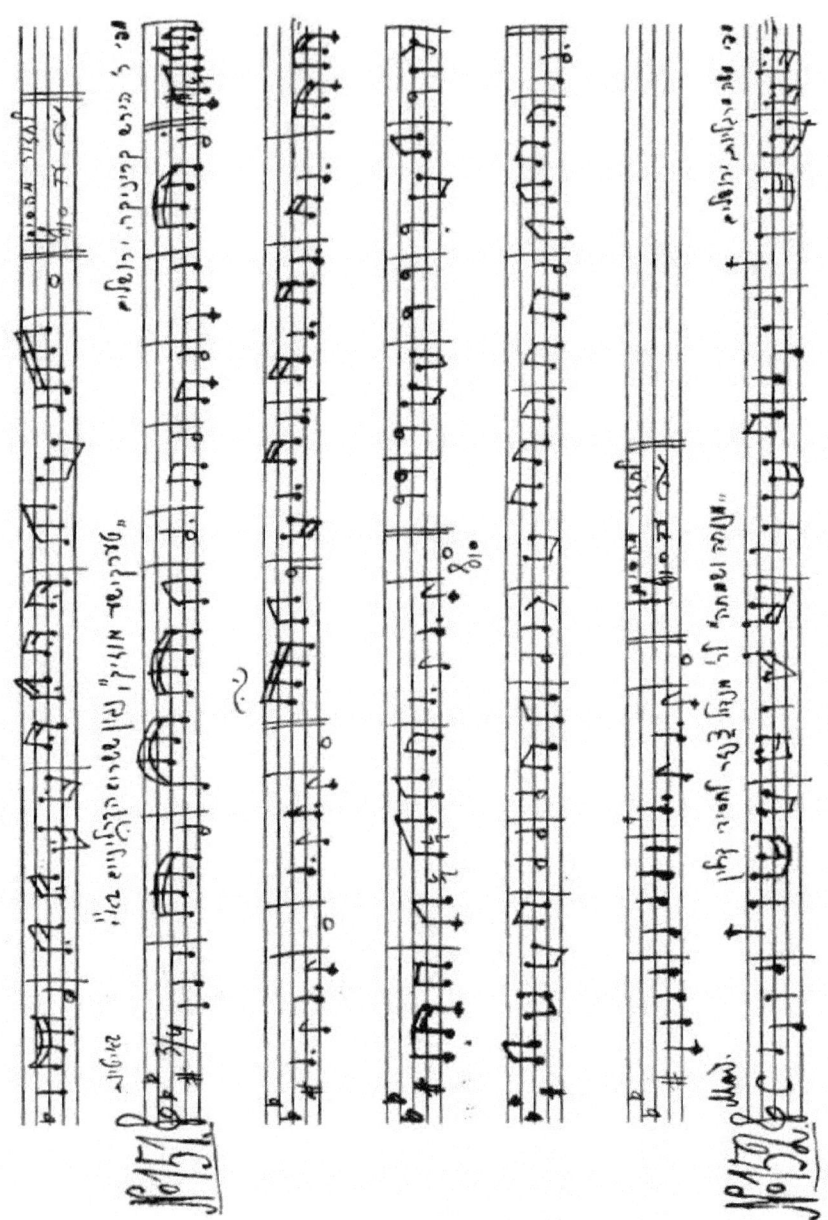

The Jewish National & University Library Jerusalem, 56 A 6
Terkischer Musik-Karlin. Manuscript from M.S. Geshuri

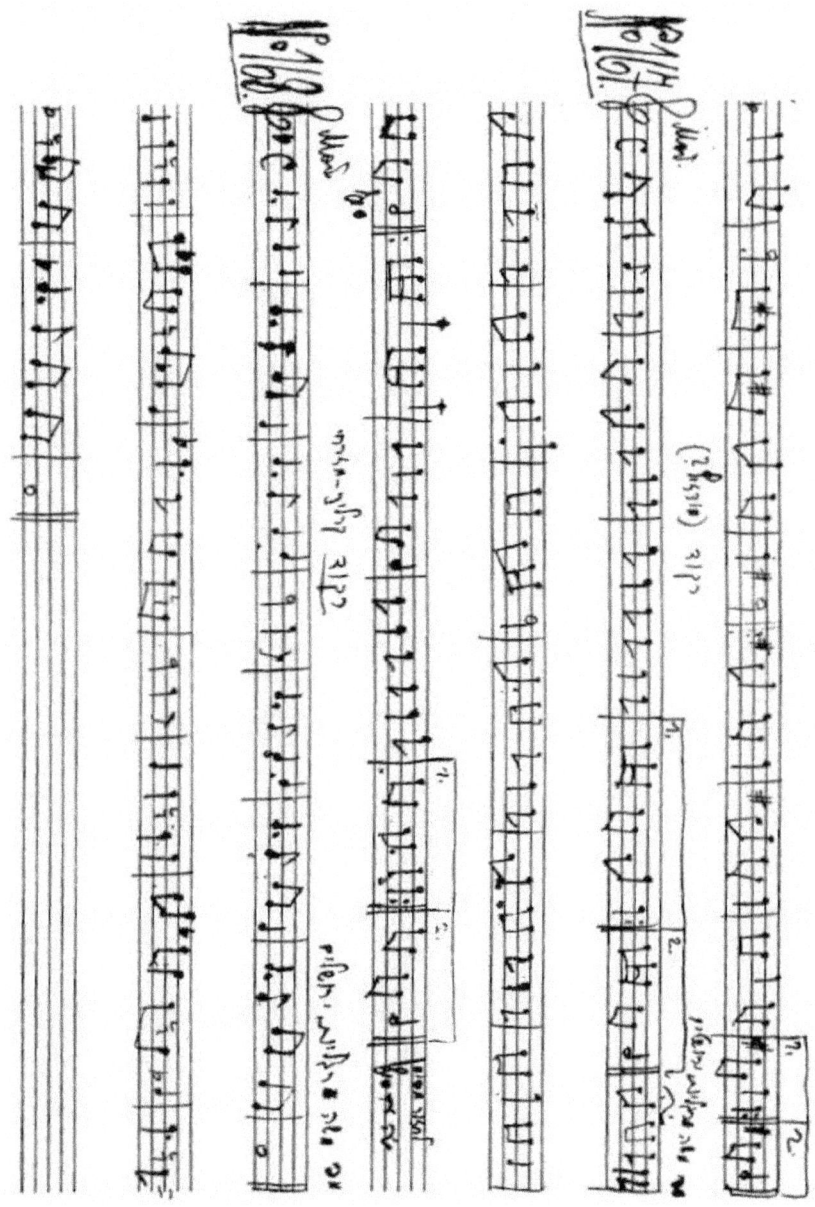

*The Jewish National & University Library Jerusalem, 56 A 7
Modzits and Karlin Dance Melody. Handwritten by M.S. Geshuri*

The 'Dvekut' Niggun of the Ger Chassidim. Handwritten by M.S. Geshuri.

Notes

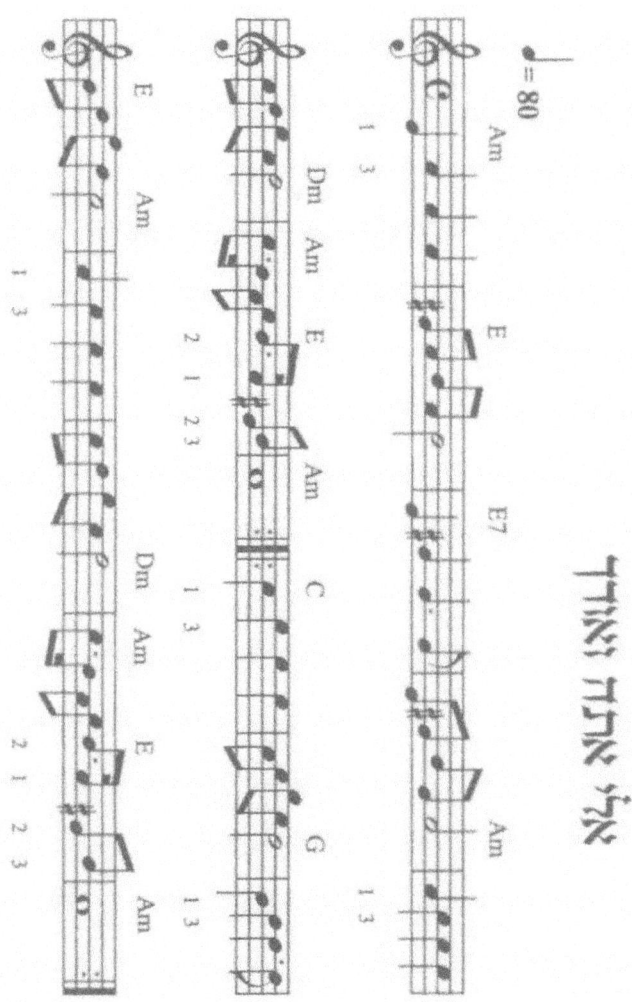

'Eli Ata Ve'Odeka' – Niggun of Rabbi Shneur Zalman of Liadi,
Niggunei Chabad 41.

'Arba Babot' – Niggun of Rabbi Shneur Zalman of Liadi, Niggunei Chabad 39.

'Ezkera' – Niggun of Rabbi Israel Taub, Modzitz
(in Neginah vaChassidut beveit Kuzmir u'Venoteha, by M.S. Geshuri)

'Ani Maamin', Ghetto song of Rabbi Ezriel David Fastag
(in Neginah vaChassidut beveit Kuzmir u'Venoteha, by M.S. Geshuri)

ניגון מיוחס להבעש"ט

*Niggun attributed to the Baal Shem Tov
(in Niggunei Chabad, 56)*

Photographs

The Besht

Rabbi Shneur Zalman of Liadi, the "Baal Hatanya"

Rabbi Saul Yedidyah Eleazar Taub, the second Modzitz Rabbi

Rabbi Israel Taub, the first Modzitz Rabbi

The Sutschke Rabbi plays the violin at the kindling of Chanukah lights

The Przemyshlan Rabbi plays the violin at the kindling of Chanukah lights

My grandfather, Rabbi Mendel Brichte, in a mitzvah-tanz with the bride

Cantor Shmuel Barzilai with his father, Rabbi Shlomo Barzilai, visiting Rabbi Israel Dan of Modzitz – May 2005

Cantor Shmuel Barzilai visits Rabbi Chaim Saul Taub of Modzitz – May 2007

With Rabbi Shlomo Carlebach, February 1994, in Vien

With Rabbi Ben Zion Shenker, August 2007, in Bnei Brak

Glossary of Rabbis and Cantors

Rabbis by date of birth

Rabbi Shlomo Ben Yitzhak (*Rashi*)	1040–1105
Rabbi Moshe ben Maimon – Maimonides (*Rambam*)	1135–1204
Rabbi Yehuda ben Shmuel heChassid (*Regensburg*)	1150–1217
Rabbi Yitzhak Berabi Moshe of Vienna (*Ohr Zarua*)	1180–1250
Rabbi Yehuda Halevi (*haKuza*ri)	1075–1140
Rabbi Isaac ben Solomon Luria (*Ari*)	1534–1572
Rabbi Judah Loew ben Bezalel (*The Maharal of Prague*)	1525–1609
Rabbi Yoel Surkis (*Bach*)	1561–1640
Rabbi Yeshayahu haLevi Horowitz (*haShla*)	1565–1630
Rabbi Moshe Azikri	1533–1600
Rabbi Josef Sagis (Azikri's Mentor)	? –1572
Rabbi Josef Karo (*Shulchan Aruch*)	1488–1575
Rabbi Jacob Bei Rav	1474–1546
Rabbi Moshe Di Trani (*Mabbit*)	1500–1580
Rabbi Josef of Trani (*Maharit*, son of the *Mabbit*)	1568–1639
Rabbi David ben Zimra (*Redvaz*)	1479–1573
Rabbi Shlomo Alkabetz	1500–1576
Rabbi Moshe Cordovero (*Ramak*)	1500–1570
Rabbi Hayim Vital	1542–1620
Rabbi Moshe Alshech	? –1593
Rabbi Israel Nagara	1550–1625
Rabbi Eliyahu ben Solomon Zalman (*Vilna Gaon*)	1720–1797
Rabbi Avraham Denzig (*Chayei Adam*)	1748–1820
Rabbi Yehuda Halevi Ashlag (*haSulam*)	1885–1954
Rabbi Baruch Shalom (son of Yehuda)	1907–1991
Rabbi Moshe Sofer (*Chatam Sofer*)	1720–1839
Rabbi Eliezer Shach	1894–2001
Rabbi Kolonymus Kalman Halevi Epstein (Cracow)	1754–1823

Chassidic Rabbis by Location[1]

Rabbi Israel ben Eliezer, the Baal Shem Tov	1700–1760

Alexander

Rabbi Hanoch haCohen of Alexander	1798–1870

Belz

Rabbi Shalom Roke'ach	1783–1855
Rabbi Aharon Roke'ach	1880–1957

Chabad/Lubavitch

Rabbi Shneur Zalman of Liadi (*Baal haTanya*)	1745–1813
Rabbi Dov Ber (*Der Mittler Rebbe*)	1773–1827
Rabbi Menahem Mendel (*Zemach Zedek*)	1789–1866
Rabbi Shmuel (*Moharash*)	1834–1882
Rabbi Shalom Dov-Ber Shneersohn (*Rashab*)	1861–1920
Rabbi Yoseph Yitzhak Shneersohn (*Harihez*)	1880–1950
Rabbi Menahem Mendel Shneersohn	1902–1994

Chernobyl

Rabbi Nahum the Great	1730–1798
Rabbi Mordechai (Motteleh) Twersky	1770–1837
Rabbi Aaron Twersky	1787–1871

Gur

Rabbi Yizhak Meir Alter (*Harim*)	1799–1866
Rabbi Menahem Mendel Morgensteren (*of Kozk*)	1787–1859
Rabbi Yacob Yitzhak Rabinovitz (*Hayehudi Hakadosh*)	1766–1813
Rabbi Simcha Bunem of Przysucha (Disciple of the Seer of Lublin, and Hayehudi Hakadosh)	1767–1827
Rabbi Avraham Mordechei Alter	1866–1948
Rabbi Israel Alter	1855–1977

---

1 Details in this book concerning the Chassidic Rabbis were extracted from the *Encyclopedia of Chassidism* by Zvi Rabinowicz

Kalev

Rabbi Yizhak Eizik Taub	1744–1821
Rabbi Menahem Mendel (Rishon Lezion)	b. 1918

Karlin

Rabbi Aharon the Great of Karlin	1736–1772
Rabbi Aharon Perlov (*Beit Aharon*)	1808–1872
Rabbi Israel Perlov (*Yanuka*)	1868–1921

Kosov

Rabbi Menahem Mendel of Kosov (son of Rabbi Jacob Koppel, Chassid and disciple of Rabbi Moshe Leib of Sassov)	1768–1825

Kozenice

Rabbi Israel Hofstin (*The Maggid of Kozenice*)	1733–1815

Kretshinev

Rabbi Menachem Eliezer Zeev	1950

Modzitz

Rabbi Ezekil of Kuzmir	1812–1856
Rabbi Shmuel Eliyahu of Zwulen	1828–1888
Rabbi Israel Taub of Modzitz	1849–1921
Rabbi Saul Yedidyah Eliazar Taub	1882–1947
Rabbi Shmuel Eliyahu Taub	1906–1984
Rabbi Israel Dan Taub	1928–2006
Rabbi Chaim Saul Taub	

Ostrowze

Rabbi Meir Yechiel	1851–1928

Radomsk

Rabbi Solomon haCohen Rabinowicz	1795–1866
Rabbi Shlomo Hanoch haCohen Rabinowicz	1882–1941

Ruzhyn

Rabbi Israel of Ruzhyn   1797–1851

Sadegura

Rabbi Abraham Jacob Friedman   1820–1883

Sassov

Rabbi Moshe Leib of Sassov   1745–1807
Rabbi Shmuel Shmelke of Sassov (Son of Moshe Leib)   1800–1869

Satmar

Rabbi Yoel Teitelbaum   1887–1979

Slonim

Rabbi Avraham Vinaverg   1804–1884
Rabbi Avraham Vinaverg (Jerusalem)   1889–1981

Disciples of the Besht

Rabbi Nahman of Bratzlav	1772–1810
Rabbi Dov Ber, The Maggid of Mezhirech	1704–1772
Rabbi Avraham Hamalakh (Son of Rabbi Dov Ber)	1741–1776
Rabbi Jacob Joseph haCohen, of Polonnoye	?–1782
Rabbi Yechiel Michael of Zloezov	1731–1786
Rabbi Pinhas of Korzec	1726–1791
Rabbi Raphael of Bershad	?–1825
Rabbi Leib Sarah's	1730–1791
Rabbi Elimelekh of Lejask	1720–1791
Rabbi Zusya of Annopoli	1717–1786
Rabbi Jacob Yizhak haHozeh, The Seer of Lublin	1745–1815
Rabbi Meir ben-Yaakov of Przemyshlan	1780–1850
Rabbi Levi Yitzhak of Berdichev	1740–1810
Rabbi Baruch Yechiel of Medziborz	1753–1811
Rabbi Naftali of Ropczyce	1760–1827
Rabbi Samuel (Shmelke) Horowitz of Nikolsburg	1726–1778
Rabbi Eliezer Horowitz of Tarnograd	1740–1806

Vizniz

Rabbi Hayim Meir Hager	1888–1972

Zanz

Rabbi Hayim Halberstam (*Divrei Hayim*)	1797–1876
Rabbi Shlomo Carlebach	1925–1994

Cantors[2]

David Koussevitsky	1899–1966
David Moshe Steinberg	1870–1941
Pinchas Spektor (Pintshik)	1872–1951
Shlomo Ravitz	1873–1983
Jacob Talmud (Gur)	?–1964
Ben Zion Shenker	b. 1925
Mordechai Hershman	1888–1940
Joseph (Yosseleh) Rosenblatt	1882–1933

2 Dates extracted from *B'ron Yachad* by Akiva Zimmerman.

References

ADLER, Israel. 2002. *Yuval,* Vol. 7, Jerusalem
AESCOLI, Aaron Ze'ev. 1998. *Hassidism in Poland,* Jerusalem
ALFASSI, Yitzchak. 1987. *Besde Hachassidut,* Tel Aviv
ALFASSI, Yizchak. 1986. *haChassudut veShivat Zion,* Tel Aviv
ALFASI, Yizchak. 2003. *Tzadikim veChassidim,* Israel
ANSHIN, Natan. 2005. *Lamishpacha Weekly Journal,* Jerusalem 31.3.2005
ARIEL, Shlomo Zalman. 1968. *Encyclopedia Meir Nativ,* Ramat Gan
AVENARY, Hanoch. 1976. *Negginot haTora beMasoret Ashkenaz 1500–1900,* Tel Aviv
BARUCH, Y. L. 1963. *Sefer haShabbat,* Tel Aviv
BEN GURION, Micha Yosef. 1928. *Aggadot Am Mimei haKabbalah vehaCHassidut,* Vol. 2, Leipzig, Germany.
BUBER, Martin. 1979. *Ohr Haganuz,* Jerusalem & Tel Aviv
BUBER, Solomon. 1911. *Siddur Raschi,* Berlin (Jerusalem 1999)
CAHANA, Dr. S. Z. 1964. El haRina ve'El haTefillah, Foreword in *Kol Israel,* Vol. 1, Tel Aviv: Bilu School
CAMPBELL, Don. 1999. *The Mozart Effect,* Israel
COHEN, David. *Lamed Vav Aggadot,* Ramat Gan
DAN, Joseph. 1989. *Sefer haZohar veDoro,* Vol. 8, Jerusalem
DAN, Joseph. 1992. *Chassidut Ashkenaz,* Tel Aviv
Die Shule un Chazzonim Velt. 1967. Association of Cantors in Argentina, April.
DOV, Eliach. *Mischulchan Gavoha*
DUBNOW, Simon. 1890. *Toldot haChassidut,* Tel Aviv
Duchan. 2000. No. 15. Jerusalem: Renanut
ELBOGEN, Yitzchak Moshe. 1972. *haTefillah beIsrael beHitpatchutah haHistorit,* Tel Aviv
Encyclopedia Ivrit. 1981. Jerusalem
Encyclopedia Judaica. 1972. Jerusalem
Encyclopedia Klalit Israel. 1951. Vol. 4, Tel Aviv
ETINGER, Shmuel. 1969. *Toldot Am Israel be'Et haChadashah,* Tel Aviv
ETKES, Immanuel. 2000. *Baal haShem,* Jerusalem
FATER, Yissachar. 1970. *Yiddisheh Music in Poland,* Federation for Polish Jews, Tel Aviv

FISKUS, Danny Moshe ben Chaim. 1983. *Mor miBsamim*, Elul
FRIEDHABER, Zvi. 2000. Rikudei Mitzva. In *Duchan,* Vol. 15, Jerusalem
FRIEDMANN, Alter Yehuda haCohen. 1994. *Otzar Pitgamei Chabad*, Brooklyn
FRIEMAN, Benjamin. 1983. *Siddur Mekor Hatfilot*, Bene Brak
GESHURI, M. S. 1970. *Kol Israel,* Bilu School, Tel Aviv
GESHURI, M. S. 1936. *laChassidim Mizmor*, Jerusalem
GESHURI, M. S. 1920. *Mefa'ane'ach haNiggun haChassidi,* Machanayim Booklet No. 46
GESHURI, M. S. 1952. *Negginah veChassidut beVeit Kuzmir uVnoteha,* Jerusalem
GESHURI, M. S. 1964. *Negginot uZmirot leShabbat,* Machanayim Booklet No. 85
GESHURI, M. S. 1963. Zemirot Chanukah etzel haChassidim. In S*efer Hamoadim,* YomTov von Levinsky, Tel Aviv
GRINBERG, Aharon Yakov. 1970. *Iturei Torah,* Tel Aviv
GRÖZINGER, Karl E. 1997. *Die Geschichten vom Ba'al Schem Tov,* Wiesbaden
GUTTMAN, Menachem. 1965. *Maayan haChassidut* , Vol. 2, Jerusalem
HORODEZKY, S. A. 1951. *haChassidut vehaChassidim*, Tel Aviv
IBEN TIBBON, Jehuda 1990. *Baal Schem Tov*, Zürich
IDEL, Moshe. 1982. *Yuval*, Vol. 4, Jerusalem
IDELSOHN, Avraham Zvi. 1931. *haNegginah haChassidit,* Jewish American Yearbook, New York
IDELSOHN, Avraham Zvi. *haNegginah haChassidit,* handwritten manuscript in Hebrew University, Jerusalem, C20MUS 4
JACOBS, Louis. 1972. *Hassidic Prayer,* New York
KAHANA, Eliezer Lippa. 1995. *Birkot Avi.* Jerusalem
KAHANA, Joseph Moshe. In newspaper: *Hamachaneh Hacharedi*, 8 February 2007
KORMAN, Avraham. 2001. *haAggadah uMashma'utah,* Tel Aviv
KRIMELOVSKY, J. Z. 1992. *Atkinu Se'udata, Zmirot leYom haShabbat*, Jerusalem
KRIMELOVSKY, J. Z. 1996. *Tehillim Pe'er Mikdoshi,* Modzitz, Jerusalem
Kuntras Tifferet Israel, Vol. Av 5708 – Iyar; 5714- Nissan, Kislev 1975; Nissan 1976
LEVINSKY, Yom Tov. 1063. S*efer haMoadim*, Tel Aviv
LEVINSKY, Yom Tov. 1970. *Encyclopedia shel Havai uMassoret beYahadut,* Tel Aviv
Likkutei Moharan miBreslav, Section 1 chapter 4
MARK, Zvi. 2003. *Mystica veShiga'on beYetzirat Rabbi Nahman miBratzlav*, Tel Aviv
MAZOR, Yaakov. 2002. Kocho shel haNiggun veTafkido beHavai haDati vehaChevrati. In *Yuval*, Vol. 7, Jerusalem

MAZOR, Yaakov. 2004. *haNiggun haChassidi beFi haChassidim*, Jerusalem
MAZOR, Yaakov. 2000. haBadchan baChevrah hachassidit. In *Duchan*, Vol. 15, Jerusalem
MAZOR, Yaakov. 2000. *Masoret haKleyzmerim b'Eretz Israel,* Jerusalem
MEIMON, Yehuda Leib Hakohen. 1951. *Sarei Hame'ah,* Jerusalem
MEIMON, Yehuda Leib Hakohen. 1960. *Sefer Habesht,* Jerusalem
MUNK, Eliahu. 1994. *Olam haTefillot,* Jerusalem
NECHT, Yaakov. 1965. *Sefer haShabbat,* Tel Aviv
NEWMAN, Louis. 1987. *The Hassidic Anthology,* New Jersey, USA: Jason Aronson
NIGGUNEI CHABAD. 2000. *Sefer Haniggunim,* Kfar Chabad
ORENSTEIN, Avraham. 1969. *haNe'um vehaDrush,* Bnei Brak
Otzar Niggunei Chabad. 1999. Y&M Music, Canada
PRAGER, Moshe. 1960. *Rabbi Israel Baal Shem Tov,* Jerusalem
RABINOWICZ, Tzvi. 1996. *Encyclopedia of Hassidim,* USA
RAZ, Simcha. 1989. *Pitgamei Chassidim,* Jerusalem
ROTENBERG, Yeshaya Meshulam Fish Halevi. 2000. *Zamru liShmoh,* Jerusalem
ROSENTAL, Avraham Israel. 2004. *Kemotzeh Shalal Rav,* Jerusalem: Machon haRav Frank
RUBIN, Yissachar Dov. 2003. *Talelei Orot,* Jerusalem
SAKMEN, Walter. 1991. *Jüdische Musikanten und Tänzer,* Innsbruck
SCHATZ, Uffenheimer Rivka. 1990. *Maggid Devarav leYa'akov: The Maggid Dov Ber of Mezhirech,* Jerusalem
SCHLEIFER, Eliyahu. 1985. *Anthology of Hassidic Music,* Jerusalem
SCHNEERSOHN, Menachem Mendel. 1993. *Sha'arey Halacha uMinhag,* Jerusalem
SHOLLEL, Judah Leib. 1950. *Minhagei heCHatam Sofer.* Pressburg
SHONWALD, Eliezer Chaim. *Kenagen Hamenagen- Negina veShirat haKodesch baYahadut,* Internet: Kippa – Tarbut Pnai.
SCHWARZ, Joel. 2003. *Perek Shira Zimra veNiggun baRe'i haYahdut,* Jerusalen
SIMON, Menachem Mendel. *BaaL Shem Tov al Hatorah –* Jerusalem
STAIMAN, Mordechei. 1994. *Niggun,* New Jersey, USA: Jason Aronson
STEINMANN, Eliezer. *Be'er haChassidut- Sefer Habesht,* Tel Aviv
STEINMANN, Eliezer. 1958. *Yalkut Mashalim, Sipurim, Imrei Chochma,* Tel Aviv
STERN, Mosche. In *Makor Rishon* Daily Newspaper, 29.9.2004
STERN, Yechiel Michel. *Otzar Hayediyot*
TA SHMA, Israel. 2003. *haTefillah haAshkenazit haKduma,* Hebrew University, Jerusalem
TAUB, Rabbi Israel, of Modzitz. 1967. *Divrei Israel,* New York USA
TAUB, Rabbi Saul Yedidyah, of Modzitz. 1960. *Imrei Saul,* Tel Aviv

TAUB, Yehuda Leib. 2004. *Simchu Tzaddikim,* Beth Shemesh, Israel.
TZOFIEF, Shlomo. 2001. *Megillat Shir haShirim haMevoeret: Shirat Shlomo.* Jerusalem
WALLACH, Shalom Meir haCohen. 1989. *beOhalei Tzaddikim: Sippurim uMa'amarim al Haggadah shel Pessach,* Bnei Brak
VINAVER, Nechemiah. 1986. *Anthology of Chassidic Music,* Dept. for Research, Hebrew University, Jerusalem: Introductions and Explanations by Prof. Eliyahu Schleifer *[see: Schleifer]*
WIGODER, Jeffrey. 1994. *Encyclopedia leYahadut,* Tel Aviv
YAKOBSON, Yoram. 1985. *Toratah shel haChassidut,* Tel Aviv
YOSEF, Chaim. 1986. *Ben Ish Chai.* Jerusalem
ZACH Ronit. In national newspaper: *Yediot Aharonot – 7 Yamim* 4.2.2005
ZALMANOV, Shmuel. 1985. *Sefer HaNigunim,* Kfar Chabad
ZEVIN, Shlomo Joseph. 1958. *Sippurei Chassidim,* Tel Aviv
ZIMMERMANN, Akiva. 1988. *B'ron Yachad,* Tel Aviv

Internet

Galili Zeev:
   http://www.makorrishon.co.il/article.php?id=868
Rat Riki:
   http://www.aish.com/hsociety/diary/Od_Avinu_Chai_-_Karlibach.asp
   http://www.aish.com/hsociety/society/Going_Up_to_Meron.asp
Sperber Elisheva:
   www.toravoda.orgil714shevi.html
   http://hydepark.hevre.co.il/hydepark/topic.asp?topic_id=1652135
Wasserman Aharon:
   www.vbm-torah.org/vtc/0055480.html

www.ingramcontent.com/pod-product-compliance
Ingram Content Group UK Ltd.
Pitfield, Milton Keynes, MK11 3LW, UK
UKHW021836210426
5322IPUK00021B/314